Benjamin Stillingfleet

Miscellaneous Tracts Relating to Natural History, Husbandry, and

Physick

To which is added, The calendar of flora

Benjamin Stillingfleet

Miscellaneous Tracts Relating to Natural History, Husbandry, and Physick
To which is added, The calendar of flora

ISBN/EAN: 9783337320997

Printed in Europe, USA, Canada, Australia, Japan

Cover: Foto ©ninafisch / pixelio.de

More available books at **www.hansebooks.com**

MISCELLANEOUS TRACTS

RELATING TO

NATURAL HISTORY,

HUSBANDRY,

AND

PHYSICK.

To which is added the

CALENDAR of FLORA.

By BENJ. STILLINGFLEET.

THE SECOND EDITION,

Corrected and augmented with additional Notes throughout, particularly on fome of the Englifh Graffes, which are illuftrated by Copper Plates;

LONDON, Printed:

And fold by R. and J. DODSLEY, in Pall-Mall; S. BAKER, in York-Street, Covent-Garden; And T. PAYNE, at the Mufe Gate.

MDCCLXII.

Homo naturæ minister et interpres tantum facit et intelligit, quantum de naturæ ordine, re vel mente obfervaverit : nec amplius fcit vel poteft.   BACON.

Primus gradus fapientiæ eft res ipfas noffe ; quæ notitia confiftit in vera idea objectorum ; objecta diftinguuntur et nofcuntur ex methodica illorum *divifione* et conveniente *denominatione* ; adeoque divifio et denominatio fundamentum noftræ fcientiæ erit.   *George Carley*   LINN.

TO THE

RIGHT HONORABLE

George, Lord Lyttelton,

Baron of FRANKLEY.

MY LORD,

BESIDES private motives of refpect and honor, there is another of a public nature, which makes me defirous to infcribe the following fheets to Your Lordfhip. I mean the zeal which You fhewed in Parliament for fecuring to this Country that noble collection of natural curiofities now repofited in the Britifh Mufeum; which cannot fail

A 2   in

DEDICATION.

in time to produce many good effects, and prove the truth of what
Your Lordſhip obſerved, that the
reputation and intereſt of the nation
were highly concerned in that pur-
chaſe. I am, with the greateſt regard,

My Lord,

Your Lordſhip's moſt Obliged

and Humble Servant,

PREFACE

TRANSLATOR.

THE following pieces were selected from many others publiſhed by ſeveral ingenious members of that great, and hitherto unrivalled ſchool of natural hiſtory, the univerſity of Upſal in Sweden, under the preſidence of Linnæus[a]. They

A 3　　　　were

[a] Linnæus Phil. Bot. p. 9. has theſe words, vid. diſſert. noſtra de ficu. Now there is a piece in Amæn. Acad. vol. 1. on this ſubject, in which the matter referred to is contained. This piece goes under the name of Cornelius Hegardt, tho' Linnæus plainly quotes

it

were felected not as the only, or even the moft valuable, but as anfwering beft the intention of the tranflator ; which was to make known more generally how far all mankind is concerned in the ftudy of natural hiftory, and thereby to incite fuch as are properly qualified to profecute, and encourage that branch of knowledge, and fpread, as far as the nature of the thing is capable of, amongft all orders of men in this nation, the improvements made in it by the excellent Linnæus. His name, it muft be confeffed, has been for fome time paft in the mouths of people, but his works, i imagine, are little known except to a few vertuofi who have a more than ordinary curiofity, and ardor to look into the minute parts of nature. It cannot indeed be otherwife. For to underftand him and to make ufe of his method, requires

it as his own. How far that may be the cafe of all the other pieces in the Amæn. Acad. i cannot pretend to fay. But it is moft likely from the practice in foreign univerfities in relation to thefes held for degrees, that they muft in great part be attributed to him, as prefident.

more

more patience and time than are likely to
fall to the fhare of the generality of the
world. My defign therefore is not to ex-
hort people indifcriminately to ftudy his
works; but, as i obferved before, to give
them fome idea how ufefull his purfuits are
likely to become in many refpects. There
will appear, i imagine, fuch great and extenfive views in relation to hufbandry, phyfic, and the general œconomy of human life
in the few fpecimens i have given, that in
this age and nation, where every art and
fcience, that can be of any ufe to the public,
are fure to meet with generous encouragers,
there will be found many who will readily
promote any rational endeavour to pufh
thefe difcoveries farther, or put in practice
fuch hints, as may feem to bear a probable
appearance of fuccefs.

I can fcarcely condemn mankind for
treating with contempt a vertuofo whom
they fee employed in poring over a mofs or
an infect day after day, and fpending his
life in fuch feemingly unimportant and barren fpeculations. The firft and moft natu-

ral reflections that will arife on this occafion muft be to the difadvantage of fuch
purfuits. Yet were the whole fcene of nature laid open to our views, were we admitted to behold the connections and dependencies of every thing on every other,
and to trace the œconomy of nature thro'
the fmaller as well as greater parts of this
globe, we might perhaps be obliged to own
we were miftaken; that the Supreme Ar-
chitect had contrived his works in fuch a
manner, that we cannot properly be faid to
be unconcerned in any one of them; and
therefore that ftudies which feem upon a
flight view to be quite ufelefs, may in the
end appear to be of no fmall importance to
mankind. Nay, were we only to look
back into the hiftory of arts and fciences,
we muft be convinced, that we are apt to
judge over haftily of things of this nature.
We fhould there find many proofs, that he
who gave this inftinctive curiofity to fome
of his creatures, gave it for good and great
purpofes, and that he rewards with ufefull
difcoveries all thefe minute refearches.

It

It is true this does not always happen to
the fearcher, or his contemporaries, nor
even, fometimes to the immediate fucceed-
ing generation; but i am apt to think that
advantages of one kind or other always accrue to mankind from fuch purfuits. Some
men are born to obferve and record what
perhaps by itfelf is perfectly ufelefs, but
yet of great importance, to another who
follows and goes a ftep farther ftill as ufelefs. To him another fucceeds, and thus
by degrees; till at laft one of a fuperior
genius comes, who laying all that has been
done before his time together brings on a
new face of things, improves, adorns, ex-
alts human fociety.

All thofe fpeculations concerning lines
and numbers fo ardently purfued, and fo
exquifitely conducted by the Grecians;
what did they aim at? or what did they
produce for ages? A little arithmetic, and
the firft elements of geometry were all
they had need of. This Plato afferts, and
tho' as being himfelf an able mathematician
and remarkably fond of thefe fciences, he

re-

recommends the study of them, yet he makes use of motives that have no relation to the common purposes of life.

When Kepler, from a blind and strong impulse merely to find analogies in nature, discovered that famous one between the distances of the several planets from the sun, and the periods in which they compleat their revolutions; of what importance was it to him or to the world?

Again; when Galileo, pushed on by the same irresistible curiosity, found out the law by which bodies fall to the earth, did he or could he foresee that any good would come from his ingenious theorems, or was any immediate use made of them?

Yet had not the Greeks pushed their abstract speculations so far; had not Kepler and Galileo made the above mentioned discoveries; we never could have seen the greatest work that ever came from the hands of man. Every one will guess that i mean Sir Isaac Newton's Principia.

Some obscure person, whose name is not so much as known, diverting himself idly

as

as a ftander-by would have thought, with
trying experiments on a feemingly contemptible piece of ftone, found out a guide for
mariners on the ocean, and fuch a guide as
no fcience, however fubtile and fublime its
fpeculations may be, however wonderful
its conclufions, would ever have arrived at.
It was bare curiofity that put Sir Thomas
Millington upon examining the minute
parts of flowers; but his difcoveries have
produced the moft perfect, and moft ufefull
fyftem of botany that the world has yet
feen.

Other inftances might be produced to
prove, that bare curiofity in one age is the
fource of the greateft utility in another.
And what has frequently been faid of chymifts, may be applyed to every other kind
of vertuofi. They hunt perhaps after
chimæras and impoffibilities, they find
fomething really valuable by the bye. We
are but inftruments under the Supreme Di-
rector, and do not fo much as know in
many cafes what is of moft importance
for us to fearch after. But we may be fure

of

of one thing, viz. that if we ftudy and follow nature, whatever paths we are led into, we fhall at laft arrive at fomething valuable to ourfelves and others, but of what kind we muft be content to remain ignorant.

I am fenfible that after all i have faid, or can fay, many people will not be perfuaded to allow that the ftudy of fome parts of natural hiftory can be worthy of a rational creature. They will never vouchfafe to look on moffes and infects in this light. Yet why may not the ftudy of thefe likewife have its ufe in future times? It ought to be confidered that the number of the latter is immenfe, that it is but lately that any great attention has been paid to them, that one of them is and has been long the means of cloathing thoufands and feeding more, that another affords us honey, another a fine dye, not to mention fome few befides, of acknowledged benefit to mankind. Laftly, that they are capable of doing us the greateft mifchief, and that it is poffible that a more thorough knowledge

of

of them may inftruct us how to fecure ourfelves againft their attacks. Whether this
be poffible we can never know, till proper
encouragement has been given to this
branch of natural hiftory. Something to
the fame purpofe might be faid concerning mofles, but as the intent of one of the
following pieces is principally to take off
fuch objections as i have been confidering,
i fhall dwell no longer on this fubject;
but proceed to give a fhort account of what
Linnæus has done towards the improvement
of natural hiftory, that the reader, who is
unacquainted with his works, may form
fome idea, tho' very imperfect, of this
great man. Firft then, he has invented a new fyftem of botany, founded on
the male and female organs of generation
in plants, a fyftem which has thrown a
new light over botany. He has defined
about 10,000 plants, ranged them into
clafles, genera and fpecies, given new and
regular generical names to many inftead of
thofe barbarous and uncouth ones which
prevailed till his time, and added fpecifical

names

names to all, fhort, eafy, and oftentimes fignificant, a thing never fo much as attempted before. He has brought into botany, a precifion, concifenefs and elegance, that were very much wanted. He has obferved and given names to fome parts of plants not taken notice of by any other botanift, parts which in fome cafes are fufficient as well as neceffary to diftinguifh the genus and the fpecies.

The Philofophia botanica [b] of this author affords throughout inftances of this reformation. Had he wrote no other book but this, he would have deferved the higheft praife from all lovers of botany. For befides the improvements juft mentioned it comprehends in a fhort compafs fome-

[b] In the year 1750. when he was writing this book, as he tells us in the preface to it, he was hindered from going on by a terrible fit of the gout, that broke the ftrength of his mind as well as body. In the year 1755, he fays, Flor. Suec. article 450. that he had been freed from the gout for fome years by eating great quantities of frefh ftrawberries. He adds that this fruit diffolves the tartar of the teeth, that it is remarkably good for people afflicted with the ftone or gout, and that it may be fafely eaten in abundance.

thing

thing of confequence in every branch of that part of natural hiftory, and affords hints for various difcoveries, hints that muft, if purfued, produce many confiderable improvements in phyfic, hufbandry, and œconomy.

He has publifhed a Materia medica fo far as relates to plants, in which he has undertaken to determine many fpecies commonly ufed but not fufficiently afcertained, adding throughout in the fhorteft manner poffible what he has found to be ufelefs or efficacious, and as he affures us never highly recommends any without being thoroughly convinced of their vertues by his own experiencé in the hofpitals where he prefided. Some of thefe medicines have not yet, i believe, been received into our fhops, but they may poffibly deferve confideration.

In the laft edition of his Syftema naturæ he has mentioned above 1500 fpecies of infeéts, has claffed them all, divided them into genera and fpecies, defcribed them as to the minuteft parts fo far as was neceffary to diftinguifh them, marked the places where

. 4

where they are to be found, the plants
they feed upon, their transformations, cited
the authors who have treated on them, given
them claffical, generical, and trivial or fpecifical names; has done the fame by birds,
fifhes, and all other known animals; has
ranged all the foffils, minerals and ftones,
to ufe his language, in a manner partly bor-
rowed, and partly founded on his own obfervations. But what improvements and
additions he has lately made to this part of
natural hiftory, as well as that of plants, we
cannot fay till the other part of his new edition of the Syftem of nature comes out,
which is expected daily. However what
we fee he has done in relation to animals,
leaves us no room to doubt but that it will
all together be the moft extraordinary book
that was ever publifhed in this or almoft
any other way.

Befides his writings, of which i have
mentioned but a fmall part, this indefatigable man, born to be nature's hiftorian,
has travelled over Lapland, all Sweden,
part of Norway, Denmark, Germany,

Holland, England, and France, in fearch of knowledge. That part of his travels which is publiſhed in Latin has many curious and uſeful obſervations relating to the purpoſes of common life. Of thoſe which are written in his own tongue i cannot give any other account, but that by fome quotations from them to be found in the writings of his diſciples it appears, that they very well deſerve to be communicated to the world in a language more generally underſtood.

Befides theſe labours of his own, the world will be one day obliged to him for what others have done. Incited by his example and perſuaſion, C. Ternſtrom went into Aſia; P. Kalmius to Penſilvania and Canada; L. Montin into one part of Lapland; D. Selander into another; F. Haſſelquiſt into Ægypt and Paleſtine; O. Toren to Malabar and Surat; P. Oſbech to China and Java; P. Loefling to Spain and America; P. J. Berg to Gothland; M. Koehler to Italy and Apulia; and D. Rolander to Surinam and St. Euſtacia; all

a   theſe

thefe with a view to the promotion of natural hiftory. When we confider him in
this light of a mafter of fuch difciples as
thefe, and many others, fome of whofe
works make up the following book, he
muft appear like Homer at the head of the
poets, Socrates at the head of Greek mo-
ralifts, and our Newton at the head of the
mathematical philofophers. Among all
thefe extraordinary qualifications there appear throughout his writings fpirit, candor,
a due regard for others, and proper mo-
defty and diffidence of himfelf.

I will give a fhort fpecimen of his way
of thinking in relation to the degree of human knowledge hitherto attained by man
on the fubject of natural hiftory. A fubject on which it was very natural for a lefs
extenfive genius to be vain, as he has had
fo great a fhare himfelf in the advancement
of it. The paflage is taken out of the introduction to the new edition of his Syftem
of nature, and is to this effect. ' How
' fmall a part of the great works of nature
' is laid open to our eyes, and how many
' things

'things are going on in secret which we
'know nothing of! How many things are
'there which this age first was acquainted
'with! How many things that we are ig-
'norant of will come to light when all
'memory of us shall be no more! For
'nature does not at once reveal all her se-
'crets. We are apt to look on ourselves as
'already admitted into the sanctuary of her
'temple, we are still only in the porch. I
'have entered, adds he, into the thick and
'shady woods of nature, which are every
'where beset with thorns and briars. I
'have endeavored as much as possible to
'keep clear of them, but experience has
'taught me that there is no man so circum-
'spect as never to forget himself, and there-
'fore i have born with patience the sneers of
'the malevolent, and the buffoneries of those
'whose vivacity is exerted only to mo-
'lest and give offence to others. I have in
'spite of these insults, kept on steadily in
'my old path, and have finished the course
'I was destined for.'

The latter part of this passage, shews that

he has not been without his enemies, and
that he hath fuffered in the fame way that
all the moft curious enquirers into nature
have done in all ages. The tartnefs of his
expreffions, which is ftill ftronger in the
original, plainly proves that they have not
ufed fair arguments againft him, but like
interefted rivals, or men of a fuperficial
underftanding, have endeavored to fubject him and his labours to ridicule. But
whatever has been his fate in his own
countrey, as far as I know, his name is
almoft univerfally mentioned with refpect
in all other parts of Europe. It is true,
objections have been made to his innova-
tions in other places befides Sweden ^c,
which

^c Having fince the firft edition of thefe tracts met with
Browellius' anfwer to Siegefbec, M. D. and botanical
profeffor at Peterfburg; who wrote againft the fexual
fyftem of Linnæus, i cannot omit quoting one of his
objections, which i imagine will divert the reader at the
fame time, that it may ferve as an inftance how far zeal
for old notions will fometimes carry men. The objection is, that the laws of nature are overturned by
Linnæus, fince polygamy and adultery would be according to his fyftem allowed in the vegetable world;
for

which muſt unavoidably happen on many
accounts, but particularly becauſe thoſe
natural hiſtorians who had been brought
up and inured to other ſyſtems, who

for in ſome plants there are many filaments to one piſtil.
This is polygamy. In others there are female flowers,
which are impregnated by the duſt of male flowers,
which have other female flowers belonging to them,
i. e. which are already married. This is plainly adultery. Now according to profeſſor Siegeſbec, it is not
credible that ſuch confuſion and deteſtable pollution
ſhould be tolerated in nature.

Browellius rightly obſerves in his anſwer, that Siegeſbec had totally overlooked many inſtances of theſe
enormities in the animal kingdom, and even the immo-
rality of farmers and their wives, ſhepherds, jockies,
ſportſmen, nay even ladies of reputation, who in their
ways promote theſe immoral and indecent practices.

However it muſt be obſerved in favor of this very
ſcrupulous profeſſor, that ſyſtems of philoſophy, founded
on facts have been anathematiſed, and the authors
and favorers of them condemned to the ſevereſt pu-
niſhments, for reaſons as little to the purpoſe as the
foregoing of Siegeſbec. To quote inſtances would be
endleſs, as every one the leaſt converſant in the hiſtory
of learning will eaſily recollect them. But ſo moderate
is the world now become, that I do not hear that the
Linnæan ſyſtem is looked on as heretical even at the
court of Rome, though the profeſſor has drawn ſome
ſhrewd arguments againſt it from the book of Geneſis.

a 3

had

had learned things by other names, and could not eafily attain the new ones, muft have ftrong prejudices arife on this occafion. This objection being perfonal i fhall not confider it any farther, but readily allow that great indulgence is due to fuch people, and that their fate is to be pitied · for coming into the world too foon to be enlightened farther on fubjects, that perhaps had employed the greateft part of their life. But there are prejudices of another fort which i cannot omit to confider more fully on this occafion.

In order to this it muft be premifed, that the ufe and intent of a claffical fyftem in any part of natural hiftory, is not to range things according to their natural connections in regard to their outward afpects, or effential qualities, or their medicinal or œconomical properties, but to range them in fuch a manner that upon a plant, mineral or animal being fhewn to a naturalift he may certainly, upon a due infpection of the object, give its true name according to fome fyftem. He who goes

farther

farther than this is not barely a naturalift, but fomething more, viz. a phyfician,
a chymift, a farmer, a gardener, &c.
And he who cannot go thus far to a certain degree, does not deferve the name of a
naturalift, however fkillfull he may be in
the vertues and properties of bodies animate and inanimate.

The ufe then and intent of a claffical fyftem is nothing more than that of a dic-
tionary, where no one complains that
words totally unconnected in fenfe are put
near one another. The queftion therefore
as to the fexual fyftem [d], v. g. in plants, is
not whether they be ranged naturally, but
whether in the beft manner poffible in order
to be known. Nay farther, it matters not
whether the fexual fyftem be founded on
nature or not, i. e. whether there be any

[d] At the end of the preface i have endeavored to explain the meaning of thefe terms in fuch a manner, that
i think any curious perfon that will be at the pains to
compare my explication with nature, cannot fail to underftand perfectly what they mean in general. I thought
this method would be more agreeable to the reader than
to be referred to other books.

propagation

propagation by feeds without male and female organs of generation. The whole to be confidered is whether thofe parts which are called, and, i believe, truly called fo, do really exift, and whether they they for the moft part exift fo uniformly, as to furnifh marks fufficient to diftinguifh the claffes, &c. by. Nor does it matter whether it be hard to diftinguifh thofe marks, but whether they can with proper care and patience be diftinguifhed, and whether we can furely diftinguifh plants, without obferving thofe nice and minute parts, and whether a fyftem has been found equally fure with the Linnæan without having regard to thofe parts. Thofe who think fo would do well to inform the world of their difcovery, and not make objections that affect only the obfcurity of nature, when they mean to condemn a fyftem which is obfcure merely from its confonancy to nature. If Providence has thought fit to write in cyphers, fhall he be blamed who endeavors to give a key to its works, becaufe

fome

fome men cannot diftinguifh one ftroke from another in the cypher ?

Thofe who have not learned to read the characters of nature for want of leifure, patience, or any other caufe, ought not to complain that Linnæus cannot make them fkillfull in a part of knowledge they are not qualified for. If a man unacquainted with the learned languages wants to know the meaning of a Greek word, will he complain of the lexicon, becaufe he cannot find it ? certainly not. Neither ought we to complain of Linnæus in a fimilar cafe.

This i think is a full anfwer to all the objections that have or can be made to his fyftem in general. What errors he has committed according to his own principles in relation to particulars is quite another queftion. I am one of thofe who think him not free from errors. Nor is it wonderfull that he fhould fall into fome, but it is truly wonderfull that one man fhould be able to invent and carry fo far fo nice and extenfive a fyftem, efpecially when we confider not only what he has done in botany, but what he has done in all the branches of

natural

natural hiftory befides, and fome of them almoft entirely neglected before his time. I fhould therefore wifh that thofe who are fond of this part of knowledge would, inftead of making frivolous objections, try by an accurate and diligent examination to rectify his miftakes, and thereby help to perfect a fyftem which deferves the utmoft attention, and commendation.

Tho' i faid above that it matters not whether the fexual fyftem be founded on nature or not; yet it was natural for the inventor of it to endeavor by all proper means to vindicate it as likely to be fo, and this he has done to the fatisfaction of the moft curious obfervers; and i will venture to add, that it is natural for others likewife to embrace with zeal a fyftem, that puts the works of Providence in fo new and beautiful a light by continuing the analogy from the animate to the inanimate creation. It feems as if Providence intended to lead men to this difcovery by ftriking our fenfes fo intenfely and fo agreeably with thofe very parts which contain the clue of this fyftem. Yet fuch is the inattention and

in-

inaccuracy of man on certain points, that even a tolerable conjecture concerning the use of thofe parts was not made till the year 1676.

Having finifhed all that I think neceffary to fay concerning Linnæus and his works, i fhall now come to what relates immediately to myfelf only. Firft then as to the tranflation, I have endeavored to avoid making it too literal, and fervile, but yet i hope without taking any undue liberties, or deviating from the fenfe of the originals.

The part which is likely to prove leaft agreeable to the reader, is that which was moft troublefome to the tranflator. I mean the names of things not generally known. Some of thefe i have been obliged to leave in Latin, not being able to find any Englifh names for them. I will not pretend to have avoided all miftakes on this head, but it is certain i fhould have committed more, as well as have had much more trouble, had it not been for the affiftance of the ingenious Mr. Hudfon, whofe fkill in all the branches of natural hiftory, and particularly

cularly thofe relating to his profeffion as an apothecary, cannot fail to recommend him to the favor of the public.   To him i like-wife owe the afcertaining of fome of the graffes, one of which, viz. the fmall bent grafs which i had in my collection, but knew not where i found it, he difcovered to be the gramen minimum anglo-bri-tanum, mentioned in the indiculus plan-tarum dubiarum at the end of Ray's Synopfis.

I muft not omit alfo on this occafion to acknowledge my obligation to that excel-lent botanift Dr. Watfon, for favoring me with the perufal of his collection of graffes, which was of no fmall fervice to me.

But to return to the tranflation ; I faid that i did not pretend to have avoided all miftakes in relation to the names of things, i will now extend this farther, and own my fufpicions that i may have made fome in re-lation to other particulars, but i hope they are of fuch a kind only as may be looked on with indulgence by the learned, efpecially when they confider the great variety of fub-

jects

jects treated on in thefe pages, of none of
which fubjects i profefs to be a mafter, and
therefore do not undertake to teach fuch
readers; but on the contrary fhall always be
ready and even defirous to receive inftruc-
tions from them.   I beg they will alfo confider that i do not aim at letting the unlearned into the myfteries of this part of
knowledge, or even teaching them the elements of it.   My bufinefs is only to excite
curiofity, and therefore fmall errors can be
of no confequence.   What I have farther
to fay will be found in notes.

   Res fummas initio deberi parvo ac debili
experientia omnium temporum teftatur.
Amænit. Acad. vol. 2. p. 266. §. 2.

End of the P R E F A C E.

IN

IN order to explain the fexual fyftem, i fhall make ufe of the lilly, as that plant is almoft every where to be found, and as the parts of generation are in that more obvious, than perhaps in any other flower. Upon opening the flower leaves there will appear in the very center, at the bottom, an oblong thickifh fubftance with fix furrows along its fides. This contains the feeds, and is called the

The germen or germ.

On this ftands a fmall kind of pillar called

The ftyle.

Which is terminated by a thickifh triangular head, called

The ftigma.

Thefe all together from the female part of the flower, and are called by one name,

The piftil.

Round this piftil grow fix long thready fubftances, called

The filaments,

Each terminated by an oblong body, that plays as on a pivot, upon the leaft motion

tion being given to the flower, and is called

The anthera.

This anthera contains the male duft, which when ripe is fcattered about by every breath of air, and what happens to fall on the ftigma, or upper part of the piftil, is fuppofed to enter thro' the ftyle into the germ, and there impregnate the feed.

This plant is called an hermaphrodite, becaufe the male and female organs of generation are contained within one flower. Moft plants are hermaphrodites, like this, and have fomething analogous to what i have defcribed above. Some plants have the male and female parts feparate on the fame individual; others have male parts on one plant and female on another.

The part of the flower that contains honey is called

The nectary.

Only a few plants have this part, the lilly; has it but as the knowledge of it is not neceffary for underftanding the following pieces, i fhall not trouble the reader with a defcription of it.

C O N-

CONTENTS.

AN oration concerning travelling in one's own countrey, by Dr. Linnæus — — — page 1

The œconomy of nature, by Ifaac Biberg — — — — 37

On the foliation of trees, by Harald Barck — — — — — 131

Of the ufe of curiofity, by Chriftoph. Gedner — — — — — 159

Obftacles to the improvement of phyfic, by J. G. Beyerftein — — 201

The calendar of Flora — — — 229

The Swedifh Pan, by Nicholas Haffelgren — — — — — 339

Obfervations on graffes, by the Tranflator — — — — — — 363

BENEFIT

OF

TRAVELLING, &c.

Miſcellaneous Tracts, &c.

An ORATION concerning the neceſſity of travelling in one's own
countrey, made by Dr. L I N N Æ U S
at Upſal, Oct. 17, anno 1741, when
he was admitted to the royal and
ordinary profeſſion of phyſic.

Amænitat. Academ. vol. ii.

MOST honorable and moſt learned auditors of all orders, i am going to undertake a province, allotted to me by the favor of
our moſt auguſt, and moſt potent monarch,
whoſe will it is that i preſide over, and direct
the ſtudy of phyſic in this Univerſity ; and
that i do my utmoſt to advance the glory of
this illuſtrious body. May his choice be
crowned with ſucceſs, and may the great and
good God favor my undertaking.

As by cuſtom, delivered down by our fore-
fathers, and preſcribed by the laws of our aca-

demy, i am obliged upon undertaking this province to fay fomething before fo illuftrious a circle of fathers and citizens; i confefs that all thofe circumftances, each of which is apt to ftrike terror into the mind of man, offer themfelves together in a croud before my eyes on this occafion. For whether i confider the amplenefs of the place, or the dignity of the audience, or the multitude of chofen people, or laftly my little talents in the arts of fpeech; all thefe circumftances, i ingenuoufly confefs, throw me into no fmall confufion.

For if the moft eloquent men, when they come to fpeak in public, have been known to tremble, and become incapable of uttering a fingle word; what muft i feel who have none of the common advantages, either from art or nature, in the readinefs and elegance of fpeech?

However, fince i am under a neceffity of faying fomething, i muft fly for refuge to that favor, and humanity, which you never refufe to thofe who fpeak on thefe occafions; and thus i doubt not but that, however deficient i may be from want of talents, or want of exercife, i fhall not wholly fail of the end i aim at. I fhall therefore, moft honorable auditors, undertake to treat on a fubjeƈt neither unfuitable to

the

the prefent occafion, nor to the office i am going
to enter into, nor to that employment which i
was lately engaged in by the will, and fuffrage
of the high, and mighty ftates of this kingdom ; and from which i am now once again
brought back to this feat of the mufes. Nay
fo far is the fubject, i am about to treat on,
from being unfuitable to any of thefe circumftances, that it feems to me particularly adapted to every one of them. The fubject is concerning the neceffity of travelling in one's own
countrey, and the advantages that may thence
accrue, efpecially to phyficians. I fhall treat
it in a plain and popular manner ; and endeavor to manage it fo, that the meannefs of my
language may be compenfated by the dignity
of the matter, and the brevity of my expreffions.

All human knowledge is built on two foundations ; reafon and experience.—Thefe two
joyned together are neceffary to make a good
phyfician.

We muft confefs indeed, that the bufinefs of
reafoning may be carried on with equal fuccefs
in our clofets, as in travelling, fuppofing we
have an opportunity of converfing with men
truly learned.

B 3   But

But it was experience, that fovereign miftrefs without which a phyfician ought to be afhamed to open his lips ; it was experience, i fay, that confecrated to immortality fo many of the antients, and amongft the reft that divine old man Hippocrates, whofe writings were publifhed many ages before chriftianity. The writings of this wonderful man alone, among fo many ingenioufly contrived fyftems, remain to this day, and will for ever remain firm, unmoved, unfhaken, untouched by any decay, by any change. It is experience that has adorned with laurels the heads of fo many celebrated phyficians in all times, and even now adorns. And hence it is that the chief and moft honorable title of phyfician is to be called a man of experience. Experience ought to go firft; reafoning fhould follow. The former furnifhes the materials of knowledge; the latter holds her confultations on the given phænomena; and when fhe has weighed with judgment every circumftance, fhe difcovers truth, and concludes, orders, and determines rightly about the point in queftion. Experience ought to be animated by reafon in all phyfical affairs; without this fhe is void of order, void of energy, void of life. On the other hand reafon with-

without experience can do nothing ; being nothing, but the mere dreams, phantafms, and meteors of ingenious men who abufe their time. The antients certainly did not, any more than we, bring experience into the world with them. There is need of much diligence and labor, before man can be thoroughly inftructed. Diofcorides confeffes, that he undertook many journies in order to increafe experience ; and the other fathers of phyfic in their writings frequently make mention of their travels either exprefsly or tacitly.

Academies were inftituted to the end, that men well verfed in all kinds of literature, and enriched befides by much experience, might be invited thither, and that the youth, who were ambitious of becoming learned, might flock together to thofe feats ; and have the advantage of improving no lefs by the experience, than by the erudition of the profeffors; and thefe qualifications combined together, which is of all alliances the moft pleafing, very juftly deferve the utmoft veneration and refpect.

Vaft and fumptuous libraries are erected in academies; in which the obfervations of the learned, like fo many legacies, and donations,

are

are preferved; that they who diligently give themfelves up to ftudy, may become endued with learning, polifhed, and confirmed by experience. Thefe libraries are the repofitories of wifdom, and their ftores are laid open to every ingenious candidate.

Hofpitals are founded that the candidates of phyfic may learn thofe things at the patients bed fide, which cannot be learned from books; for here practice, and experience fhew their force by means of the eyes, and hands; as he paints any object moft accurately, who paints from the idea, which his own eyes afford him, and not from that, which he gets by the relation of another.

Anatomy fchools are erected, that we may behold in another's body, as it were in a glafs, the nature, and conftitution of our own; as thofe conceive more clearly the fituation of countries, diftricts, and cities, and the manners, rites, and cuftoms of their inhabitants, who themfelves have been there, and have feen what is remarkable amongft them with their own eyes, than he who relies folely upon the vague and imperfect maps, and relations of travellers.

Phyfic

Phyſic gardens are here cultivated ; where the plants of various kinds are collected from all parts of the globe, that we may by this means behold, as it were, the great in the little world.

Hither inſtruments for experimental philo-ſophy are brought together, that the abſtruſe forces of the elements, which otherwiſe would eſcape our ſenſes, may be made manifeſt, and that ſo we may ſuccefsfully be let into the very receſſes of nature ; as far as human pe-netration will admit of.

All theſe things are inſtituted in academies, that the youth may arrive at knowledge by experience ; all tend to this end, that tho' we be confined to one ſpot, one corner of the earth, we may examine the great and various ſtores of knowledge, and therein behold the immenſe domains of nature, and get acquaint-ed with ſuch things, as otherwiſe muſt be ſought for, and oftentimes in vain, over the whole globe.

In my opinion therefore ſtudying at acade-mies ought by no means to be neglected, but rather ſhould be looked on as neceſſary to thoſe, who are ambitious of attaining wiſdom, ſupported by experience. And thoſe who en-deavor

deavor to inftill into the minds of young people a contempt for univerfities, and to with-
draw the ftudious from thefe feats of learning,
fuggeft very pernicious advice; not confidering that in thefe ftorehoufes of knowledge
much greater, and more excellent things may
be attained by means of experience in a very
fhort fpace of time, than by the moft multifa-
rious, moft indefatigable, and moft extenfive
reading at home all one's life.

If i may be allowed to fpeak what is really
fact, this our univerfity may contend with any
foreign one whatever for true, and folid learning in all thofe parts of knowledge, which i
have enumerated, owing to our noble, and
exemplary inftitutions. For we begin to excell in botanical gardens, in hofpitals, in apparatus's for experimental philofophy, in ana-
tomical preparations, and other helps for arts
and fciences, and to excell fo much that we
are likely in time, by the blefling of the almighty, to be inferior to no univerfity.

Although fome univerfities excell others on
account of certain advantages peculiar to
themfelves; for in proportion as one kind of
knowledge in this, or that nation is held
in greater, or lefs efteem, and is therefore
more

more or lefs cultivated, fo the profeffors of
it will be more or lefs fkillful; as at this
time the hofpitals at London both for
number and goodnefs exceed all others, at
Paris chirurgical operations, at Leyden, ana-
tomical preparations, at Oxford botanical collections; tho', i fay, this may be the cafe, yet
i cannot think, that thofe act prudently, or
enough confult the good of themfelves, and
countrey, who feek for that abroad, which may
be had at home, and who travel to foreign univerfities, before they have laid a fufficient
foundation in their own countrey. And there
is no doubt but that they who do fo will at
laft repent of their error. He, who goes
abroad raw, and ignorant, feldom returns more
learned. Whereas, he, who has fpent his time
well at his own univerfity, will never find reafon to repent. Whoever has employed himfelf properly in the ftudy of the arts, and fciences will become an ufefull, and folid man in
every branch of bufinefs. Whoever, before he
fets out to vifit regions warmed by other funs,
has laid the firft foundations of his ftudies in
his native countrey, will be moft likely to bring
back materials of far greater price, than we
ufually fee amongft the greateft part of our

tra-

travellers, who feldom return home laden with
any thing, but fine founding, and empty words
collected out of the European languages. What
do they learn, but to prate about theatres, and
plays, and the modes of drefs amongft the Ita-
lians, the Spaniards, the Germans, and above
all the French? If they were well advifed they
would not ftir a foot out of their own countrey; that they might not deftroy their fortunes, their time, their health, nay their very
life itfelf by luxury, and voluptuoufnefs. They
would not then return, as too frequently happens, entirely ufelefs to themfelves, and countrey, and a burthen upon the face of the earth.
But whither am i hurried?

My defign was, in the little time allotted me,
to fpeak to you, gentlemen, not of the peculiar
advantages of univerfities, or of fojourning at
this, rather than any foreign one; but chiefly
of travelling in one's own countrey, thro' its
fields, and roads; a kind of travelling, i confefs, hitherto little ufed, and which is looked upon as fit only for amufement. I once more, moft
honorable auditors, beg your patience, and that
i may not forfeit all right to your favor, and
benevolence, i promife to be as fhort as poffible.
You know what the poet fays,

The

The farmer talks of graſſes and of grain,
The ſailor tells you ſtories of the main.
You ought not therefore to wonder, that i
chooſe to make travelling in one's own countrey the ſubject of my diſcourſe. Every one
thinks well of what belongs to himſelf, and
every one has pleaſures peculiar to himſelf. I
have travelled about, and paſſed over on foot
the froſty mountains of Lapland, have climbed up the craggy ridges of Norland, and wandered along its ſteep hills, and almoſt impe-
netrable woods. I have made large excurſions
into the foreſts of Dalecarlia, the groves of
Gothland, the heaths of Smoland, and the
unbounded plains of Scania. There is ſcarcely any conſiderable province of Sweden, which
i have not crawled thro' and examined; not
without great fatigue of body and mind. My
journey to Lapland was indeed an undertaking
of immenſe labor; and i muſt confeſs, that i
was forced to undergo more labor, and danger
in travelling thro' this one tract of the northern world, than thro' all thoſe forreign coun-
treys put together, which I have ever viſited;
tho' even theſe have coſt me no ſmall pains,
and have not a little exhauſted my vigor. But
love to truth, and gratitude towards the ſu-
preme

preme being oblige me to confefs, that no
fooner were my travels finifhed, but, as it were,
a Lethæan oblivion of all the dangers, and
difficulties came upon me ; being rewarded by
the ineftimable advantages, which i reaped
from thofe devious purfuits. Advantages, the
more confpicious for that i became daily more
and more fkillful, and gained a degree of experience, which I hope will be of ufe to myfelf, and others; and, what i efteem above all
other confiderations; as it comprehends in one
all other duties, and charities; to my countrey, and the public.

Good God! how many, ignorant of their
own countrey, run eagerly into forreign regions, to fearch out and admire whatever curiofities are to be found; many of which are
much inferior to thofe, which offer themfelves
to our eyes at home. I have yet beheld no
forreign land, that abounds more with natural
curiofities of all kinds, than our own. None
which prefents fo many, fo great, fo wonderfull works of nature; whether we confider the
magazines of fnow heaped up for fo many ages
upon our Alps, and amongft thefe vaft tracks
of fnow green meadows, and delicious vallies
here and there peeping forth, or the lofty
heads

heads of mountains, the craggy precipices of rocks, or the fun lying concealed from our eyes for fo many months, and thence a thick Cimmerian darknefs fpread over our hemifphere, or elfe at another feafon darting his rays continually along the horizon. The like to all which in kind, and degree, neither Holland, nor France, nor Britain, nor Germany, nor laftly any countrey in Europe can fhew; yet thither our youth greedy of novelty flock in troops. But it was not my intent to fpeak of thefe things at prefent. I come now clofer to my purpofe, being about to fhew by inftances, that the natural philofopher, the mineralogift, the botanift, the zoologift, the phyfician, the farmer, and all others, initiated in any part of natural knowledge, may find in travelling thro' our own countrey things, which they will own they never dreamed of before. Nay things which to this day were never difcovered by any perfon whatever. Laftly fuch things, as may not only gratify, and fatiate their curiofity; but may be of fervice to themfelves, their countrey, and all the world.

To give a few examples. The fagacious fearcher after nature will find here, wherewithall to fharpen, and exercife his attention in beholding

holding the top of mount Swucku, of so immenfe a height, that it reaches above the
clouds. The wonderfull ftructure of mount
Torfburg, the horrid precipices of the rock
Blakulla in an ifland of that name, fituated near
Oeland, and that prefents by its name, ftill
ufed among the Suegothic vulgar, no lefs than
by its difmal afpect, an idea of the ftupidity,
and fuperftition of that antient people.

Befides the wonderfull vaults, and caverns of
the Skiula mountains, the high plains of the
ifland Carolina, the unufual form and ftructure
of the Kierkerfian fountains in Oeland; to pafs
over numberlefs other ftrange works of nature,
the like to which perhaps are no where to be
met with.

Where can we have greater opportunities,
than in this Suegothic tract, of confidering the
intenfe rigor, and vehemence of winter, the
incredible marble-like ftrength of ice ? And
yet in this inclement climate grain of all forts
is obferved to fpring forth fooner, grow quicker, and ripen in lefs time than in any other part
of the world.*

* Vid. a treatife concerning the foliation of trees publifhed in this collection, and the prolegomena to the Flora
Lapponica of this author, where he fays that at Purkyaur
in Lapland anno 1732. barley fown May 31. was ripe
July 28. i. e. in 58 days; and rye fown May 31. was
ripe, and cut Aug. 5. i. e. in 66 days.

Whoever defires to contemplate the ftupendous metamorphofes of fea, and land, will
fcarcely find any where a more convenient opportunity, than in the fouth, and eaft parts of
Gothland; where the rock-giants, as they are
called, feem to threaten heaven, and where
the epocha's of time, the ages, the years, if
i may fo fay, are as it were carved out in a
furprifing feries upon the fea-fhore, and the
ground above the fhore.

The philofopher will find room to exercife
his ingenuity fufficiently in the Oeland-ftone,
by trying to difcover how to overcome its moift
nature, and quality; which whoever could ac-
complifh would do no fmall fervice to his
countrey, and above all would infinitely oblige
the inhabitants of that place.

I fhall fay no more than what is known, and
confeffed by all the world, when i fay that
there is no countrey in the habitable part of
the globe, where the mineralogift may make
greater progrefs in his art, than in this our
countrey. Let any one, that can, tell me, in
what regions, more rich, and ample mines of
metal are found, than in Sweden, and where
they dig deeper into the bowels of the earth
than here.

C   Let

Let the mines of Norburg, the ridge of Taburga, the pits of Dannemore, Bitſberg, Grengia, and laſtly the immenſe treaſures of Salbergen, and Fahluna be my witneſs, which exceed all in the known world.

Where do the poſſeſſors ſuffer forreigners more freely to approach their furnaces, and obſerve their operations? where are there men more ready to communicate their knowledge? Strangers are received by us with civility, and even preſſed to ſtay.

Who would not ſhudder on beholding thoſe forges, vomiting forth immenſe clouds of fire and ſmoak, where our iron ores are melted? who would not behold with pleaſure the ſimple countreyman in the thick pine-groves of Dalecarlia, without furnace, without any apparatus, extracting an iron ſo very ſo fit for uſe, that it yields to no other, tho' prepared with the fierceſt fires, and greateſt expence?

Who ten years ago would have imagined, that the *lapis calaminaris* was to be had in Dalecarlia? or mines of the very beſt kind of *gold* in Smolandia?

You will perhaps ſcarce believe me when i tell you, that there are whole mountains full of *petroleum* in Dalecarlia. Yet doubt not. This thing

thing hitherto unheard of, unfeen, i myfelf faw
with thefe eyes, and was furprifed.

We admire the abundance of *coral* on the
Indian fhores, yet the port of Capellus in
Gothland alone equals, nay exceeds thofe riches
of the eaft. I have feen deep ftrata of *corals* ex-
tending many furlongs, many miles along its
fhores.

Botanifts, who have travelled over the
greateft part of the globe in fearch of the treafures of the vegetable kingdom, have yet left
many plants for us and our pofterity to difcover in thefe our regions. For there is fcarce
any where a greater variety of *moffes*, *lichens*,
fuci, and *fungi*, than with us; and the moft
curious botanifts are now diligently employed
in contemplating thefe minute plants.

Whoever beheld, or defcribed our *diapen-
fia?* who the *blafia* unlefs Micheli alone?
Thefe two kinds of plants grow with us, and
the latter efpecially is found in great plenty
about Fahluna. What traveller, that is not
totally ignorant in botany, does not go from
Paris to Fontainebleau to fee thofe very rare
orchis's, fome of which reprefent helmets,
others knats, others flies; all of them fo exactly, fo wonderfully, that there feems nothing

C 2 want-

wanting to make them the very animals themfelves, but noife, and motion? Who imagined
thefe flowers grew in our countrey, and in fuch
plenty in Oeland, than they are to be met with
in every field?

Who would ever have thought of looking
in our countrey for the following exotics. The
winged pea, the *great burnet*, the *perennial let-*
tuce, the *dwarf carline thiftle*, the *middle flea-*
bane, the *black hellebore*, the Illyric *crowfcot*,
much lefs the *riccia*, and herb *terrible*, and
efpecially the *fcorpion fena*, that moft beautiful
fhrub, which in winter is carefully guarded
againft the frofts in the ftoves of our botanifts;
yet all thefe have lately been obferved to grow
in Oeland and Gothland.

We ufed to purchafe at a great price from
forreigners the following medicinal plants, *ver-*
vain, *moneywort*, &c. which all are natives of
Sweden, and yet ten years ago nobody knew
this.

What expences have we been at yearly to
get the *glafs-wort*, of whofe afhes and falt,
glafs is made. The *dyers weed* and *woad* were
purchafed yearly at a very high price; plants
that we have at laft found grow every where
about our provinces.

Lapland

Lapland alone furnifhed me fome time ago
with a hundred rare plants. I have gathered
lately as many in the iflands of the Baltic, and
in Scania as many more, never before obferved in Sweden. Nor can it be doubted,
but that our other provinces conceal in their
unfrequented corners other new plants, valuable for ufe or beauty, tho' hitherto overlooked, if a diligent and acute inquirer be
not wanting. I will not fay with the poet,
" Happy the rural inhabitant," but " happy
" the Swedifh inhabitant if he knew but what
" good he is poffeffed of [b]."

The zoologift will no where meet with a
place more delightful, and more fuitable to
his views, than that where flocks of all kinds
of birds in fpring time, and fummer, gather

[b] Our countrey has been fearched by fo many able botanifts
for plants, that what is faid here cannot be applied to us.
But a curious traveller might be of great fervice in relation
to plants even here, by obferving, and making generally
known what plants are peculiarly cultivated in fome countries. Thus for inftance they fow *lotus*, 13. Linn. *birds-
foot trefoil*, *Ray fyn.* 334. in Herefordfhire, which grows all
over England on dry paftures, and is found very good for
fheep, tho' every where elfe, as far as i know, neglected.
Again they make great ufe of the *common vetch* in Glo-
celterfhire, chiefly for horfes, feeding them with it upon
the fpot, and eating it up time enough for turneps the fame
year.

C 3   toge-

together to breed. This is the cafe in the woody, and mountainous parts of Sweden, more than in any other spot of the earth; the Lapland *plover* called *pago*, the Norland *pied chaffinch*, the Oeland *tringa* called *alwar-grim*, the Gothland *duck* called *eider*, the artic *duck* of he ifland Carolina called *torde*, the Ottenbyenfian *cobler's awl* called *fierfloecha*, the *picus tridactylus* of the Darlecarlians are all more rare in other countries than pheafants are with us. I may venture to affirm that no countrey upon the face of the earth abounds more with birds and infects, than Sweden. Wild *reindeer*, *flying fquirrels*, and the Norway *rat* that pours down in troops from the mountains into the plains below are unknown, and perhaps happily unknown, any where elfe.

Forreigners come into the Dalecarlian mountains to catch *falcons*, as is well known.

In the ifland Farô, fituated near Gothland, *whale* and *falmon* fifhery is very conveniently carried on, and no where with greater profit.

How many fpecies of fifhes furnifh our tables very common in Sweden, efpecially of the foftmouthed kind; fuch as the *afp*, the *wimba*, the *faren*, the *biorkna*, the *mudd*, and others,

others, unknown, undefcribed, unfeen in forreign countries. Who ever diffected, examined, defcribed thofe minute *red ferpents* called *afps*, or *æfpingar* by the fouthern Swedes,
whofe bite communicates a deadly poifon ?

It would be tedious were i to defcend to
the fpecies of infects. The great Reaumur,
who has fhewn a fagacity, and accuracy, before him unknown, in examining infects, upon feeing my collection of Swedifh infects
owned ingenuoufly, that my countrey alone
contained more fpecies of thofe animals, than
any other known in the world.

The curious diætetic, whofe bufinefs it is
to inquire into the various ways of living
among men, will fcarcely find any place,
where there are fo many different kinds of
food, as here. Here men vary in their food,
as they vary in fortune, fituation, and condition. And what is very remarkable, the inhabitants of this northern world have their
peculiar cuftoms, and rules of eating in every
province, and territory. In Lapland they
live without corn, or wine, without falt or
any made liquor. Water, and flefh, and preparations of thefe are their only fuftenance.

In fome places the countreyman lives in his fmoaky, and footy ftove on the ᶜ *coregonus* when ftinking; and bread made of the roots of the *calla*, or of the hufks, and beards of grain pounded.

In fome places they live upon ftinking *herring*, and *ropy* whey called *fyra*; in other places on a food called *affu*, and *artfau*, and ftinking *fiſh*; and yet they undergo much labor. In fome places their food is *turneps*, and their drink made of *juniper berries*. Some live upon *peas*, others on *buck wheat*, others grow fat upon *whale*'s flefh, to the aftonifhment of ftrangers.

In travelling thro' other countries you will hardly ever fee fo many different ways of living in this refpect, as in the Swedifh dominions, and where confequently the diætetic phiiofopher may have fo many opportunities of making his experiments.

The pathologift, who inquires into the caufes of diftempers, will not lofe his time in travelling into thefe countries; as in every dif-

---

ᶜ A general name of fifhes, fome fpecies of which are known in England and Wales, as the *fchelley*, the *grayling*, the *gwiniad*, &c. Vid. Artedi ichthyolog.

ferent

ferent province men are fubject to peculiar
difeafes, which arife in a great meafure from
the different kinds of food, that prevail among
them. He will no doubt hence be empower-
ed to affign the true caufes; why the Norlan-
der is infected with the fcurvy, and why the
Laplander on the contrary is free from it :
why the fame Laplander is fubject to thofe terrible gripes, called by them *ullem*; why the
Gothlander is chiefly afflicted with the hypo-
chondriacal colic; why the Weft-Bothnians,
who are more prolific than any other people
in our part of the world, lofe moft of their
children in the cradle; why fo many people
are liable to the epilepfy in the territory of
Verns, for the caufe is flight in appearance,
but very fingular in its nature.

Why almoft all the males in Orfobæa dye
of confumptions before the age of 30.

To enumerate all the things, which we have
particular opportunities of obferving in relation to thefe affairs in our countrey, would require no fhort treatife.

I am fully perfuaded that it is abfolutely neceffary for the young phyfician to travel thro'
his own countrey, were it only for this reafon, that relying upon his own ftrength he
might

might daily become more diligent, gain experience, without which there can be no skill in
physic, and bring the art which he professes
to some degree of perfection. For it happens
amongst us, and perhaps no where so frequently, that our common people have confidence in their physicians, and run in crouds
to consult any one, that is known to have taken
a doctor's degree; in other countries they will
scarcely trust a young physician with a favorite dog.

By following this course, and entering into
practice, the young physician will perceive,
whether medicines, oftentimes celebrated beyond all bounds of moderation, have that effect upon the patient, which we find mentioned in practical books. He will hear of many
domestic remedies, unknown elsewhere, in use
among the countrey people, that are looked
upon as specifics, and preferred to the most
costly prescriptions; for during the consulta-
tion, the patient may reveal the secret, if the
physician is prudent, and makes use of a
little art.

What are those famous exotic remedies
brought from either Indies, and purchased
at so great a price. v. g. *sarsaparilla*, a
spe-

species of *smilax, ipecacuanha,* a species of *honey-suckle, acmella,* a species of *hemp agrimony,* contrayerva of *dorstenia,* and *simoruba* of *pistacia,* which in some diseases are reckoned specifics? what are all these, I say, but remedies approved by long use amongst the vulgar? and are not innumerable remedies used among our own countrey people of the same nature? were not all those I have enumerated found out by [d] barbarians, and when experience had shewn, that they were useful, and efficacious in many diseases, were they not thought worthy to be communicated to the rest of mankind? Let our young physician then learn,

[d] Vid. *Vires plantarum Amœnitat. academ.* vol. i. p. 403. where Brunnerus is quoted for saying, that barbarians have done more towards the advancement of physic, than the learned of all ages. In the same passage the following words of Tournefort are quoted, *que tout le travail des hommes n'a encore rien produit de si assuré que deux ou trois drogues que les sauvages trouvent dans les bois.* The author subjoins to these quotations a list of twenty medicines with an &c. taken from barbarous nations, now used in our shops.

The curious reader may find in Dampier's voyages a very extraordinary instance of the skill of the savages of America in the chirurgical way. Wafer there gives an account of a cure performed upon himself by these people, and his testimony is the stronger, as he was a surgeon himself.

not to contemn, but accurately to remark thofe remedies, which are cried up amongft the common people. For he who boafts of knowing more of the virtues of fimples, than what ᵉ tafte, fmell, ᶠ fructification, and experiments will fuggeft, vehemently deceives, or is deceived.

Ye who intend one of thefe days to cultivate your native foil with advantage, and profit, may be affured that you will find nothing in all the books of hufbandry, that will be of fuch affiftance to you in that art, as travelling thro' the different provinces of this kingdom. In fome parts, and thofe the moft barren, you

---

ᵉ Vid. *Amænit. academ.* vol. 2. p. 371. in an exprefs treatife on this fubject the author quotes feveral eminent phyficians both ancient and modern, who maintained the fame opinion as to taftes. And vol. 3. p. 183. where the affiftance to be had from fmell is confidered, and the effects of odors amply treated on.

ᶠ Fructification. The reader perhaps may be at a lofs to underftand this. The meaning of it is, that plants which agree in the genus and even in the clafs agree alfo in their vertues. Thus the leaves of all the graffes are good for cattle, the leffer feeds for fmall birds, the greater for man, and this without exception. The ftellated plants of Ray are diuretic, the rough-leaved plants of the fame author are aftringent and vulnerary. Plants with a pea-flower are all wholefome for cattle and man, &c. Vid. a curious treatife on this fubject, in the *Academ.* vol. 1. p. 389.

will

will fee very confiderable crops produced by the force of fkill, and induftry. In others, tho' by nature extremely fertile, you will fcarcely fee any appearance of crops ; and the inhabitants live poorly, and in a miferable condition, merely from careleffnefs, and indolence. You may obferve how far the Cuprimontani exceed all others in the management of hay, and grafs, and the Gothlanders in relation to cattle, and particularly fheep.

You will have an opportunity of noting the different ways in different places of ploughing, manuring, harrowing, fowing, reaping, gathering, drying, and threfhing, from whence a prudent traveller may judge which way is beft.

It would be abfurd indeed to apply to our lands forreign methods of hufbandry in every particular, v. g. forreign grafs feed would not fucceed fo well as our own. Yet i will venture to fay one could fcarcely travel a day in any of our countries without learning fomething of ufe in œconomy. Many things that will occur, may appear trifling at firft fight, which yet upon a more mature confideration, you will own may be turned to very great advantage ; fuch as the various ways of cloathing, preparing vic-
tuals,

tuals, feeding cattle, not to mention the marí-
ners, commerce and numberlefs other particulars.

Laftly, however neceffary and incumbent
upon us it may be to take a view of our countrey, it will be in vain to undergo this trouble,
if we do not lay the foundation of our ftudies
at the univerfity, as to natural philofophy,
natural, and medical hiftory; without which
preparation for travelling to advantage every
thing that occurs, will appear trite, common,
and not worth our attention. The traveller
however, above all men, ought to keep in
mind that famous principle of Defcartes, viz.
to doubt about every thing. He muft alfo be
very cautious not to fuffer his mind, from too
eager a defire of knowledge, to be overwhelmed at the beginning by the number of
things to be obferved [e]. * * * * * *
* * * * * * * * * * * *

We ought to travel in the flower of our age,
while the mind, and body are in vigor, while
our ftrength is unimpaired, and alacrity at its
height; before a family, houfhold affairs,

---

[e] Here follow fome few lines in the original, which not
underftanding i have omitted.

and

and conjugal tyes have engroffed our affections.

When by this method you have laid the firft
foundation of travelling in your own countrey,
you will then be qualified to go farther, and
become ferviceable to yourfelves, and the public, by learning thofe things abroad, which
could not be learned at home ; and thus, having made a fair examination, you may be enabled to judge, whether our own cuftons may
be improved by the help or forreign ones, and
how far ; and thus you will not be apt rafhly
to imagine, that every fafhion which prevails
at Paris, is fit to be introduced into our cottages ; laftly, thus you will not be better acquainted with the manners and cuftoms in
France, England, Germany, and other countries, than with thofe of your own ; .i. e. you
will not, as the proverb fays, for want of common fenfe,

Invert all order, and become

Lynxes abroad, mere moles at home.

But not to abufe your patience any longer,
i here break off the thread of my difcourfe,
that what time remains may be employed by
me in expreffing my wifhes and thanks. Firft,
to thee, O omnipotent God, i humbly offer

up

up my thankſgiving, for the immenſe benefits,
that have been heaped upon me thro' thy gra-
cious protection, and providence. Thou from
my youth upwards haſt ſo led me by the hand,
haſt ſo directed my footſteps, that i have grown
up in the ſimplicity, and innocence of life,
and in the moſt ardent purſuit after knowledge. I give thee thanks for that thou haſt
ever preſerved me in all my journies thro' my
native and forreign countries, amidſt ſo many
dangers, that ſurrounded me on every ſide.
That in the reſt of my life, amidſt the heavieſt
burthens of poverty, and other inconveniences,
thou waſt always preſent to ſupport me with thy
almighty aſſiſtance. Laſtly that amidſt ſo many
viciſſitudes of fortune, to which I have been
expoſed, amongſt all the goods, i ſay, and evils,
the joyfull and gloomy, the pleaſing, and diſ-
agreeable circumſtances of life, thou endow-
edſt me with an equal, conſtant, manly, and
ſuperior ſpirit on every occaſion.

   To our moſt auguſt, and potent prince Fre-
derick the firſt, as becomes a dutifull, and obe-
dient ſubject, i give moſt humble thanks for
his favorable kindneſs in beſtowing upon me
this honorable poſt. May the almighty grant,
that his majeſty, and his moſt ſerene conſort,

                                      thoſe

thofe fhining ftars of the north, may long, very long illuminate, and adorn this region with the brightnefs of their rays.

To thee, moft mighty count Gyllenbourg, illuftrious chancellor of this univerfity, to thee, though abfent, i return the moft fincere, and humble thanks for the great, and even endlefs benefits beftowed upon me; amongft which, exceeding all number, this muft not be reckoned the leaft, that, when I was called hither by this academy, you recommended me in the moft indulgent manner to our great monarch. It fhall be my conftant care that you may never repent of this favor, and by reverence, refpeft, and duty, to teftify my gratitude to my lateft breath.

To the moft reverend the archbifhop, to the vice-chancellor, to the magnificent rector, and to you illuftrious and celebrated profeffors, i return alfo moft grateful acknowledgments, who honored me by your unanimous votes, and affifted in bringing me to this chair. As th's your benevolence laid me under the greateft obligation to you, to employ every office of regard and friendfhip towards you, fo by the grace of God i fhall omit no opportunity of fhewing i am not unworthy of your favor.

D   Whilft

Whilft i am thus employed in teftifying the feelings of a grateful mind, i ought not to forget your name, moft illuftrious Roberg, my -predeceffor highly worthy of the utmoft veneration. As i am one of thofe who have had the happinefs of being educated in your fchool, i fhould be the moft ungratefull of men, if i were ever to fuffer the remembrance of fuch a benefit to flip out of my mind.

It has been your lot, venerable fir, to furvive all your brethren; and you may juftly boaft, what every phyfician now in Sweden will gratefully confefs, that to you, as to their faithful inftructor, they owe the beginning, the increafe, and the finifhing of their art. Nay not only the faculty at Upfal, but the whole circle here prefent ought to falute, and reverence you as fuperior to them all in age.

Suffer then at laft your difciple to eafe you of that burthen, which for forty years, and more, you have fuftained, with honor; that now, time having laid his heavy hand upon you, you may enjoy that reft, which his facred majefty has kindly granted to your wifhes. My fincere prayers are not wanting to the almighty, that he may grant you a chearfull, and vigorous old age, and that
every

every thing may fucceed to the utmoft of your defires.

Nor is it fit, ye florifhing and chofen youth, that on this folemn occafion i fhould pafs you over in filence. I have been long fenfible of your regard for me, by many, and undoubted proofs; i have been long fenfible, i fay, and i gratefullyacknowledge it. Many of you defired, ardently defired to have me in this ftation, though perhaps never feen by you before. For this alone, i know, i am called hither, that i may be ufeful to you. On you therefore my fortune turns. My induftry, my ftudies, my labors, my watchings, i willingly, and chearfully confecrate to your fervice, and by the affiftance of God, i will exert the utmoft of my power to fatisfy your expectations, that you may not be difappointed in the hopes you have conceived of me.

D 2   THE

THE
OECONOMY
OF
NATURE.

THE
OECONOMY
OF
NATURE.

BY
ISAAC J. BIBERG.

Upsal, 1749. *March* 4.

Amænitat. Academ. vol. ii.

Æternæ funt vices rerum. Sen. nat. 3. 1.

§. I.

BY the Œconomy of Nature we underſtand the all-wiſe diſpoſition of the Creator in relation to natural things, by which they are fitted to produce general ends, and reciprocal uſes.

All things contained in the compaſs of the univerſe declare, as it were, with one accord the infinite wiſdom of the Creator. For whatever ſtrikes our ſenſes, whatever is the objeƈt

D 4   of

of our thoughts, are fo contrived, that they concur to make manifeft the divine glory, i. e. the ultimate end which God propofed in all his works. Whoever duly turns his attention to the things on this our terraqueous globe, muft neceffarily confefs, that they are fo connected, fo chained together, that they all aim at the fame end, and to this end a vaft number of intermediate ends are fubfervient. But as the intent of this treatife will not fuffer me to confider them all, i fhall at prefent only take notice of fuch as relate to the prefervation of natural things, In order therefore to perpetuate the eftablifhed courfe of nature in a continued feries, the divine wifdom·has thought fit, that all living creatures fhould conftantly be employed in producing individuals; that all natural things fhould contribute and lend a helping hand to preferve every fpecies; and laftly, that the death and deftruction of one thing fhould always be fubfervient to the reftitution of another. It feems to me that a greater fubject than this cannot be found, nor one on which laborious men may more worthily employ their induftry, or men of genius their penetration.

I am

I am very fenfible, being confcious of my own weaknefs, how vaft and difficult a fubject it is, and how unable i am to treat it as it deferves; a fubject which would be too great a tafk for the ability of the moft experienced and fagacious men, and which properly performed would furnifh materials for large volumes, My defign therefore is only to give a fummary view of it, and to fet forth to the learned world, as far as i am able, whatever curious, worthy to be known, and not obvious to every obferver occurs in the triple kingdom of nature. Thus if what the induftry of others fhall in future times difcover in this way be added to thefe obfervations, it is to be hoped, that a common ftock may thence grow, and come to be of fome importance. But before i examine thefe three kingdoms of nature, it will not, i think, be amifs to fay fomething concerning the earth in general, and its changes.

§. 2.

The world, or the terraqueous globe, which we inhabit, is every where furrounded with elements, and contains in its fuperficies the three kingdoms of nature, as they are called; the *fof-*
fil,

fil, which conftitutes the cruft of the earth, tho *vegetable*, which adorns the face of it, and draws the greateft part of its nourifhment from the *foffil* kingdom, and the *animal*, which is fuftained by the *vegetable* kingdom. Thus thefe three kingdoms cover, adorn and vary the fuperficies of our earth. It is not my defign to make any inquiry concerning the center of the terraqueous globe. He, who likes hypothefes, may confult Defcartes, Helmont, Kircher, and others. My bufinefs is to confider the external parts of it only, and whatever is obvious to the eye.

As to the *ftrata* of the earth and mountains, as far as we have hitherto been able to difcover, the upper parts confift of *rag-ftone*, the next of *ftate*, the third of *marble* filled with petrifactions, the fourth again with *ftate*, and laftly the loweft of *free-ftone*. The habitable part of the earth, though it is fcooped into various inequalities, yet is every where high in comparifon with the water, and the farther it is from the fea, it is generally higher. Thus the waters in the lower places are not at reft, unlefs fome obftacle confines them, and by that means form lakes, and marfhes.

The fea furrounds the continent, and takes up the greateft part of the earth's fuperficies,

as

as geography informs us. Nay, that it once spread over much the greateſt part, we may be convinced by its yearly decreaſe, by the rubbiſh left by the tides, by *ſhells, ſtrata,* and other circumſtances.

The ſea-ſhores are uſually full of dead teſtaceous animals, wrack, and ſuch like bodies, which are yearly thrown out of the ſea. They are alſo covered with ſand of various kinds, ſtones, and heaps of other things not very common. It happens moreover, that while the more rapid rivers ruſh through narrow vallies, they wear away the ſides, and thus the friable, and ſoft earth falls in, and its ruins are carried to diſtant, and winding ſhores; whence it is certain, that the continent gains no ſmall increaſe, as the ſea ſubſides.

The clouds collected from exhalations, chiefly from the ſea, but likewiſe from other waters, and moiſt grounds, and condenſed in the lower regions of the atmoſphere, ſupply the earth with rain; but ſince they are attracted by the mountainous parts of the earth, it neceſſarily follows, that thoſe parts muſt have, as is fit, a larger ſhare of water than the reſt. Springs, which generally ruſh out at the foot of mountains, take their riſe from

this

this very rain water, and vapours condenfed, that trickle through the holes, and interftices of loofe bodies, and are received into caverns.

Thefe afford a pure water purged by ftraining, which rarely dry up in fummer, or freeze in winter, fo that animals never want a wholefome and refrefhing liquor.

The chief fources of rivers are fountains, and rills growing by gradual fupplies into ftill larger and larger ftreams, till at laft, after the conflux of a vaft number of them, they find no ftop, but falling into the fea with leffened rapidity, they there depofit the united ftores they have gathered, along with foreign matter, and fuch earthy fubftances, as they tore off in their way. Thus the water returns in a circle, whence it firft drew its origin, that it may act over the fame fcene again.

Marfhes arifing from water retained in low grounds are filled with moffy tumps, which are brought down by the water from the higher parts, or are produced by putrifyed plants.

We often fee new meadows arife from marfhes dryed up. This happens fooner when the ᵍ _fphagnum_ F. S. 864.* has laid a founda-

ᵉ A kind of mofs.

* This refers to the firft Edition of the _Flora Suecica_. It is 958 in the fecond Edition.

tion;

tion; for this in procefs of time changes into a very porous mould, till almoft the whole marfh is filled with it. After that the *rufh* ftrikes root, and along with the *cotton graffes* conftitutes a turf, raifed in fuch a manner, that the roots get continually higher, and thus lay a more firm foundation for other plants, till the whole marfh is changed into a fine and de-lightfull meadow; efpecially if the water hap-pens to work itfelf a new paffage.

Hillocks, that abound in low grounds, oc-cafion the earth to increafe yearly, more than the countreyman would wifh, and feem to do hurt: but in this the great induftry of nature deferves to be taken notice of. For by this means the barren fpots become fooner rich meadow, and pafture land. Thefe hillocks are formed by the ant, by ftones, and roots, and the trampling of cattle; but the principal caufe is the force of the winter cold, which in the fpring raifes the roots of plants fo high above the ground, that being expofed to the air they grow, and perifh; after which the *golden maidenhairs* fill the vacant places.

Mountains, hills, vallies, and all the ine-qualities of the earth, though fome think they take away much from its beauty, are fo far

4   from

from producing fuch an effect, that on the contrary they give a more pleafing afpect, as well as great advantages. For thus the terreftrial fuperficies is larger; different kinds of plants thrive better, and are more eafily watered, and the rain-waters run in continual ftreams into the fea, not to mention many other ufes in relation to winds, heat and cold. Alps are the higheft mountains, that reach to the fecond region of the air, where trees cannot grow erect. The higher thefe Alps are, the colder they are *cæteris paribus*. Hence the Alps in Sweden, Siberia, Swifferland, Peru, Brafil, Armenia, Afia, Africa, are perpetually covered with fnow; which becomes almoft as hard as ice. But, if by chance the fummer heats be greater than ordinary, fome part of thefe ftores melts, and runs through rivers into the lower regions; which by this means are much refrefhed.

It is fcarcely to be doubted, but that the rocks and ftones difperfed over the globe were formed originally in, and from the earth; but when torrents of rain have foftened, as they eafily do, the foluble earth, and carried it down into the lower parts, we imagine it happens that thefe folid, and heavy bodies, being

laid

laid bare, ftick out above the furface. We might alfo take notice of the wonderfull effects of the tide, fuch as we fee happen from time to time on the fea-fhore, which being daily and nightly affaulted with repeated blows, at length gives way, and breaks off. Hence we fee in moft places the rubbifh of the fea, and fhores.

The winter by its froft prepares the earth, and mould, which thence are broken into very minute particles, and thus, being put into a mouldering ftate, become more fit for the nourifhment of plants; nay by its fnow it covers the feeds, and roots of plants, and thus by cold defends them from the force of cold. I muft add alfo that the piercing froft of the winter purifies the atmofphere, and putrid waters, and makes them more wholefome for animals.

The perpetual fucceffion of heat and cold with us renders the fummers more pleafing; and though the winter deprives us of many plants, and animals, yet the perpetual fummer within the tropics is not much more agreeable, as it often deftroys men, and other animals by its immoderate heat; though it muft be con-

feffed

fcffed that thofe regions abound with moft exquifite fruits. Our winters, though very troublefome to a great part of the globe, on account of their vehement, and intenfe cold, yet are lefs hurtfull to the inhabitants of the northern parts, as experience teftifies. Hence it happens, that we may live very conveniently on every part of the earth, as every different countrey has different advantages from nature.

The feafons, like every thing elfe, have their viciffitudes, their beginnings, their progrefs, and their end.

The age of man begins from the cradle, pleafing childhood fucceeds, then active youth, afterwards manhood firm, fevere and intent upon felf-prefervation, laftly old age creeps on, debilitates, and at length totally deftroys our tottering bodies.

The feafons of the year proceed in the fame way. Spring, the jovial, playfull infancy of all living creatures, reprefents childhood and youth ; for then plants fpread forth their luxuriant flowers, fifhes exult, birds fing, every part of nature is intent upon generation. The fummer, like middle age, exhibits plants, and trees every where cloathed with green ; it

gives

gives vigor to animals, and plumps them up, fruits then ripen, meadows look cheerfull, every thing is full of life. On the contrary autumn is gloomy, for then the leaves of trees begin to fall, plants to wither, infects to grow torpid, and many animals to retire to their winter quarters. The day proceeds with juft fuch fteps, as the year. The morning makes every thing alert, and fit for bufinefs ; the fun pours forth his ruddy rays, the flowers which had, as it were, flept all night, awake and expand themfelves again; the birds with their fonorous voices, and various notes make the woods ring, meet together in flocks, and facrifice to Venus. Noon tempts animals into the fields, and paftures ; the heat puts them upon indulging their eafe, and even neceffity obliges them to it. Evening follows, and makes every thing more fluggifh ; flowers fhut up, [h] and animals retire to their lurking

---

[h] Of fuch flowers as fleep by night fome account is given by Linnæus in Philof. Botan. p. 88. where the curious may alfo find p. 274. a lift of plant, one or other of which fhut their flowers at every hour of the day without regard to the weather. One plant is fo remarkable for this property, that it is generally known in our countrey by the name of go-to-bed-at-noon. Its botanical name is tragopogon or goat's-beard. See a Differtation in the Amæn. acad. vol. 4. where this fubject is treated at large.

E

places.

places. Thus the spring, the morning, and youth are proper for generation; the summer, noon, and manhood are proper for preservation; and autumn, evening, and old age are not unfitly likened to destruction.

§. 3.
The fossil kingdom.
Propagation.

It is agreed on all hands, that stones are not organical bodies, like plants, and animals; and therefore it is as clear that they are not produced from an egg, like the tribes of the other kingdoms. Hence the variety of fossils is proportionate to the different combinations of coalescent particles, and hence the species in the fossil kingdom are not so distinct, as in the other two. Hence also the laws of generation in relation to fossils have been in all ages extremely difficult to explain; and lastly hence have arisen so many different opinions about them, that it would be endless to enumerate them all. We therefore for the present will content ourselves with giving a very few observations on this subject.

That

That clay is the fediment of the fea is fufficiently proved by obfervation, for which reafon it is generally found in great plenty along
the coafts.

The journals of feamen clearly evince, that
a very minute fand covers the bottom of the
fea, nor can it be doubted, but that it is daily
cryftallifed out of the water.

It is now acknowledged by all, that teftaceous bodies and petrifactions refembling
plants were once real animals or vegetables ; [i]
and it feems likely that fhells being of a calcareous nature have changed the adjacent clay,
fand, or mould into the fame kind of fubftance.
Hence we may be certain that marble may be
generated from petrifactions, and therefore it
is frequently feen full of them.

Rag-ftone the moft common matter of our
rocks appears to be formed from a fandy kind
of clay, but this happens more frequently,
where the earth is impregnated with iron.

Freeftone is the product of fand, and the
deeper the bed, where it is found, the more
compact it becomes ; and the more denfe the

---

[i] I have taken the liberty not to follow the original
text in this place. The learned will fee the reafon at firft
fight.

fand,

fand, the more eafily it concretes. But if an *alcaline* clay chances to be mixed with the fand, the *freeftone* is generated more readily, as in the *freeftone* called *cos friatilis, particulis argillo-glarenfis*, S. N. 1. 1.

The *flint*, S. N. 3. 1. is almoft the only kind of *ftone*, certainly the moft common in *chalky* mountains. It feems therefore to be produced from *chalk*. Whether it can be reduced again to *chalk*, i leave to others to inquire.

Stalactites, S. N. 33. 1. or *drop-ftone* is compofed of calcareous particles, adhering to a dry and generally a vegetable body.

The incruftations S. N. 32. 5, 6, 7, 8. are often generated, where a vitriolic water connects claiey and earthy particles together.

Slate by the vegetables, that are often inclofed in it, feems to take its origin from a marfhy mould.

Metals vary according to the nature of the matrix, to which they adhere, e. g. the *pyrites cupri Fahlunenfis* contains frequently *fulphur, arfenic, iron, copper,* a little *gold, vitriol, alum,* fometimes *lead ore, filver* and *zinck.* Thus *gold, copper, iron, zinck, arfenic, pyrites, vitriol* come out of the fame vein. That very rich *iron* ore at Normark in Vermelandia, where

4   it

it was cut tranfverfly by a vein of clay, was changed into a pure *filver*. The number therefore of fpecies, and varieties of *foffils*, each ferving for different purpofes, according to their different natures, will be in proportion, as the different kinds of earths and *ftones* are varioufly combined.

§. 4.

Prefervation.

As *foffils* are deftitute of life, and organifation, are hard, and not obnoxious to putrefaction; fo they laft longer, than any other kind of bodies. How far the air contributes to this duration it is eafy to perceive, fince air hardens many *ftones* upon the fuperficies of the earth, and makes them more folid, compact, and able to refift the injuries of time. Thus it is known from vulgar obfervation that *lime*, that has been long expofed to the air, becomes hardened. The *chalky marl*, which they ufe in Flanders for building houfes, as long as it continues in the quarry, is friable; but when dug up and expofed to the air, it grows gradually harder. In the fame way our old walls, and towers gain a firmnefs in procefs of time,

E 3 and

and therefore it is a vulgar miftake, that our anceftors excelled the modern architects in the art of building as to this point [k].

However ignorant we may be of the caufe, why large rocks are every where to be feen fplit, whence vaft fragments are frequently torn off; yet this we may obferve, that fiffures are clofed up by water, that gets between them, and is detained there; and are confolidated by *cryftal* and *fpar*. Hence we fcarcely ever find *cryftal*, but in thofe *ftones*, which have for fome time in its chinks water loaded with ftony particles. In the fame manner *cryftals* fill the cavities in mines, and concrete into *quartz* or a debafed *cryftal*.

It is manifeft that *ftones* are not only generated, augmented, and changed perpetually

[k] Too great ftrefs ought not, I think, to be laid on this obfervation of our author, though it may be in part true; for without fuppofing that our anceftors had more fkill in building, we may fuppofe, what was likely to be the cafe, that they ufed more care in the choice of their materials, and had them wrought up with more labor; which muft add confiderably to the firmnefs of the cement. Where thefe circumftances have happened to be wanting, time alone has not been able to produce the fame effect. I have feen a houfe about fourfcore years old, where one might rub out the mortar from between the bricks without fcarcely ufing any force.

from

from incruftations brought upon mofs, but are alfo increafed by *cryftal* and *fpar*. Not to mention that the adjacent earth, efpecially if it be impregnated with iron particles, is commonly changed into a folid *ftone*.

It is faid, that the *marble quarries* in Italy, from whence fragments are cut, grow up again. *Ores* grow by little and little, whenever the mineral particles, conveyed by the means of water through the clefts of mountains, are retained there; fo that adhering to the homogeneous matter a long while, at laft they take its nature, and are changed into a fimilar fubftance.

§. 5.

Deftruction.

Foffils, although they are the hardeft of bodies, yet are found fubject to the laws of deftruction, as well as all other created fubftances. For they are diffolved in various ways by the elements exerting their force upon them, as by water, air and the folar rays, as alfo by the rapidity of rivers, violence of cataracts, and eddies which continually beat upon and at laft reduce to powder the hardeft *rocks*. The agi-

E 4 tations

tations of the fea, and lakes, and the vehemence of the waves, excited by turbulent
winds pulverife *ftones*, as evidently appears by
their roundnefs along the fhore. Nay as the
poet fays,

The hardeft ftone infenfibly gives way
To the foft drops, that frequent on it play.

So that we ought not to wonder, that thefe
very hard bodies moulder away into powder,
and are obnoxious like others to the confum-
ing tooth of time.

Sand is formed of *freeftone*, which is deftroyed partly by froft, making it friable,
partly by the agitation of water, and waves;
which eafily wear away, diffolve, and reduce
into minute particles, what the froft had made
friable.

Chalk is formed of rough *marble*, which the
air, the fun, and the winds have diffolved, as
appears by Iter. Goth. 170.

The *flate* earth or *humus fchifti* Syf. Nat. 511.
owes its origin to *flate*, diffolved by the air,
rain and fnow.

Ochre is formed of metals diffolved, whofe
fæces prefent the very fame colours, which
we always find the *ore* tinged with, when
expofed to the air. *Vitriol* in the fame

man-

manner mixes with water from *ores* deftroyed.

The *muria faxatilis* Syf. Nat. 14. 6. a kind
of talky ftone yielding falt in the parts that
are turned to the fun, is diffolved into fand,
which falls by little and little upon the earth,
till the whole is confumed; not to mention
other kinds of *foffils*. Laftly from thefe there
arife new *foffils*, as we mentioned before, fo
that the deftruction of one thing ferves for
the generation of another.

Teftaceous worms ought not to be paffed over
on this occafion, for they eat away the hardeft
rocks. That fpecies of *fhell fifh* called the *razor
fhell* bores thro' ftones in Italy, and hides itfelf
within them; fo that the people who eat
them are obliged to break the ftones, before
they can come at them. The *cochlea* F. S.
1299. a kind of *fnail* that lives on craggy
rocks, eats, and bores through the chalky
hills, as worms do through wood. This is
made evident by the obfervations of the celebrated de Geer.

§. 6.

§. 6.

The Vegetable Kingdom,

Propagation.

Anatomy abundantly proves, that all *plants* are *organic*, and living bodies; and that all *organic* bodies are propagated from an egg has been fufficiently demonſtrated by the induſtry of the moderns. We therefore the rather, according to the opinion of the ſkilfull, rejeċt the æquivocal generation of *plants*; and the more ſo, as it is certain that every living thing is produced from an egg. Now the ſeeds of *vegetables* are called eggs; thefe are different in every different *plant*, that the means being the fame, each may multiply its ſpecies, and produce an offspring like its parent. We do not deny, that very many *plants* puſh forth from their roots freſh offsets for two or more years. Nay not a few *plants* may be propagated by branches, buds, fuckers and leaves fixed in the ground, as likewife many trees. Hence their ſtems being divided into branches, may be looked on as roots above ground; for in the fame way the roots creep under ground;

and

and divide into branches. And there is the more reason for thinking so, because we know that a tree will grow in an inverted situation, viz. the roots being placed upwards, and the head downwards, and buried in the ground; for then the branches will become roots, and the roots will produce leaves, and flowers. The *lime-tree* will serve for an example, on which gardeners have chiefly made the experiment. Yet this by no means overturns the doctrine, that all *vegetables* are propagated by seeds; since it is clear that in each of the foregoing instances nothing vegetates but what was part of a plant, formerly produced from seed, so that, accurately speaking, without seed no new *plant* is produced.

Thus again *plants* produce seeds, but they are entirely unfit for propagation, unless fœcundation precedes, which is performed by an intercourse between different sexes, as experience testifies. *Plants* therefore must be provided with *organs* of generation; in which respect they hold an analogy with *animals*. Since in every *plant* the flower always precedes the fruit, and the fœcundated seeds visibly arise from the fruit; it is evident that the *organs* of generation are contained in the flower, which

which *organs* are called *antheræ*, and *ſtigmata*,
and that the impregnation is accompliſhed
within the flower. This impregnation is performed by means of the duſt of the *antheræ*
falling upon the moiſt *ſtigmata*, where the duſt
adheres, is burſt, and ſends forth a very ſub-
tle matter, which is abſorbed by the *ſtyle*, and
is conveyed down to the rudiment of the ſeed,
and thus renders it fertile. When this opera-
tion is over, the *organs* of generation wither
and fall, nay a change in the whole flower en-
ſues. We muſt however obſerve, that in the
vegetable kingdom one, and the ſame flower does
not always contain the *organs* of generation of
both ſexes, but oftentimes the male *organs* are
on one *plant*, and the female on another. But
that the buſineſs of impregnation may go on
ſucceſsfully, and that no plant may be deprived of the neceſſary duſt, the whole moſt
elegant *apparatus* of the *antheræ* and *ſtigmata*
in every flower is contrived with wonderful
wiſdom.

    For in moſt flowers the *ſtamina* ſurround
the *piſtills*, and are about the ſame height;
but there are many *plants*, in which the *piſtill* is longer than the *ſtamina*, and in theſe
it is wonderfull to obſerve, that the Creator

                                                    has

has made the flowers recline, in order that the duſt may more eaſily fall into the *ſtigma*, e. g. in the *campanula*, *cowſlip* [1], &c. But when the fœcundation is compleated the flowers riſe again, that the ſeeds may not fall out before they are ripe, at which time they are diſperſed by the winds. In other flowers on the contrary the *piſtill* is ſhorter, and there the flowers preſerve an erect ſituation, nay when the flowering comes on they become erect; tho' before they were drooping, or immerſed under water. Laſtly, whenever the male flowers are placed below the female ones, the leaves are exceedingly ſmall, and narrow, that they may not hinder the duſt from flying upwards, like ſmoak; as we ſee in the *pine*, *fir*, *yew*, *ſea-grape*, *juniper*, *cy-preſs*, &c. and when in one and the ſame ſpecies one plant is male, and the other female, and conſequently may be far from one another, there the duſt, without which there is no impregnation, is carried in abundance by the help

[1] This curious phænomenon did not eſcape the poetical eye of Milton, who was ſo very much ſtruck with the beauty of it, that he thought it worth deſcribing in the following enlivened imagery,

With cowſlips *wan that hang the penſive head.*

of

of the wind from the male to the female; as in the whole *dioicous* [m] clafs. Again a more difficult impregnation is compenfated by the longævity of the individuals, and the continuation of life by buds, fuckers and roots, fo that we may obferve every thing moft wifely difpofed in this affair. Moreover we cannot without admiration obferve that moft flowers expand themfelves when the fun fhines forth, whereas when clouds, rain, or the evening comes on, they clofe up, left the genital duft fhould be coagulated, or rendered ufelefs, fo that it cannot be conveyed to the *ftigmata*. But what is ftill more remarkable and wonderfull! when the fœcundation is over, the flowers neither upon fhowers, nor evening coming on clofe themfelves up. Hence when rain falls in the flowering time, the hufbandman and gardener foretell a fcarcity of fruits. I could and would iluftrate all this by many remarkable inftances, if the fame fubject had not lately been explained, in this very place [n] in a manner equal to its

[m] i.e. where one plant bears male flowers, and the other female ones.

[n] I fuppofe the author here alludes to a treatife publifhed in Amœn. academ. vol. 1. entitled, *Sponfalia plantarum*, in which are contained fo many proofs of the reality of the different fexes of plants, that to me there feems to remain no room for doubt.

im-

importance. I cannot help remarking one particular more, viz. that the organs of generation, which in the animal kingdom are by nature generally removed from fight, in the vegetable are expofed to the eyes of all, and that when their nuptials are celebrated, it is wonderfull what delight they afford to the fpectator by their moft beautiful colours and delicious odors. At this time bees, flies, and other infects fuck honey out of their nectaries, not to mention the humming bird; and that from their effete duft the bees gather wax.

§. 7.

As to the diffemination of feeds, after they come to maturity, it being abfolutely neceffary; fince without it no crop could follow; the Author of nature has wifely provided for this affair in numberlefs ways. The ftalks and ftems favor this purpofe, for thefe raife the fruit above the ground, that the winds, fhaking them to and fro, may difperfe far off the ripe feeds. Moft of the [n] *pericarps* are fhut at

---

[n] Whatever furrounds the feeds is called by botanical writers a *pericarpium*, and as we want an Englifh word to exprefs this, i have taken the liberty to call it a pericarpy.

top,

top, that the feeds may not fall, before they are ſhook out by ſtormy winds. Wings are given to many *feeds*, by the help of which they fly far from the mother plant, and oftentimes ſpread over a whole countrey. Theſe wings conſiſt either of a down, as in moſt of the compoſite flowered plants, or of a membrane, as in the *birch*, *alder*, *aſh*, &c. Hence *woods*, which happen to be conſumed by fire, or any other accident, will ſoon be reſtored again by new plants, diſſeminated by this means. Many kinds of fruits are endued with a remarkable elaſticity, by the force of which, the ripe *pericarps* throw the *feeds* to a great diſtance, as the *wood-forrel*, the *fpurge*, the *phyllanthus*, the *dittany*. Other *feeds* or *pericarps* are rough, or provided with hooks; ſo that they are apt to ſtick to animals, that paſs by them, and by this means are carried to their holes where they are both ſown, and manured by nature's wonderfull care ; and therefore the plants of theſe *feeds* grow, where others will not, as *hounds-tongue*, *agrimony*, &c.

Berries and other *pericarps*, are by nature allotted for aliment to animals, but with this condition, that while they eat the pulp they ſhall ſow their *feeds* ; for when they feed upon

it

it they either difperfe them at the fame time, or, if they fwallow them, they are returned with intereft; for they always come out unhurt. It is not therefore furprifing, that if a field be manured with recent mud or dung not quite rotten, various other plants, injurious to the farmer, fhould come up along with the grain, that is fowed. Many have believed that *barley*, or *rye* has been changed into *oats*, altho' all fuch kinds of metamorphofes are repugnant to the laws of generation, not confidering that there is another caufe of this phæ-nomenon, viz. that the ground perhaps has been manured with horfe-dung, in which the *feeds* of *oats*, coming entire from the horfe, lye hid and produce that grain. The *mifletoe* always grows upon other trees, becaufe the thrufh that eats the feeds of it, cafts them forth with its dung, and as bird-catchers make their bird-lime of this fame plant, and daub the branches of trees with it, in order to catch the thrufh, the proverb hence took its rife;

The thrufh, when he befouls the bough,
Sows for himfelf the feeds of woe.

It is not to be doubted, but that the greateft part of the *junipers* alfo, that fill our woods,

F   are

are fown by thrufhes, and other birds in the
fame manner; as the berries, being heavy,
cannot be difperfed far by the winds. The
crofs-bill that lives on the fir-cones, and the
hawfinch that feeds on the pine-cones, at the
fame time fow many of their *feeds*, efpecially
when they carry the *cone* to a ftone, or trunk
of a tree, that they more eafily ftrip it of its
fcales. Swine likewife, by turning up the
earth, and moles by throwing up hillocks,
prepare the ground for feeds in the fame manner, as the ploughman does.

I pafs over many other things, which might
be mentioned concerning the fea, lakes, and
rivers, by the help of which oftentimes *feeds*
are conveyed unhurt to diftant countries ; nor
need I mention in what a variety of other
ways nature provides for the diffemination of
plants, as this fubject has been treated on at
large in our illuftrious prefident's oration concerning the augmentation of the habitable
earth. ᵖ

§. 8.

ᵖ As there is fomething very ingenious, and quite new
in the treatife here referred to, i will for the fake of thofe,
who cannot read the original, give a fhort abftract of it.
His defign is to fhew that there was only one pair of all
living things, created at the beginning. According to the
account

§. 8.

Prefervation.

The great Author and Parent of all things, decreed, that the whole earth fhould be covered with plants, and that no place fhould be

F 2   void,

account of Mofes, fays the author, we are fure, that this was the cafe in the human fpecies; and by the fame account we are informed that this firft pair was placed in Eden, and that Adam gave names to all the animals. In order therefore that Adam might be enabled to do this, it was neceffary that all the fpecies of animals fhould be in paradife; which could not happen unlefs alfo the fpecies of vegetables had been there likewife. This he proves from the nature of their food, particularly in relation to infects, moft of which live upon one plant only. Now had the world been formed in its prefent ftate, it could not have happened that all the fpecies of animals fhould have been there. They muft have been difperfed over all the globe, as we find they are at prefent, which he thinks improbable for other reafons which I fhall pafs over for the fake of brevity. To folve all the phænomena then he lays down a principle, that at the beginning all the earth was covered with fea, unlefs one ifland large enough to contain all animals and vegetables. This principle he endeavors to eftablifh by feveral phænomena which make it probable, that the earth has been and is ftill gaining upon the fea, and does not forget to mention *foffil fhells*, and *plants* every where found, which he fays cannot be accounted for by the deluge. He then undertakes to fhew

how

void, none barren. But fince all countries
have not the fame changes of feafons, and
every foil is not equally fit for every plant, He
therefore, that no place fhould be without

how all vegetables and animals might in this ifland have a
foil and climate proper for each, only by fuppofing it to be
placed under the æquator, and crowned with a very high
mountain. For it is well known that the fame *plants* are
found on the Swifs, the Pyrenean, the Scotch alps, on
Olympus, Lebanon, Ida, as on the Lapland and Green-
land alps. And Tournefort found at the bottom of mount
Ararat the common plants of Armenia, a little way up
thofe of Italy, higher thofe which grow about Paris, afterwards the Swedifh plants, and laftly on the top the
Lapland *alpine plants*; and i myfelf, adds the author, from
the plants growing on the Dalecarlian alps could collect
how much lower they were than the alps of Lapland. He
then proceeds to fhew how from one plant of each fpecies
the immenfe number of individuals now exifting might
arife. He gives fome inftances of the furprifing fertility of
certain plants, v. g. the elecampane, one plant of which
produced 3000 feeds, of fpelt, 2000, of the funflower
4000, of the poppy 3200, of tobacco 40320. But fuppofing any annual plant producing yearly only two feeds,
even of this after 20 years there would be 1,048,576 individuals. For they would increafe yearly in a duple proportion, viz. 2, 4, 8, 16, 32, &c. He then gives fome inftances of plants brought from America, that are now
become common over many parts of Europe. Laftly he
enters upon the fubject for which he is quoted in the
text, where the detail he gives of the feveral methods
which nature has taken to propagate vegetables is extremely curious, but too long to infert in this place.

fome,

fome, gave to every one of them fuch a nature, as might be chiefly adapted to the climate; fo that fome of them can bear an intenfe cold, others an equal degree of heat; fome delight in dry ground, others in moift, &c. Hence the fame plants grow only where there are the fame feafons of the year, and the fame foil.

The *alpine* plants live only in high, and cold fituations, and therefore often on the *alps* of Armenia, Switzerland, the Pyreneans, &c. whofe tops are equally covered with eternal fnows, as thofe of the Lapland *alps*, plants of the fame kind are found, and it would be in vain to feek for them any where elfe. It is remarkable in relation to the *alpine* plants, that they blow, and ripen their *feeds* very early, otherwife the winter would fteal upon them on a fudden, and deftroy them.

Our northern plants, altho' they are extremely rare every where elfe, yet are found in Sibiria, and about Hudfon's bay, as the *arbutus, Flor.* 339. *bramble* 412. *wintergreen,* &c.

Plants impatient of cold live within the torrid zones; hence both the Indies tho' at fuch a diftance from one another have plants in com-

F 3   mon.

mon. The Cape of Good Hope, i know not from what caufe, produces plants peculiar to itfelf, as all the *mefembryanthema*, and almoft all the fpecies of *aloes*. *Graffes*, the moft common of all plants, can bear almoft any temperature of air, in which the good providence of the Creator particularly appears; for all over the globe they above all plants are neceffary for the nourifhment of cattle, and the fame thing is feen in relation to our moft common grains.

Thus neither the fcorching fun, nor the pinching cold hinders any countrey from having its vegetables. Nor is there any foil, which does not bring forth many kinds of plants; the *pond-weeds*, the *water-lily*, *lobelia* inhabit the waters. The *fluviales*, *fuci*, *confervæ* cover the bottoms of rivers, and fea. The *fphagna* ⁹ fill the marfhes. The *brya* ʳ cloath the plains. The dryeft woods and places fcarce ever illuminated by the rays of the fun are adorned with the *hypna*. Nay ftones and the trunks of trees are not excepted, for thefe are covered with various kinds of *liverwort*.

The defart, and moft fandy places have their peculiar trees, and plants; and as rivers or

---

⁹ Kind of mofs.   ʳ Kind of mofs.

brooks

brooks are very feldom found there, we cannot without wonder obferve that many of them di-ftill water, and by that means afford the great-eft comfort both to man, and beafts that tra-vel there. Thus the ' *tillandfia*, which is a *parafitical plant*, and grows on the tops of trees in the defarts of America, has its leaves turned at the bafe into the fhape of a pitcher, with the extremity expanded ; in thefe the rain is collected, and preferved for thirfty men, birds, and beafts.

The *water-tree* in Ceylon produces cylindri-cal bladders, covered with a lid ; into thefe is fecreted a moft pure, and refrefhing water, that taftes like nectar to men, and other ani-mals. There is a kind of *cuckow-pint* in New-France, that if you break a branch of it, will afford you a pint of excellent water. How wife, how beautiful is the agreement between the plants of every countrey, and its inhabi-tants, and other circumftances.

ˢ A kind of *mifletoe.*

F 4 §. 9.

§. 9.

Plants oftentimes by their very ſtructure contribute remarkably both to their own preſervation, and that of others. But the wiſdom of the Creator appears no where more, than in the manner of growth of *trees*. For as their roots deſcend deeper, than thoſe of other *plants*, proviſion is thereby made, that they ſhall not rob them too much of nouriſhment ; and what is ſtill more, a ſtem not above a ſpan in diameter often ſhoots up its branches very high ; theſe bear perhaps many thouſand buds, each of which is a *plant* with its *leaves, flowers* and *ſtipulæ*. Now if all theſe grew upon the plain, they would take up a thouſand times as much ſpace, as the *tree* does, and in this caſe there would ſcarcely be room in all the earth for ſo many *plants*, as at preſent the *trees* alone afford. Beſides *plants* that ſhoot up in this way are more eaſily preſerved from cattle by a natural defence, and farther their leaves falling in autumn cover the *plants* growing about againſt the rigor of the winter, and in the ſummer they afford a pleaſing ſhade, not only to animals, but to *plants*, againſt the intenſe heat of the ſun. We may add that

trees

trees like all other *vegetables* imbibe the water from the earth, which water does not circulate again to the root, as the ancients imagined [t]; but being difperfed, like fmall rain, by the tranfpiration of the leaves, moiftens the *plants* that grow about. Again, many *trees* bear flefhy fruits of the *berry* or *apple* kind, which, being fecure from the attack of cattle, grow ripe for the ufe of man, and other animals, while their feeds are difperfed up and down after digeftion. Laftly the particular ftructure of *trees* contribute very much to the propagation of infects; for thefe chiefly lay their eggs upon their leaves, where they are fecure from the reach of cattle.

Ever-green trees, and *fhrubs* with us are chiefly found in the moft barren woods, that they may be a fhelter to animals in the winter. They lofe their leaves every third year, as their feeds are fufficiently guarded by the *moffes,* and do not want any other covering. The *palms* in the hot countries perpetually keep their leaves, for there the feeds ftand in no need of any fhelter whatever.

[t] See *Vegetable Statics* by that great philofopher Dr. Hales, where this fubject is treated in a mafterly way.

Many

Many *plants*, and *fhrubs* are armed with thorns, e. g. the *buck-thorn*, *floe*, *carduus*, *cot-ton-thiftle*, &c. that they may keep off the animals, which otherwife would deftroy their fruit. Thefe at the fame time cover many other *plants*, efpecially of the annual kind, under their branches ᵘ. So that while the adjacent grounds are robbed of all *plants* by the voracity of animals, fome may be preferved, to ripen flowers and fruit, and ftock the parts about with feeds, which otherwife would be quite extirpated.

All *herbs* cover the ground with their leaves, and by their fhade hinder it from being totally deprived of that moifture, which is neceffary to their nourifhment. They are moreover an ornament to the earth, efpecially as leaves have a more agreable verdure on the upper, than the under fide.

The *moffes*, which adorn the moft barren places, at the fame time preferve the leffer plants, when they begin to fhoot, from cold and drought. As we find by experience in our

ᵘ This obfervation may be extended farther; for it is conftantly feen upon commons, where *furze* grows, that wherever there was a bufh left untouched for years by the commoners, fome *tree* has fprung up, being fecured by the prickles of that *fhrub* from the bite of the cattle.

gar-

gardens, that *plants* are preferved in the fame way. They alfo hinder the fermenting earth from forcing the roots of *plants* upwards in the fpring ; as we fee happen annually to trunks of trees, and other things put into the ground. Hence very few *moffes* grow in the warmer climates, as not being fo neceffary to that end in thofe places.

The Englifh *fea mat-weed* or *marran* will bear no foil but pure fand, which nature has allotted to it. Sand the produce of the fea, is blown by winds oftentimes to very remote parts, and deluges, as it were, woods and fields. But where this grafs grows, it frequently fixes the fand, gathers it into hillocks, and thrives fo much, that by means of this alone, at laft an entire hill of fand is raifed. Thus the fand is kept in bounds, other *plants* are preferved free from it, the ground is increafed [w],

---

[w] This obfervation is found in Linn. Flor. Lapp. p. 62. where he fays the Dutch fow this grafs on their fand banks, that the fand may not overwhelm the neighboring parts. I do not fee why this experiment fhould not be tryed on the barren fands in Norfolk, where I am affured by credible witneffes, that the fmall cottages are fometimes totally buried under fand during high winds. This grafs grows plentifully along the fea fhores in England. Vid. Ray, 393. 1.

and

and the fea repelled by this wonderful difpofition of nature.

How folicitous nature is about the prefervation of graffes is abundantly evident from
hence, that the more the leaves of the perennial graffes are eaten, the more they creep by
the roots, and fend forth off-fets. For the
Author of nature intended, that *vegetables* of
this kind, which have very flender, and erect
leaves, fhould be copious, and very thick-fet,
covering the ground like a carpet; and thus
afford food fufficient for fo vaft a quantity of
grazing animals. But what chiefly increafes
our wonder is, that although the graffes are
the principal food of fuch animals, yet they
are forbid, as it were, to touch the flower, and
feed-bearing ftems; that fo the feeds may
ripen and be fown.

The *caterpillar* or *grub* of the *moth*, Faun.
Sue. 826. called *graefmafken*, although it feeds
upon graffes, to the great deftruction of them,
in meadows; yet it feems to be formed, in order to keep a due proportion between thefe
and other plants; for graffes, when left to
grow freely, increafe to that degree, that they
exclude all other plants; which would confequently be extirpated, unlefs this infect fometimes

times prepared a place for them, Hence
always more fpecies of *plants* appear in thofe
places where this caterpillar has laid wafte
the paftures the preceding year, than at any
other time.

§. 10.

Deftruction.

Daily experience teaches us, that all *plants*
as well as all other living things, muft fubmit
to death.

They fpring up, they grow, they florifh,
they ripen their fruit, they wither, and at laft,
having finifhed their courfe, they die, and return to the duft again, from whence they firft
took their rife. Thus all black mould, which
every where covers the earth, for the greateft
part is owing to dead *vegetables*. For all roots
defcend into the fand by their branches, and
after a *plant* has loft its ftem the root remains;
but this too rots at laft, and changes into
mould. By this means this kind of earth is
mixed with fand, by the contrivance of nature, nearly in the fame way as dung thrown
upon fields is wrought into the earth by the
induftry of the hufbandman. The earth thus

pre-

prepared offers again to *plants* from its bo-
fom, what it has received from them. For
when feeds are committed to the earth, they
draw to themfelves, accommodate to their
nature, and turn into *plants*, the more fubtile parts of this mould by the co-operation
of the fun, air, clouds, rains, and winds ; fo
that the talleft tree is, properly fpeaking, nothing but mould wonderfully compounded
with air, and water, and modified by a vertue communicated to a fmall feed by the
Creator. From thefe *plants*, when they die,
juft the fame kind of mould is formed, as
gave birth to them originally ; but in fuch a
manner, that it is in greater quantity than
before. *Vegetables* therefore increafe the black
mould, whence fertility remains continually uninterrupted. Whereas the earth could
not make good its annual confumption, unlefs it were conftantly recruited by new fupplies.

The cruftaceous *liverworts* are the firft foundation of *vegetation*, and therefore are *plants*
of the utmoft confequence in the œconomy
of nature, though fo defpifed by us. When
rocks firft emerge out of the fea, they are fo
polifhed by the force of the waves, that
scarce

fcarce any herb can find a fixed habitation
upon them; as we may obferve every where
near the fea. But the very minute cruftaceous *liverworts* begin foon to cover thefe dry
rocks, although they have no other nourifhment, but that fmall quantity of mould, and
imperceptible particles, which the rain and air
bring thither. Thefe *liverworts* dying at laft
turn into a very fine earth; on this earth the
x imbricated *liverworts* find a bed to ftrike
their roots in. Thefe alfo dye after a time, and
turn to mould; and then the various kinds of
moffes, e. g. the *hypna*, the *brya, politricha* find
a proper place, and nourifhment. Laftly thefe
dying in their turn, and rotting afford fuch a
plenty of new formed mould, that herbs and
fhrubs eafily root, and live upon it.

That trees when they are dry or are cut
down may not remain ufelefs to the world, and
lye, as it were, melancholy fpectacles, nature
haftens on their deftruction in a fingular way:
firft the *liverworts* begin to ftrike root in them;
afterwards the moifture is drawn out of them;

---

x I have ufed this word becaufe we have no Englifh
one of the fame meaning unlefs it be the word *fcaly*, that
i know of. However imbricated means parts lying over
parts like tiles, as in the cup of the *thiftle flower*.

whence putrefaction follows. Then the *mush-room* kinds find a fit place for nourishment on them, and corrupt them still more. The *beetle* called the *dermestes*, next makes himself a way between the bark, and the wood. The *musk-beetle*, the *copper talc beetle*, and the *caterpillar* or *coffus* 812. bores an infinite number of holes through the trunk. Lastly the *woodpeckers* come, and while they are seeking for insects, wear away the tree, already corrupted; till the whole passes into earth. Such industry does nature use to destroy the trunk of a tree! Nay trees immersed in water would scarcely ever be destroyed, were it not for the worm that eats ships, which performs this work; as the sailor knows by sad experience.

Thistles, as the most usefull of plants, are armed, and guarded by nature herself. Suppose there were a heap of clay, on which for many years no plant has sprung up; let the seeds of the *thistle* blow there, and grow, the *thistles* by their leaves attract the moisture out of the air, send it into the clay by means of their roots, will thrive themselves, and afford a shade. Let now other plants come hither, and they will soon cover the ground. St, Bielke.

All

All fucculent plants make ground fine, of a good quality, and in great plenty, as *fedum*, *craffula*, *aloe*, *algæ* [1]. But dry plants make it more barren, as *ling* or *heath*, *pines*, *mofs* ; and therefore nature has placed the fucculent plants on rocks, and the dryeft hills.

§. I I .

The ánimal kingdom.

Propagation.

The generation of animals holds the firft place among all things, that raife our admiration, when we confider the works óf the Creator ; and that appointment particularly, by which he has regulated the conception of the *fœtus*, and its exclufion, that it fhould be adapted to the difpofition, and way of living of eách ánimal, is moft worthy of our attention.

We find no fpecies of anímals exempt from the ftings of love, which is put into them to the end, that the Creator's mandate may be executed, *increafe and multiply*; and that thus

---

[1] A kind of *grafs wrack*.

the egg, in which is contained the rudiment of the *fœtus* may be fœcundated ; for without fœcundation all eggs are unfit to produce an offspring.

Foxes and *wolves*, ftruck with thefe ftings, every where howl in the woods.; crowds of *dogs* follow the female ; *bulls* fhew a terrible countenance, and very different from that of *oxen*. *Stags* every year have new horns, which they lofe after rutting time. Birds look more. beautifull than ordinary, and warble all day long through lafcivioufnefs. Thus *fmall birds* labour to outfing one another, and *cocks* to outcrow. *Peacocks* fpread forth again their gay, and glorious trains. *Fifhes* gather together, and exult in the water ; and *grafhoppers* chirp, and pipe as it were, amongft the herbs. The *ants* gather again into colonies, and repair to their citadels ᶻ. I pafs over many other particulars, which this fubject affords, to avoid prolixity.

ᶻ See this fubject treated with great fpirit in Thomfon's Spring and in Virgil's Georgics.

§. 12.

§. 12.

The fœcundated egg requires a certain, and proportionate degree of heat for the expanfion of the *ftamina* of the *embryo*. That this may be obtained, nature operates in different manners, and therefore we find in different claffes of animals a different way of excluding the *fœtus*.

The females of *quadrupeds* have an *uterus*, contrived for eafy geftation, temperate and cherifhing warmth, and proper nourifhment of the *fœtus*, as moft of them live upon the earth, and are there fed.

Birds, in order to get fubfiftence, and for other reafons, are under a neceffity of fhifting place ; and that not upon their feet but wings. Geftation therefore would be burthenfome to them. For this reafon they lay eggs, covered with a hard fhell. Thefe they fit upon by a natural inftinct, and cherifh till the young one comes forth.

The *oftrich* and *caffowary* are almoft the only birds, that do not obferve this law ; thefe commit their eggs to the fand, where the intenfe heat of the fun excludes the *fœtus*.

Fifhes

Fishes inhabit cold waters, and most of them have cold blood; whence it happens that they have not heat sufficient to produce the *fœtus*. The all-wife Creator therefore has ordained, that most of them should lay their eggs upon the shore; where, by means of the solar rays, the water is warmer, and also fitter for that purpose; becaufe it is there lefs impregnated with falt, and confequently milder; and alfo becaufe water-infects abound more there, which afford the young fry a nourifhment.

Salmons in the like manner, when they are about to lay their eggs, are led by inftinct to go up the ftream, where the water is frefh and more pure.

The *butterfly fifh* is an exception, for that brings forth its *fœtus* alive.

The *fifhes of the ocean*, which cannot reach the fhores by reafon of the diftance, are alfo exempt from this law. The Author of nature to this kind has given eggs that fwim; fo that they are hatched amidft the fwimming *fucus*, called *fargazo*. Flor. Zeilon. 389.

The *cetaceous* fifh have warm blood, and therefore they bring forth their young alive, and fuckle them with their teats.

Many

Many *amphibious* animals bring forth live *fœtuses*. As the *viper*, and the *toad*, &c. But the fpecies that lay eggs, lay them in places, where the heat of the fun fupplies the warmth of the parent.

Thus the reft of the *frog* kind and the *lizard* kind, lay their eggs in warm waters; the common *fnake* in dunghills, and fuch-like warm places, and give them up to nature, as a provident nurfe, to take care of them. The *crocodile*, and *fea tortoifes* go afhore to lay their eggs under the fand, where the heat of the fun hatches them.

Moft of the *infeél* kind neither bear young nor hatch eggs; yet their tribes are the moft numerous of all living creatures; infomuch that if the bulk of their bodies were proportionate to their quantity, they would fcarce leave room for any other kinds of animals. Let us fee therefore with what wifdom the Creator has managed about the propagation of thefe minute creatures. The females by natural inftinél meet and copulate with the males; and afterwards lay their eggs, but not indifcriminately in every place; for they all know how to choofe fuch places as may fupply their offfpring in its tender age with nourifhment, and

other

other things neceſſary to ſatisfy their natural
wants; for them other, ſoon after ſhe has laid her
eggs, dyes, and were ſhe to live ſhe would not
have it in her power to take care of her young.

Butterflies, *moths*, ſome *beetles*, *wevils*,
bugs, *cuckow-ſpit inſeƐts*, *gall-inſeƐts*, *tree
bugs*, &c. lay their eggs, on the leaves of
plants, and every different tribe chooſes its
own ſpecies of plant *. Nay there is ſcarce any
plant, which does not afford nouriſhment to
ſome inſeƐt; and ſtill more, there is ſcarcely
any part of a plant, which is not preferred by
ſome of them. Thus one inſeƐt feeds upon the
flower; another upon the trunk; another upon the root; and another upon the leaves. But
we cannot help wondering particularly, when
we ſee how the leaves of ſome trees, and plants,
after eggs have been let into them, grow into
galls; and form dwellings, as it were, for
the young ones, where they may conveniently
live. Thus when the *gall-inſeƐt* called *cynips*,
Fn. 947. has fixed her eggs in the leaves of
an oak, the wound of the leaf ſwells, and a
knob like an apple ariſes, which includes and
nouriſhes the embryo.

---

* Vid. Syſt. Nat. Edit. 10. Fauna Suecica; and Hoſpita
InſeƐtorum Flora Aman. Academ. vol. 3.

When

When the *tree-bug*, Faun. Suec. 700. has
depofited its eggs in the boughs of the fir tree,
excrefences arife fhaped like peas. When another fpecies of the *tree-bug*, Fn. 695. has
depofited its eggs in the *moufe-ear chickweed*
or the *fpeedwell*, Fl. 12. the leaves contract in
a wonderfull manner into the fhape of a head.
The *water-fpider*, Fn. 1150. excludes its eggs
either on the extremities of the *juniper*, which
from thence forms a lodging, that looks like
the *arrow-headed grafs*, or on the leaves of the
poplar, from whence a red globe is produced.
The *tree-loufe*, Fn. 1355. lays its eggs on
the leaves of black poplar, Fl. 821. which
from thence turn into a kind of inflated bag,
and fo in other inftances. Nor is it upon plants
only that infects live, and lay their eggs. The
knats, Fn. 1116. commit theirs to ftagna-
ting waters. The water infect called *monoculus*, Fn. 1182. often increafes fo immenfely
on pools, that the red legions of them have
the appearance of blood. Others lay their eggs
in other places, e. g. the *beetle* in dunghills.
The *dermeftes* in fkins. The *flefh fly* in putrifyed flefh. The *cheefe-maggot* in the cracks
of cheefe, from whence the *caterpillars* iffuing
forth oftentimes confume the whole cheefe,

G 4   and

and deceive many people, who fancy the worms are produced from the particles of the cheefe itfelf, by a generation called æquivocal, which is extremely abfurd. Others exclude their eggs upon certain animals. The *mill-beetle* Fn. 618. lays its eggs betwen the fcales of fifhes. The *fpecies of glad-fly* Fn. 1024. on the back of cattle. The *fpecies* 1025 on the back of the rhen deer. The *fpecies* 1026 in the nofes of fheep. The *fpecies* 1028 lodges during the winter in the inteftinal tube, or the throat of horfes, nor can it be driven out till the fummer comes on. Nay *infeƈts* themfelves are often furrounded with the eggs of other infeƈts, infomuch that there is fcarcely an animal to be found, which does not feed its proper infeƈt, not to fay any more of all the other places, where they depofit their eggs. Almoft all the eggs of *infeƈts*, when laid, are ordained to undergo, by a wonderfull law of nature, various metamorphofes, e. g. the egg of the *butterfly* being laid in the cabbage firft of all becomes a *caterpillar*, that feeds upon the plant, crawls, and has fixteen feet. This afterwards changes into a *nymph*, that has no feet, is fmooth, and eats nothing ; and laftly this burfts into a *butterfly*, that flies, has variety of colours, is rough,

and

and lives upon honey. What can be more worthy of admiration, than that one, and the fame animal fhould appear on the ftage of life under fo many characters, as if it were three diftinct animals [a].

The laws of generation of *worms* are ftill very obfcure, as we find they are fometimes produced by eggs, fometimes by offsets, juft in the fame manner as happens to trees. It has been obferved with the greateft admiration, that the *polypus* or *hydra* S. N. 221. lets down fhoots and live branches, by which it is multiplied. Nay more, if it be cut into many parts, each fegment, put into the water, grows into a perfect animal; fo that the parts which were torn off are reftored from one fcrap.

§. 13.

The multiplication of animals is not tyed down to the fame rules in all; for fome have a remarkable power of propagating, others are

[a] Linnæus Amæn. academ. vol. 2. in a treatife on the wonders relating to infects, fays, " as furprifing as thefe " transformations may feem, yet much the fame happens " when a chicken is hatched, the only difference is, that " the chicken breaks all three coats at once, the butterfly " one after another.

con-

confined within narrower limits in this refpect. Yet in general, we find, that nature
obferves this order, that the leaft animals, and
thofe which are ufefull, and ferve for nourifhment to the greateft number of other animals,
are endued with a greater power of propagating than others [b].

Mites, and many other infects will multiply
to a thoufand within the compafs of a very few
days. While the *elephant* fcarcely produces
one young in two years.

The *hawk* kind generally lay not above two
eggs, at moft four, while the *poultry* kind rife
to 50.

The *diver* or *loon*, which is eaten by few
animals, lays alfo two eggs, but the *duck* kind,
the *moor game*, *partridges*, &c. and *fmall birds*
lay a very large number.

If you fuppofe two *pigeons* to hatch nine
times a year, they may produce in four years
14672 young [c]. They are endued with this

[b] Herodotus fpeaking of the flying ferpents in Arabia
makes the fame reflection, and attributes this courfe of nature to the divine providence. Thal.

[c] I have given this paffage as it ftands in the original.
The numbers ought to have been 14760, or the expreffion
fhould have been altered ; for he includes the firft pair.

He fuppofes it generally known that pigeons hatch but
two eggs at a time, and that they pair.

remark-

remarkable fertility, that they may ferve for food, not only to man, but to hawks and other birds of prey *. Nature has made harmlefs and efculent animals fruitfull. Plin. Nature has forbid the *bird* kind to fall fhort of the number of eggs allotted to each fpecies, and there- fore if the eggs which they intend to fit upon, be taken away a certain number of times, they prefently lay others in their room, as may be feen in the fwallow, duck, and fmall birds.

§. 14.

Prefervation.

Prefervation follows generation; this appears chiefly in the tender age, while the young are unable to provide for their own fupport. For then the parents, though otherwife ever fo fierce in their difpofition, are affeted with a wonderfull tendernefs or fenfe of love towards their progeny, and fpare no pains to provide for, guard, and preferve them, and that not by an imaginary law, but one given by the Lord of nature himfelf.

Quadrupeds give fuck to their tender young and fupport them by a liquor, perfetly eafy of digeftion, till their ftomachs are able to digeft,

* Vid. Mufchenbr. Orat. de Sap. Divin.

and

and their teeth are fit to chew more folid food. Nay their love toward them is fo great, that they endeavour to repell with the utmoft force every thing, which threatens danger, or de-ftruction to them. The *ewe* which brings forth two *lambs* at a time, will not admit one to her teats, unlefs the other be prefent, and fuck alfo; left one fhould famifh, while the other grows fat.

Birds build their nefts in the moft artificial manner, and line them as foft as poffible, for fear the eggs fhould get any damage. Nor do they build promifcuoufly in any place; but there only, where they may quietly lye con-cealed and be fafe from the attacks of their enemies.

The *hanging bird*, Act. Bonon. vol. 2. makes its neft of the fibres of withered plants, and the down of the poplar feeds, and fixes it upon the bough of fome tree hanging over the water; that it may be out of reach.

The *diver*, Fn. 123. places its fwimming neft upon the water itfelf amongft the rufhes. I de-fignedly pafs over many other inftances of the like kind.

Again birds fit on their eggs with fo much patience, that many of them choofe to perifh

with

with hunger, rather than expofe the eggs to danger by going to feek for food.

The male *rooks* and *crows* at the time of incubation bring food to the females.

Pigeons, fmall birds, and other *birds*, which pair, fit by turns; but where polygamy prevails, the males fcarcely take any care of the young.

Moft of the *duck* kind pluck off their feathers in great quantity, and cover their eggs with them, left they fhould be damaged by the cold, when they quit their nefts for the fake of food; and when the young are hatched, who knows not how folicitous they are in providing for them, till they are able to fly, and fhift for themfelves?

Young *pigeons* would not be able to make ufe of hard feeds for nourifhment, unlefs the parents were to prepare them in their crops, and thence feed them.

The *eagle owl* makes its neft on the higheft precipices of mountains, and in the warmeft fpot, facing the fun; that the dead bodies brought there may by the heat melt into a foft pulp, and become fit nourifhment for the young.

The

The *cuckow* lays its eggs in the neft of other fmall birds, generally the *wagtail*, [d] or [e] *hedge-fparrow*, and leaves the incubation, and prefervation of the young to them. But that thefe young, when grown up, degenerate into hawks, and become fo ungratefull, that they deftroy their nurfes, is a mere vulgar error, for it is contrary to their nature to eat flefh.

Amphibious animals, *fifhes* and *infects*, which cannot come under the care of their parents, yet owe this to them, that they are put in places, where they eafily find nourifhment, as we have obferved.

[d] This cuftom of the cuckow is fo extraordinary, and out of the common courfe of nature, that it would not be credible, were it not for the teftimony of the moft knowing and curious natural hiftorians, fuch as Ray, Willughby, Gefner, Aldrovandus, Ariftotle, &c.

Much has been faid by the writers on birds about the fate of the young birds, in whofe neft the cuckow is hatched, but as i find nothing but mere conjecture, it would not be worth while tranfcribing.

[e] Hedge fparrow. Linnæus feems to have taken the white-throat for the hedge-fparrow.

§. 15.

As foon as animals come to maturity, and want no longer the care of their parents, they attend with the utmoft labor, and induftry, according to the law and œconomy appointed for every fpecies, to the prefervation of their lives. But that fo great a number of them, which occur every where, may be fupported, and a certain and fixed order may be kept up amongft them, behold the wonderfull difpofition of the Creator, in affigning to each fpecies certain kinds of food, and in putting limits to their appetites. So that fome live on particular fpecies of plants, which particular regions, and foils only produce. Some on particular animalcula, others on carcafes, and fome even on mud and dung. For this reafon Providence has ordained, that fome fhould fwim in certain regions of the watery element, others fhould fly ; fome fhould inhabit the torrid, the frigid, or the temperate zones, and others fhould frequent defarts, mountains, woods, pools or meadows, according as the food proper to their nature is found in fufficient quantity. By this means there is no terreftrial tract,

tract, no fea, no river, no countrey, but what contains, and nourifhes various kinds of animals. Hence alfo an animal of one kind cannot rob thofe of another kind of its aliment; which, if it happened, would endanger their lives or health; and thus the world at all times affords nourifhment to fo many, and fo large inhabitants, at the fame time that nothing, which it produces, is ufelefs or fuperfluous.

I think it will not be amifs to produce fome inftances, by which it will appear, how providentially the Creator has furnifhed every animal with fuch cloathing, as is proper for the countrey where they live, and alfo how excellently the ftructure of their bodies is adapted to their particular way of life; fo that they feem to be deftined folely to the places, where they are found.

Monkies, *elephants*, and *rhinocerofes* feed upon vegetables, that grow in hot countries, and therefore therein they have their allotted places. When the fun darts forth its moft fervid rays, thefe animals are of fuch a nature, and difpofition, that it does them no manner of hurt; nay with the reft of the inhabitants of thofe parts they go naked, whereas were

I   they

they covered with hairy fkins they muft perifh with heat.

On the contrary the place of *rhen deer* is fixed in the coldeft part of Lapland, becaufe their chief food is the *liverwort*, Fl. 980. which grows no where fo abundantly as there; and where, as the cold is moft intenfe, the *rhen deer* are cloathed, like the other northern animals, with fkins filled with the denfeft hair; by the help of which they eafily defy the keennefs of the winter. In like manner the *rough-legged partridge* paffes its life in the very Lapland alps, feeding upon the feeds of the *dwarf birch*, and that they may run up and down fafely amidft the fnow, their feet are feathered.

The *camel* frequents the fandy, and burning defarts, in order to get the barren *camel's hay*. Mat. Med. 31. How wifely has the Creator contrived for him! he is obliged to go thro' the defarts, where oftentimes no water is found for many miles about. All other animals would perifh with thirft in fuch a journey; but the camel can undergo it without fuffering; for his belly is full of cells, where he referves water for many days. It is reported by travellers, that the Arabians, when in travelling they want water, are forced to kill their camels; and take

H   water

water out of their bellies, that is perfectly good to drink, and not at all corrupted.

The *pelican* likewise lives in defart, and dry places; and is obliged to build her neft far from the fea, in order to procure a greater fhare of heat to her eggs. She is therefore forced to bring water from afar for herfelf and her young; for which reafon Providence has furnifhed her with an inftrument moft adapted to this purpofe; v. g. fhe has a very large bag under her throat, which fhe fills with a quantity of water fufficient for many days; and this fhe pours into the neft to refrefh her young, and teach them to fwim. The wild beafts, lions, and tigers, come to this neft to quench their thirft, but do no hurt to the young.

Oxen delight in low grounds, becaufe there the food moft palatable to them grows.

Sheep prefer naked hills, where they find a particular kind of grafs called the *feftuca*, Fl. 95. which they love above all things.

Goats climb up the precipices of mountains, that they may browfe on the tender fhrubs, and in order to fit them for it, they have feet made for jumping*.

---

* Vid. Derham's Phifyco-Theol. p. 319. not 7.

Horfes chiefly refort to woods, and feed upon leafy plants.

Nay, fo various is the appetite of animals,
that there is fcarcely any plant, which is not
chofen by fome, and left untouched by others.
The *horfe* gives up the *water hemlock* to the
goat. The *cow* gives up the *long-leaved water hemlock* to the fheep. The *goat* gives up
the *monks-hood* to the horfe, &c. for that
which certain animals grow fat upon, others
abhor as poifon. Hence no plant is abfolutely
poifonous, but only refpectively. Thus the
fpurge, that is noxious to man, is a moft wholefome nourifhment to the *caterpillar*, Fn. 825.
That animals may not deftroy themfelves for
want of knowing this law, each of them is
guarded by fuch a delicacy of tafte and fmell,
that they can eafily diftinguifh what is pernicious from what is wholefome ; and when it happens that different animals live upon the fame
plants, ftill one kind always leaves fomething
for the other, as the mouths of all are not
equally adapted to lay hold of the grafs ; by
which means there is fufficient food for all.
To this may be referred an œconomical experiment well known to the Dutch, that when
eight cows have been in a pafture, and can no

H 2   longer

longer get nourifhment, two horfes will do very well there for fome days, and when nothing is left for the horfes, four fheep will live upon it.

Swine get provifion by turning up the earth; for there they find the fucculent roots, which to them are very delicious.

The leaves and fruits of trees are intended as food for fome animals, as the floth ᶠ, the

ᶠ There is fo curious an account of this animal in Kircher's Mufurgia, that i think the reader will excufe my tranfcribing it. That author fays thus : ' The defcription of ' this animal i had from fatherTorus, provincial of theJefuites ' in America, who had animals of this kind in his poffeffion, ' and made many experiments in relation to their nature ' and qualities. Its figure is extraordinary ; it is about the ' bignefs of a cat, of very ugly countenance, and has claws ' extended like fingers. The hinder part of the head and ' neck are covered with hair. It fweeps the ground with ' its fat belly, never rifes upon its feet, and moves fo ' flowly, that it would fcarce go the length of a bow-fhot ' in 15 days, tho' conftantly moving, and it is therefore ' called the Sloth. It is not known what it feeds upon, ' not being ever obferved to take any food. It lives gene- ' rally upon tops of trees, and employs two days to crawl ' up, and as many to get down again. Nature has doubly ' guarded this animal againft its enemies. Firft by giving ' it fuch ftrength in its feet that whatever it feizes, it holds ' fo faft, that it never can be freed from its claws, but muft ' there dye of hunger. Secondly in giving it fuch a moving
' afpect,

the fquirrel, and thefe laft have feet given them fit for climbing.

Befides myriads of fifhes, the *caftor*, the *fea calf*, and others inhabit the water, that they may there be fed, and their hinder feet are fit for

' afpeft, when it looks at any man who fhould be tempted
' to hurt it, that it is impoffible not to be touched with
' compaffion ; befides that at the fame time it fheds tears,
' and upon the whole perfuades one, that a creature fo de-
' fencelefs, and of fo unhappy a body ought not to be tor-
' mented. To make an experiment of this, the above-
' mentioned father procured one of thefe animals to be
' brought to our college at Carthagena. He put a long
' pole under his feet, which it feized upon very firmly, and
' would not let it go again. The animal therefore thus voluntari-
' ly fufpended was placed between two beams along with the
' pole, and there it remained without meat, drink, or fleep,
' forty days; its eyes being always fixed on people that
' looked at it, who were fo touched, that they could not
' forbear pitying it. At laft being taken down they let loofe
' a dog on it, which after a little while the Sloth feized with
' his feet, and held him four days, till he dyed of hunger.
' This was taken from the mouth of the father. They add,
' continues Kircher, that this creature makes no noife but
' at night, but that very extraordinary. For by interrup-
' tions, that laft about the length of a figh or femipaufe
' it goes thro' the fix vulgar intervals of mufic ut, re, mi,
' fa, fol, la. La, fol, fa, mi, re, ut, afcending and defcend-
' ing, and thefe perfectly in tune. So that the Spaniards,
' when they firft got poffeffion of this coaft, and heard thefe

' notes,

for fwimming, and perfectly adapted to their manner of life.

The whole order of the *goose* kind, as ducks, merganfer, &c. pafs their lives in water as feeding upon water-infects, fifhes, and their eggs [g]. Who does not fee, that attends ever fo little, how exactly the wonderfull for-

‘ notes, they imagined that fome people brought up to our ‘ mufic, were finging. This animal is called by the na- ‘ tives Haut, certainly becaufe going thro' thefe mufical ‘ intervals, it repeats, Ha, ha, ha, ha, ha, &c.

This account feems very wonderfull, and i leave it as it ftands without entering into any difcuffion about its credibility. I will only add, that Linnæus feems in the new edition of the Syft. Nat. to give credit to it. For he fays in his fhort way of defcription among other things, ‘ It utters ‘ an afcending hexacord. Its noife is horrible, its tears pi- ‘ teous.’ He quotes Mangrave, Clufius, Gefner, &c. But not having an opportunity of confulting thefe books i cannot tell how far thefe authors confirm the foregoing account; if it be true, it would furnifh fome obfervations, but this would not be a place for them.

[g] Many opinions, fays the author in the note, have been ftarted in order to account how it happens that fifhes are found in pools, and ditches, on high mountains and elfewhere. But Gmelin obferves that the *duck* kind fwallow the eggs of fifhes, that fome of thefe eggs go down, and come out of their bodies unhurt, and fo are propagated juft in the fame manner, as has been obferved of plants. Biberg.

Gmelin adds, that the Sibirians themfelves account for this phænomenon in the manner above mentioned.

mation

mation of their beaks, their necks, their feet, and their feathers fuit their kind of life, which obfervation ought to be extended to all other birds.

The way of living of the *fea-fwallow* Fn. 129. deferves to be particularly taken notice of; for as he cannot fo commodioufly plunge into the water and catch fifh, as other aquatic birds, the Creator has appointed the *fea-gull* to be his caterer in the following manner. When this laft is purfued by the former, he is forced to throw up part of his prey, which the other catches; but in the autumn, when the fifhes hide themfelves in deep places, the mergan-fer, Fn. 113. fupplies the gull with food, as being able to plunge deeper into the fea. Act. Stock.

The chief granary of *fmall birds* is the *knot-grafs*, Fol. Suec. 322. that bears heavy feeds, like thofe of the *black bindweed.* It is a very common plant, not eafily de-ftroyed, either by the road fide by trampling upon it, or any where elfe, and is extremely plentifull after harveft in fields, to which it gives a reddifh hue by its numerous feeds. Thefe fall upon the ground, and are gather-ed all the year round by the fmall birds.

ʰ Thus bountifull nature feeds the fowls of the air.

The Creator has taken no lefs care of fome *amphibious animals*, as the fnake and frog kind, which, as they have neither wings to fly, nor feet to run fwiftly, and commodioufly, would fcarcely have any means of taking their prey, were it not that fome animals run, as it were of their own accord, into their mouths. When the *rattle-fnake* a native of America, with open jaws fixes his eyes on a bird, fly, or fquirrel, fitting on a tree, they fly down his throat, being rendered ftupid, and giving themfelves up ⁱ, as deftitute of all refuge. On the other hand we cannot but adore the Creator's great goodnefs towards man, when we

---

ʰ To which we may add, that many fmall birds feed upon the feeds of *plantain*, particularly linnets. It is generally known that the goldfinch lives upon the feed of *thiftles*, from which he has its name in Greek, Latin and French.

ⁱ How dreadfull this ferpent is to other animals will appear by an account we have in a treatife intitled, Radix Senega. Where the author Amæn. academ. vol. 2. fays, one of thefe terrible ferpents got clandeftinely into the houfe of governor Blake at Cacolina ; where it would have long laid concealed, had it not been that all the domeftic animals, as dogs, hogs, turkies and fowls admonifhed the family by their unufual cries, equally fhewing their horrror and confternation, their hair, briftles and crefts ftanding up an end.

confider

confider the rattle which terminates this ferpent's tail. For by the means of that we have an opportunity of guarding againft this dreadfull enemy; the found warning us to fly, which if we were not to do, and we fhould be wounded by him, the whole body would be turned into a putrid corruption in fix hours, nay fometimes in half an hour.

The limits of this differtation will not permit me to produce more examples of this kind. But whoever will be at the pains to take ever fo flight a view of the wonderfull works of the Creator, will readily fee, how wifely the plan, order and fitnefs of things to divine ends are difpofed.

§. 16.

We cannot without the utmoft admiration behold how providently the Creator has acted as to the prefervation of thofe animals, which at a certain time of the year, are by the rigor of the feafon excluded from the neceffaries of life. Thus the *bear* in the autumn creeps into the *mofs*, which he has gathered, and there lies all winter; fubfifting upon no other nourifhment but his fat, collected during the fummer in the cellulous membrane, and which

without

without doubt, during his faſt, circulates thro'
his veſſels, and ſupplies the place of food; to
which perhaps is added that fat juice which
he ſucks out of the bottom of his feet.

The *hedge-hog*, *badger* and *mole* in the
ſame manner fill their winter quarters with vegetables, and ſleep during the froſts.

The *bat* ſeems cold, and quite dead all
the winter. Moſt of the *amphibious animals* get
into dens, or to the bottom of lakes and pools.

In the autumn, as the cold approaches, and
infects diſappear, *ſwallows* [k] ſeek for an aſylum
againſt the violence of the cold in the bottom

of

[k] I never had but one credible teſtimony that ſwallows
paſs the winter at the bottom of lakes or ponds; and this
from a gentleman of character, who ſaw a ſwallow ſo found
brought to life by warmth. On the other hand, i know of
no author but Herodotus who mentions their being ſeen in
any countrey during the winter. He lib. 2. p. 109. edit.
Steph.ſays, that ſwallows and kites continue all the year about
the ſprings of the Nile. What he mentions concerning kites
deſerves ſome notice, viz. that they lye concealed in holes a few
days. Pliny ſays a few months. Geſner repeats the ſame, adding that they have been found in hollow trees ſomewhere in
Upper Germany, but he ſeems to relate this upon hearſay
only. Aldrovandus gives the ſame account as Geſner, and
adds that they winter in Ægypt, but whether upon the authority of Bellonius or any other credible writer, does not
appear.

of lakes amongst the reeds and rushes; from whence by the wonderfull appointment of nature they come forth again. The periftaltic motion of the bowels ceases in all these animals, while they are obliged to faft, whence the appetite is diminished, and so they suffer less from hunger. To this head may be referred the obfervation of the celebrated Lifter concerning those animals; that their blood, when let into a bafon, does not coagulate, as that of all other animals, and so is no less fit for circulation than before.

The *moor-fowls* work themfelves out walks under the very fnow. They moult in the fummer, so that about the month of Auguft they

appear. He quotes a paffage from that author concerning the appearance of a vaft number of kites at the mouth of the Bofphorus, but this happened at the latter end of May, and feems to prove nothing; for the time marked for their appearance by Calippus, who obferved near the Hellefpont, is the month of March. Willughby fays that kites are fuppofed to be birds of paffage, and then quotes from Bellonius the place abovementioned.

From what has been faid it appears evident, that nothing certain is known by the moderns about the difappearance of thefe remarkable birds, yet their coming was regularly noted by the antient writers, and coincided with that of fwallows, as appears by the old calendars of Geminus, and Ptolemy from the obfervations of Eudoxus, Euctemous, Calippus, and Dofitheus.

can-

cannot fly, and are therefore obliged to run into the woods ; but then the moor-berries and
bilberries are ripe, from whence they are
abundantly fupplied with food. Whereas the
young do not moult the firft fummer, and
therefore, tho' they cannot run fo well, are
able to efcape danger by flight.

The *reft of the birds* who feed upon infects
migrate every year to forreign regions, in order to feek for food in a milder climate; while
all the northern parts, where they live well in
the fummer, are covered with fnow.

Infects in the winter generally lye hid within their cafes, and are nourifhed by the fur-
rounding liquor like the fœtus of other animals, from whence at the approach of fpring
they awake, and fly forth to the aftonifhment
of every one.

However all animals which lye hid in winter, do not obferve thefe laws of fafting. Some
provide ftore-houfes in fummer, and autumn,
from which they take what is neceffary, as
mice, jays, fquirrels, bees.

§. 17.

What i have obferved in a few words concerning the migration of birds into forreign
coun-

countries, gives me an opportunity of illuftrating this fubject farther by inftances.

The *ftarling*, Fn. 183. finding with us after the middle of fummer worms in lefs plenty, yearly goes inot Schonen, Germany and Denmark.

The *female chaffinches* every winter about Michaelmas go in flocks to Holland ; but as the males ftay with us, they come back the next fpring, unlefs fuch as choofe to breed no more.

In the fame manner the female *Caroline yellow-hammer* in the month of September, while the rice, on which fhe feeds, is laid up in granaries, goes towards the fouth, and returns in the fpring to feek her mate.

Our *aquatic birds* are forced by neceffity to fly towards the fouth every autumn before the water is frozen. Thus we know that the lakes of Poland and Lithuania are filled with *fwans* and *geefe* every autumn, at which time they go in great flocks along many rivers as far as the Euxine. But in the beginning of fpring, as foon as the heat of the fun molefts them, they turn back, and go again to the northern pools, and lakes, in order to lay their eggs. For there, and efpecially in Lapland, there is a vaft abundance of knats Fn. 1116. which afford them

excellent

excellent norifhment, as all of this kind live in the water, before they get their wings.

The *woodcock* Fn. 141. lives in England in winter, and departs from thence at the coming on of fpring after they have paired.

The *fwallow-tail'd fheldrake* Fn. 96. croffes Sweden in April, and does not ftop till fhe has reached the White fea.

The *coblers awl* Fn. 137. goes every autumn into Italy.

The *arētic driver* Fn. 121. goes into Germany every fpring, and autumn.

The *miffel thrufh* Fn. 189. fills our woods in the fpring, but leaves us in the winter.

The *pied chaffinch* Syf. Nat. 10. 97. 1. during the winter, being obliged to leave the alps *, haftens into Sweden, and often into Germany.

The *gulls* vifit Spain and Italy.

The *raven* [1] goes into Schonen.

By thefe migrations birds alfo become ufeful to many different countries, and are diftributed over almoft all the globe. I cannot forbear expreffing my admiration here, that all

---

* The Author means the Northern alps.

[1] I have tranflated the word corvus by raven, becaufe Linnæus does not mention the carrion crow at all, either in the Faun. Suec. nor in the Syft. Nat. before the late edition.

of

of them exactly obferve the times of coming and
going, and that they do not miftake their way.
There is a very large fhell-fifh in the Medi-
terranean called the *pinna*, blind as all of that
genus, but furnifhed with very ftrong calcareous valves. (Bell. aquat. 401. t. 401. Jonft.
exfang. t. 16. f. 5, 6. Gualt. ind. t. 79, 79.)
The *fcuttle-fifh* (Bell. aquat. 330. t. 331. Jonft.
exfang. t. 1. f. 1.) is an inhabitant of the fame
fea, and a deadly enemy to the former; as
foon as the *fcuttle-fifh* fees the *pinna* open its
fhell, he rufhes upon her like a lion, and devours her. The *pinnoteres* or *pinnophylax*
(Jonft. exfang. t. 20. f. 3.) is of the crab kind
naked, like the hermit, and very quick-fight-
ed. This *cancer* or *crab* the *pinna* receives
into her covering, and when fhe opens her
valves in queft of food, lets him out to look for
prey. During this the *fcuttle-fifh* approaches;
the *crab* returns with the utmoft fpeed and
anxiety to his hoftefs, who being thus warned
of the danger fhuts her doors, and keeps out
the enemy. That very fagacious obferver D.
D. Haffelquift in his voyage towards Paleftine
beheld this curious phænomenon, which tho'
well known to the antients had efcaped the
moderns. Arift. hift. lib. 5. c. 15. relates,

that

that the *pinna* kept a guard to watch for her. That there grew to the mouth of the *pinna* a ſmall animal, having claws, and ſerving as a caterer, which was like a *crab*, and was called the *pinnophylax*. Plin. lib. 9. 51. ſays, the ſmalleſt of all the kinds is called the *pinnoteres*, and therefore liable to injury; this has the prudence to hide itſelf in the ſhells of *oyſters*. Again lib. 9. 66. he ſays ᵐ the *pinna* is of the genus of ſhell-fiſh; it is produced in muddy waters, always erect, nor ever without a companion, which ſome call the *pinnoteres*, others the *pinnophylax*. This ſometimes is a ſmall *ſquill*, ſometimes a *crab*, that follows the *pinna* for the ſake of food. The *pinna* is blind, and

ᵐ This is taken out of Ariſtotle, who ſeems to have thought, that the pinna grew from that which really is its beard, and which it throws out upon the adjoyning bodies in order to fix itſelf. For he ſays the pinna is produced from the byſſus, which is generally ſuppoſed to mean the beard of this ſhell-fiſh, and to have been uſed for making the fineſt of ſtuffs, frequently mentioned by antient writers under the name of Byſſine garments, and of which they now in ſome countries make ſtockings as i am informed. This notion of the pinna growing from the byſſus or beard is of the ſame kind with that which prevailed formerly in relation to the gooſe tree, mentioned by many writers, of whom a long liſt may be ſeen in the tenth edition of the Syſt. Nat.

3   when

when upon opening its fhell it expofes itfelf as a prey to the fmalleft kind of fifhes, thefe immediately affault her, and growing bolder upon finding no refiftance venture in. The guard watching its time gives notice by a bite; upon which the *pinna* clofing its fhell, fhuts in, kills, and gives part of whatever happens to be there to its companion.

The *pinna*, and the *crab* together dwell,
For mutual fuccour in one common fhell.
They both to gain a livelihood combine ;
That takes the prey, when this has given the fign.
From hence this *crab* above his fellows famed,
By antient Greeks was *pinnoteres* named.

OPPIAN.

§. 18.

Deftruction.

We have obferved above that all animals do not live upon vegetables, but that there are fome which feed upon certain animalcula. Nay there are fome which fubfift only by ra-pine, and daily deftroy numbers of the peace-able kind.

Thefe animals are deftroyed, but in fuch a

I manner

manner that the weaker generally are infefted by the ftronger in a continued feries. Thus the *tree-loufe* lives upon plants. The fly called *mufca aphidivora* lives upon the *tree-loufe.* The *hornet* and *wafp fly* upon the *mufca aphidivora.* The *dragon fly* upon the *hornet* and *wafp fly.* The *fpider* on the *dragon fly.* The *fmall birds* on the *fpider.* And laftly the *hawk* kind on the *fmall birds.*

In like manner the ⁿ *monoculus* delights in putrid waters, the *knat* eats the *monoculus,* the *frog* eats the *knat,* the *pike* eats the *frog,* the *fea calf* eats the *pike.*

The *bat* and *goat-fucker* make their excurfions only at night, that they may catch the *moths* which at that time fly about in vaft quantities.

The *wood-pecker* pulls out the *infects,* which lye hid in the trunks of trees.

The *fwallow* purfues thofe which fly about in the open air.

The *mole* purfues the *worms.* The large fifhes devour the fmall. Nay we fcarcely know an animal, which has not fome enemy to contend with.

ⁿ An infect that has no name in Englifh as far as i can find.

Amongft

Amongſt quadrupeds *wild beaſts* are moſt
remarkably pernicious and dangerous to others,
as the *hawk* kind among birds. But that they
may not, by too atrocious a butchery, deſtroy
whole ſpecies; even theſe are circumſcribed
within certain bounds. Firſt, as to the moſt
fierce of all, it deſerves to be noted how few
they are in proportion to other animals. Secondly, the number of them is not equal in
all countries. Thus France and England breed
no *wolves*, and the northern countries no *tigers*
or *lions*. Thirdly, theſe fierce animals ſometimes fall upon, and deſtroy one another. Thus
the *wolf* devours the *fox*. The *dog* infeſts
both the *wolf* and *fox*; nay *wolves* in a body
will ſometimes venture to ſurround a *bear*.
The *tiger* often kills its own male whelps.
Dogs are ſometimes ſeized with madneſs and
deſtroy their fellows, or with the mange deſtroy
themſelves.

Laſtly, wild beaſts ſeldom arrive at ſo great
an age as animals, which live on vegetables.
For they are ſubject from their alcaline diet to
various diſeaſes, which bring them ſooner to
an end.

But although all animals are infeſted by their
peculiar enemies, yet they are often able to

elude

elude their violence by ftratagems and force. Thus the *hare* often confounds the dog by her windings.

When the *bear* attacks *fheep* and cattle, they draw up together for mutual defence. *Horfes* joyn heads together, and fight with their heels. *Oxen* joyn tails, and fight with their horns.

Swine get together in herds, and boldly op-pofe themfelves to any attack, fo that they are not eafily overcome; and it is worth while to obferve, that all of them place their young, as lefs able to defend themfelves, in the middle, that they may remain fafe during the battle.

Birds by their different ways of flying often-times efcape the *hawk* If the *pigeon* had the fame way of flying as the *hawk* fhe would hardly ever efcape his claws °.

It deferves alfo to be remarked, how much fome animals confult their fafety by night. When *horfes* fleep in woods, one by turns re-mains awake, and, as it were, keeps watch. When *monkies*, S. N. 2. 10. in Brafil fleep

upon

° As i have, when opportunities offered, meafured and weighed feveral kinds of birds, i fhall here fubjoyn a table of fome of them with the proportions of the weight to the fail. N. B. By fail i mean the extent of the wings and tail.

I do

upon trees, one of them keeps awake, in order to give the fign, when the *tiger* creeps towards them,

I do not pretend to accuracy, and i imagine it will not be expected on a fubject of this nature.

		Weight Avoidupois.		Proportion of fquare inches to the ounce.
		l.	oz.	
Turkey	——	8	8	$2\frac{1}{4}$
Pheafant	——	2	8	$2\frac{1}{4}$
Coot	——	2	8	$2\frac{1}{4}$
Black cock	——	2 .	6	$3\frac{1}{2}$
Puttock	——	1	14	18
Rook	——	1	3	$10\frac{1}{4}$
Partridge	——	1	1	3
Ivy owl	——	0	15	9
Ring-dove	——	0	14	10
Woodcock	——	0	10	6
Small hawk	—	0	$6\frac{3}{4}$	26
Wood-pecker	—	0	4	9
Cuckow	——	0	4	18
Miffel bird	——	0	4	14
Snipe	——	0	4	$9\frac{1}{4}$
Redfhank	——	0	4	9
Crofs bill	——	0	$1\frac{1}{2}$	$11\frac{3}{4}$
Houfe fwallow	—	0	1	18
Houfe fparrow	—	0	1	12
Wheat-ear	——	0	1	14
Linnet	——	0	$0\frac{1}{2}$	$20\frac{3}{4}$
Black cap	——	0	$0\frac{1}{2}$	18
Stone fmich	——	0	$0\frac{1}{2}$	25
Beccafigo	——	0	$0\frac{1}{2}$	24
White throat	—	0	$0\frac{1}{2}$	17
			grains.	
Long tailed titmoufe		0	95	25
Regulus criftatus		0	76	23

It

them, and in cafe the guard fhould be caught
afleep, the reft tear him to pieces*. Hence the
hunting of rapacious animals is not always fuc-
cefsfull, and they are often obliged to labor for
a whole day to no purpofe. For this reafon the
Creator has given them fuch a nature, that they
can bear fafting a long time. Thus the *lion*
lurks in his den many days without famifhing,
and the *wolf*, when he has once well fatisfied
his hunger, can faft many weeks without any
difficulty.

It appears by this table that the fmaller birds in general
have more fail in proportion than the larger of the efculent
kind, fuch as the pheafant, partridge, woodcock, ring-dove,
&c. and that it fhould be fo contrived appears reafonable on
more accounts than one. Firft, becaufe fmall birds living,
many of them, amongft fhrubs and bufhes, are obliged to
make fhort and quick motions in hopping from bough to
bough, at which time they always make ufe of their wings;
fome of them live chiefly on worms and flies, which are not
to be caught without great nimblenefs, and frequent gardens
and houfes and are more liable to the attacks of cats and
other animals. And thofe which live in the open fields are
expofed to the hawk, and were they not quick at turning
they would fcarcely ever efcape.

Again the different proportions of the bulk to the furface
in large and fmall birds is to the difadvantage of the latter,
on account of the greater proportional refiftance of the air,
and this wanted fome compenfation.

More might be added on this fubject, but i am afraid moft
readers will think what i have already faid is more than
enough.

* Maregraf. Braf. 227. Biberg.

If

If we confider the end for which it pleafed
the Supreme Being to conftitute fuch an order
of nature, that fome animals fhould be, as it
were, created only to be miferably butchered
by others, it feems that his Providence not
only aimed at fuftaining, but alfo keeping a
juft proportion amongft all the fpecies; and fo
prevent any one of them increafing too much,
to the detriment of men, and other animals.
For if it be true, as it is moft affuredly, that
the furface of the earth can fupport only a certain number of inhabitants, they muft all perifh, if the fame number were doubled, or
tripled, Derh. Phyf. Theol. p. 237.

There are fome viviparous *flies*, which bring
forth 2000 young. Thefe in a little time would
fill the air, and like clouds intercept the rays
of the fun, unlefs they were devoured by birds,
fpiders, and many other animals.

Storks, and *falcons* free Ægypt from *frogs*,
which after the inundation of the Nile, cover
all the countrey. The fame birds alfo clear
Paleftine of *mice*. Bellonius on this fubject
fays as follows. " The *ftorks* come to Ægypt
" in fuch abundance, that the fields, and mea-
" dows are white with them. Yet the Ægyp-
" tians are not difpleafed with this fight; as

* Mufchenbr.

I 4 " *frogs*

" *frogs* are generated in fuch numbers there,
" that did not the *ftorks* devour them, they
" would over-run every thing. Befides they
" alfo catch, and eat *ferpents*. Between Belba
" and Gaza the fields of Paleftine are often
" defert on account of the abundance of *mice*,
" and *rats*; and were they not deftroyed by the
" *falcons*, that come here, by inftinct, the in-
" habitants could have no harveft.

The *white fox* S. N. 8. 7. is of equal advantage
in the Lapland alps; as he deftroys the Norway
rats, F. N. 26. which are generated there in great
abundance; and thus hinders them from increafing too much in proportion, which would
be the deftruction of vegetables.

It is fufficient for us, that nothing is made
by Providence in vain, and that whatever is
made, is made with fupreme wifdom. For it
does not become us to pry too boldly into all the
defigns of God. Let us not imagine, when
thefe rapacious animals fometimes do us mifchief, that the Creator planned the order of nature according to our private principles of œconomy; for the Laplanders have one way of
living; the European hufbandman another;
the Hottentots and favages a third, whereas
the ftupendous œconomy of the Deity is one
through-

throughout the globe, and if Providence does not always calculate exactly according to our way of reckoning, we ought to confider this affair in the fame light, as when different feamen wait for a fair wind, every one, with refpect to the part he is bound to, who we plainly fee cannot all be fatisfied.

§. 19.

The whole earth would be overwhelmed with carcafes, and ftinking bodies, if fome animals did not delight to feed upon them. Therefore when an animal dyes, *bears, wolves, foxes, ravens,* &c. do not lofe a moment till they have taken all away. But if a *horfe* e. g. dyes near the public road, you will find him, after a few days, fwoln, burft, and at laft filled with innumerable *grubs* of carnivorous *flies,* by which he is entirely confumed, and removed out of the way, that he may not become a nufance to paffengers by his poifonous ftench.

When the carcafes of fifhes are driven upon the fhore, the voracious kinds, fuch as the *thornback,* the *hound fifh,* the *conger eel,* &c. gather about and eat them. But becaufe the flux, and

reflux

reflux foon change the ftate of the fea, they themfelves are often detained in pits, and become a prey to the wild beafts, that frequent the fhores. Thus the earth is not only kept clean from the putrefaction of carcafes, but at the fame time by the œconomy of nature the neceffaries of life are provided for many animals. In the like manner many *infects* at once promote their own good, and that of other animals. Thus *knats* lay their eggs in ftagnant, putrid and ftinking waters, and the *grubs* that arife from thefe eggs clear away all the putrefaction; and this will eafily appear, if any one will make the experiment by filling two veffels with putrid water, leaving the *grubs* in one, and taking them all out of the other. For then he will foon find the water, that is full of *grubs*, pure and without any ftench, while the water that has no *grubs* will continue ftinking.

Lice increafe in a wonderfull manner in the heads of children, that are fcabby, nor are they without their ufe, for they confume the redundant humours.

The *beetle* kind in fummer extract all moift and glutinous matter out of the dung of cattle,

fo

fo that it becomes like duft, and is fpread by the wind over the ground. Were it not for this, the vegetables that lye under the dung, would be fo far from thriving, that all that fpot would be rendered barren.

As the excrements of *dogs* is of fo filthy and feptic a nature, that no *infect* will touch them, and therefore they cannot be difperfed by that means, care is taken that thefe animals fhould exonerate upon ftones, trunks of trees, or fome high place, that vegetables may not be hurt by them.

Cats bury their dung. Nothing is fo mean, nothing fo little, in which the wonderfull order, and wife difpofition of nature does not fhine forth.

§. 20.

Laftly, all thefe treafures of nature fo artfully contrived, fo wonderfully propagated, fo providentially fupported throughout her three kingdoms, feem intended by the Creator for the fake of man. Every thing may be made fubfervient to his ufe, if not immediately, yet mediately, not fo to that of other animals. By the help of reafon man tames the fierceft animals,

mals, purſues and catches the ſwifteſt, nay he is able to reach even thoſe, which lye hid in the bottom of the ſea.

By the help of reaſon he increaſes the number of vegetables immenſely, and does that by art, which nature, left to herſelf, could ſcarcely effeƈt. By ingenuity he obtains from vegetables whatever is convenient or neceſſary for food, drink, cloathing, medicine, navigation, and a thouſand other purpoſes.

He has found the means of going down into the abyſs of the earth, and almoſt ſearching its very bowels. With what artifice has he learned to get fragments from the moſt rocky mountains, to make the hardeſt ſtones fluid like water; to ſeparate the uſefull metal from the uſeleſs droſs, and to turn the fineſt ſand to ſome uſe! In ſhort when we follow the ſeries of created things, and conſider how providentially one is made for the ſake of another, the matter comes to this, that all things are made for the ſake of man; and for this end more eſpecially, that he by admiring the works of the Creator ſhould extoll his glory, and at once enjoy all thoſe things, of which he ſtands in need, in order to paſs his life conveniently and pleaſantly.

§. 20.

§. 21.

This subject concerning the œconomy of nature, a very small part of which i have lightly touched upon, is of such importance and dignity, that if it were to be properly treated in all its parts, men would find wherewithal to employ almost all the powers of the mind. Nay time itself would fail before even the most acute human sagacity would be able to discover the amazing œconomy, laws, and exquisite structure of the least insect, since as Pliny observes, nature no where appears more herself, than in her most minute works. Every species of created beings deserves to engross one examiner.

If according to gross calculation we reckon in the world 20000 species of *vegetables*, 3000 of *worms*, 12000 of *insects*, 200 of *amphibious animals*, 2600 of *fishes*, 2000 of *birds* [p], 200 of *quadrupeds*; the whole sum of the species of living creatures will amount to 40000. Out of these our countrey has scarcely 3000,

[p] How the author came to reckon 2000 species of birds in the world i cannot guess, for in the Syst. Nat. Linn. edit. 6. there are only about 150 mentioned, and in the last edition of that book not above 550.

for

for we have difcovered only about 1200 native plants, and about 1400 fpecies of animals. We of the human race, who were created to praife and adore our Creator, unlefs we choofe to be mere idle fpectators, fhould and in duty ought to be affected with nothing fo much as the pious confideration of this glorious palace. Moft certainly if we were to improve and polifh our minds by the knowledge of thefe things; we fhould befides the great ufe which would accrue to our œconomy, difcover the more excellent œconomy of nature, and more ftrongly admire it when difcovered.

Omnium elementorum alterni recurfi funt,
Quicquid alteri perit in alterum tranfit.
Senec. Nat. III. 10.

THE foregoing piece, though on a fubject often treated by learned and ingenious men, feems to me to contain many things new and curious, and to give a more comprehenfive and diftinct view, as it were in a map, of the feveral parts of nature, their connections and dependencies, than is any where elfe to be found. But exclufive of this or any other comparative merit, it certainly conveys an ufefull

3

leffon,

leſſon, and ſuch an one as the beſt of us often want to have inculcated.

From a partial conſideration of things, we are very apt to criticiſe what we ought to admire; to look upon as uſeleſs what perhaps we ſhould own to be of infinite advantage to us, did we ſee a little farther; to be peeviſh where we ought to give thanks; and at the ſame time to ridicule thoſe, who employ their time and thoughts in examining what we were, i. e. ſome of us moſt aſſuredly were, created and appointed to ſtudy. In ſhort we are too apt to treat the Almighty worſe than a rational man would treat a good mechanic; whoſe works he would either thoroughly examine, or be aſhamed to find any fault with them. This is the effect of a partial conſideration of nature; but he who has candor of mind and leiſure to look farther, will be inclined to cry out:

How wond'rous is this ſcene! where all is form'd
With number, weight, and meaſure! all deſign'd
For ſome great end! where not alone the plant
Of ſtately growth; the herb of glorious hue,
Or food-full ſubſtance; not the laboring ſteed,
The herd, and flock that feed us; not the mine
That yields us ſtores for elegance, and uſe;

The

The fea that loads our table, and conveys
The wanderer man from clime to clime, with all
Thofe rolling fpheres, that from on high fhed
    down
Their kindly influence; not thefe alone,
Which ftrike ev'n eyes incurious, but each mofs,
Each fhell, each crawling infect holds a rank
Important in the plan of Him, who fram'd
This fcale of beings; holds a rank, which loft
Wou'd break the chain, and leave behind a gap
Which nature's felf would rue. Almighty Being,
Caufe and fupport of all things, can i view
Thefe objects of my wonder; can i feel
Thefe fine fenfations, and not think of thee?
Thou who doft thro' th' eternal round of time;
Doft thro' th' immenfity of fpace exift
Alone, fhalt thou alone excluded be
From this thy univerfe? Shall feeble man
Think it beneath his proud philofophy
To call for thy affiftance, and pretend
To frame a world, who cannot frame a clod?—
Not to know thee, is not to know ourfelves—
Is to know nothing—nothing worth the care
Of man's exalted fpirit—all becomes
Without thy ray divine, one dreary gloom;
WHERE lurk the monfters of phantaftic brains,
Order bereft of thought, unclus'd effects,

                      Fate

Fate freely acting, and unerring Chance:
WHERE meanlefs matter to a chaos finks
Or fomething lower ftill, for without thee
It crumbles into atoms void of force,
Void of refiftance — it eludes our thought:
WHERE laws eternal to the varying code
Of felf-love dwindle. Intereft, paffion, whim
Take place of right, and wrong; the golden chain
Of beings melts away, and the mind's eye
Sees nothing but the prefent. All beyond
Is vifionary guefs — is dream — is death.

K   O N

FOLIATION of TREES.

✗✗✗✗✗✗✗✗✗✗✗✗✗✗✗✗✗✗✗✗✗✗✗✗

ON THE

FOLIATION of TREES;

O R,

The time when they put out their leaves.

By *HARALD BARCK.*

Upsal, 1753. May 3.

Amæn. Acad. vol. iii.

§. I.

BOtanifts in every age have not only taken great pains to difcover and give names to plants, but have alfo defcribed them with all poffible accuracy. But this part of knowledge has been, till this prefent age, confined to narrower bounds than it deferved; for an opinion has prevailed amongft almoft all the men of learning, that it is of no ufe out of the re-

gions

gions of medicine. From whence it has happened, that we find very few that have cultivated botany, but phyficians; nor have even thefe carried their inquiries farther than to obtain a moderate knowledge of officinal plants. But in our times fome, who are worthy of the higheft regard from all true lovers of this ftudy, have endeavoured to find out, and inveftigate the vertues of plants with greater care, and induftry. For thefe men befides medical ufes have difcovered great, and remarkable advantages accruing from fuch refearches.

However i do not intend to give a catalogue of them here, but fhall content myfelf with juft touching upon fome few things, that have been done in this way, in our own univerfity. In the *Philofophia Botanica* our illuftrious prefident has fhewn, that every foil has its own peculiar plants, which we fhould feek for in vain any where elfe ; and that certain plants keep, as it were, their watches, i. e. expand their flowers and clofe them again at ftated times [q]. The differtation on the *efpoufals of plants* has imparted to the learned world the ufe of various phænomena, which

[q] Vid. Philof. Botan. p. 263. 273. Barck. This curious fubject is amply treated in Amæn. Acad. vol. 4.

occur

occur in the fœcundation of plants. The *Flora œconomica* has faithfully fet forth the ufe of plants in private life. The differtation on the *buds of plants* has opened to us the caufe, why various trees cannot bear the fnows, and frofts of our part of the world. From the effay on the *efculent plants* of our countrey we find, that there are many plants growing with us, which are proper for food, hitherto overlooked. In the *Swedifh Pan* it is fhewn, that certain plants only are deftined for fuftenance to certain animals. From the *Hofpita Infeéto-rum Flora* we are informed that certain vegetables are eat by certain fpecies of infeéts.

It is now the fourth year fince our illuftrious prefident exhorted his countreymen to obferve with all care and diligence, at what time every tree expands its buds, and unfolds its leaves; imagining, and not without good reafon, that our countrey would fome time or other, from obfervations of this kind made in different places, reap fome new, and perhaps unexpeéted advantage. Upon this admonition, i at that time living in Smoland with that noble perfon G. A. Witting major, and knight of the military order, was incited to obferve for the fpace of three years, beginning from the year

1750, the days when different trees began to put out their leaves, when the countreymen fowed their fields, and how much time there paffed between feed time, and harveft. This i did with intent, if poffible, to find out fixed laws by which to regulate the proper feed-time in every province. But the few obfervations, which i was able to make, were not fufficient for this purpofe ; that the work therefore which i meditated might not reft upon too flight a foundation, our prefident communicated all the papers fent to him from different places for my examination. Such then is the defign of this effay, and i fubmit it to the candid reader, hoping that he will look upon it with an indulgent eye.

§. 2.

Our lands, which lye under a cold fky, are bound up with froft all the winter. Hence the roots of our plants oppreffed, as it were, with a drowfy fleep, are benummed, and many herbs, that remain above ground, dye [r]. But when

---

[r] We have had five winters remarkably fevere in Sweden, viz. 1665, $\frac{1683}{1684}$, $\frac{1708}{1709}$, $\frac{1739}{1740}$, and 1751. The cold of which laft Feb. 1. N S. was extremely intenfe, and fuch as has

when the fun by its mild rays at the beginning
of fpring refrefhes the earth, the fnows melt,
the

has fcarcely been known in this age, for the botanic thermometer funk to 32 degrees. Barck.

In that thermometer the freezing point is o, and that of
boiling water 100. So that taking it for granted that the
author muft mean 32 below o, this point would anfwer to 57
below 32 or the freezing point of Farenheit, which is a degree of cold never known in this countrey. I am affured
from good authority, that in the year 1739 the thermometer did not fink nine degrees below freezing point in England.
They who are curious to fee much more furprizing inftances
of cold than that in Sweden, may confult the preface to
Gmelin's Flora Sibirica, where they will find how very apt
philofophers are to fall into miftakes about the powers of
nature, when they truft to theory, inftead of confulting
experience. Monf. Maupertuis fays, that the mercury in
Reaumur's thermometer in Lapland funk to 37 degrees below
freezing point, which is equal to 67 degrees in Farenheit.

Perhaps, fays Linnæus in the Flora Lapponica, the
curious reader will wonder how the people in Lapland
during the terrible cold, that reigns there in winter, can
preferve their lives; fince almoft all birds, and even
fome wild beafts, defert it at that time. The Laplander
not only in the day, but thro' whole winter nights is
obliged to wander about in the woods with his herds of
rhen deer. For the rhen deer never come under cover, nor
eat any kind of fodder, but a particular kind of *liverwort*.
On this account the herdfmen are under a neceffity of living continually in the woods, in order to take care of their
cattle, left they fhould be devoured by wild beafts. The
Lap-

the ice gives way, the froft is diffolved, and a
joyfull face of things returns. Immediately we
fee

Laplander eafily does without more light, as the fnow re-
flects the rays that come from the ftars, and as the *aurora
borealis* illuminates the air every night with a great variety
of figures. The cold is fo great that forreigners are kept
aloof, and even deterred from their moft happy woods. No
part of our body is more eafily deftroyed by cold than the
extremities of the limbs, which are moft remote from the
fun of this microcofm, the heart. The kibes that happen
to our hands, and feet, fo common in the northern parts
of Sweden, prove this. In Lapland you will never fee fuch
a thing, altho' were we to judge by the fituation of the
countrey we fhould imagine juft the contrary, efpecially as
the people wear no ftockings, as we do, not only fingle but
double, and triple. The Laplander guards himfelf againft
the cold in the following manner. He wears breeches made
of rhen deer fkins with the hair on, reaching down to his
heels; and fhoes made of the fame materials, the hairy
part turned outwards. He puts into his fhoes *flender-eared
broad-leaved cyperus grafs*, carex veficaria, Spec. Pl. that is cut
in fummer and dryed. This he firft combs, and rubs in his
hands, and then places it in fuch a manner, that it not only
covers his feet quite round, but his legs alfo; and being thus
guarded, he is quite fecured againft the intenfe cold. With
this grafs they ftuff their gloves likewife in order to
preferve their hands. As this grafs keeps off the cold in
winter, fo in fummer it hinders the feet from fweating, and
at the fame time preferves their feet from being annoyed by
ftriking againft ftones, &c. for their fhoes are very thin,
being made, not of tanned leather, but the raw hide. It
was

fee the vernal flowers begin to celebrate their nuptials, and the trees, one after another, open their buds, and cloath themfelves with leaves. It is a matter of wonder why the *wood plants*, as the *fpurge laurel*, the *wood anemone*, the *noble liverwort*, the *vernal vetch*, the *broom rape*, the *pafque flower*, the *colts-foot*, the *fage of Jerufa-lem*, *pilewort*, *violets*, &c. and the garden plants, as the *affara bacca*, *fnow drops*, *bulbous violet*, *vernal crocus*, &c. fhould flower in the very beginning of fpring; when we cannot by any pains, or care bring them to flower in the autumn, or after the fummer folftice. For it is remarkable that thefe plants, which are fo very patient of the cold in the fpring, are yet in the autumn fo tender, and weak, that they dye like the Indian plants upon the firft hoar froft [s], e. g. the

was difficult for me to find what particular kind of grafs they prefer for this purpofe, as not being every where the fame, tho' always one of the *cyperus graffes*, but i perceived at laft that it was what i mentioned above. Thus far Linnæus. I will add, that this grafs grows with us.

[s] The iron nights, as they are called in the Swedifh language, i. e. fharp nights, happen generally at Upfal between the 19th and 31ft of Auguft. e. g. 1746 they began the 19th, 1748 the 17th, 1749 the 1ft of Sept. 1750 the 20th of Auguft, 1751 the 27th, 1752 the 20th. They feldom

the *blue mountain thiftle*, *touch-me-not*, &c. On the contrary we fee *fuccories* and *thiftles* never flower before the fame folftice, whence the hufbandman judges from their flowers, as from a calendar that cannot deceive, that the folftice is paft. From hence it is evident, that there is fomething elfe befides moifture and heat which promotes the fertility of plants.

§. 3.

In the fame manner trees obferve fixed laws, and a certain order in their leafing; fo that he, who is but moderately verfed in this affair,

feldom laft above three or four nights. After thefe barley does not grow, and about the time they come on, the gardeners do not venture to truft their green-houfe and other tender plants any longer to the open air. At that time the leaves of the *fig*, the *mulberry*, the *walnut*, the *vine*, the *toxicodendrum* and even of the *beech* are fhrivelled up. The Indian plants, fuch as the *kidney bean*, the *African marygold*, the *cucumber*, the *amaranth*, the *convolvulus*, the *tobacco*, the *thorn apple*, &c. dye. Nay fometimes even our native plants, as the *noli me tangere*, the *leffer burdock*, the *bryony*, the *vipers buglos*, the *pimpernel*, the *blue mountain fow-thiftle*, the *goofewort*, &c. wither. But before this happens, the *meadow faffron* puts forth its flowers, and that fometimes fooner, fometimes later, according as thefe iron nights come fooner or later. Barck,

may

may immediately know, when he fees one fpecies of trees in leaf, what fpecies will be next
in leaf. Nor do we hardly ever find this order
of Flora tranfgreffed. He who fhould imagine
he had found the true caufe of this phænomenon in the different depths of the roots of different trees would be miftaken; for then fhrubs
would always be in leaf before trees of one,
and the fame kind; which yet rarely happens.
This phænomenon therefore arifes without
doubt from fome other caufe, hitherto undif-
covered, and perhaps explicable only by the
different texture of the tree.

The order of the leafing of trees with us is
as follows.

1 *Red elder*	12 The *ofier*
2 *Honey fuckle*	13 *Alder*
3 *Goofeberry*	14 *Sea buckthorn*
4 *Red currant*	15 *Apple tree*
5 *Spiræa frutex*	16 *Cherry tree*
6 *Bird cherry*	17 *Water elder*
7 *Spindle tree*	18 *Birch*
8 *Shrub cinquefoil*	19 *Hafel*
9 *Common elder*	20 *Elm*
10 *Privet*	21 *Dog rofe*
11 *Quicken tree*	22 *Pear tree*

23 *Plum*

23 *Plum tree*   28 *Aria Theophrafti*

24 *Buckthorn*   29 *Afp*

25 *Berry-bearing alder* 30 *Maple*

26 *Lime tree*   31 The *oak*

27 *Beech*   32 The *afh* [t]

With the firſt ſoft breeze, ſays Pliny, the *cornelian cherry* puts forth its buds, next the *bay* a little before the æquinox. The *lime*,

---

[t] As i do not know that any thing of this kind has ever been publiſhed in England, i will ſubjoyn the order of the leafing of ſome trees and ſhrubs, as obſerved by me in Norfolk, Ann. 1755.

1 Honey ſuckle	Jan. 15	19 Marſh elder	Apr. 11
2 Gooſeberry	March 11	20 Wych elm	12
3 Currant	11	21 Quicken tree	13
4 Elder	11	22 Hornbeam	13
5 Birch	April 1	23 Apple tree	14
6 Weeping willow	1	24 Abele	16
7 Raſberry	3	25 Cheſnut	16
8 Bramble	3	26 Willow	17
9 Briar	4	27 Oak	18
10 Plumb	6	28 Lime	18
11 Apricot	6	29 Maple	19
12 Peach	6	30 Walnut	21
13 Filberd	7	31 Plane	21
14 Sallow	7	32 Black poplar	21
15 Alder	7	33 Beech	21
16 Sycomore	9	34 Acacia robinia	21
17 Elm	10	35 Aſh	22
18 Quince	10	36 Carolina poplar	22

the

the *maple*, the *poplar*, the *elm*, the *fallow*, the *alder*, the *filberd* and *hafel* are among the firft that put out leaves; the *plane tree* alfo is very early. Nat. Hift. lib. 16. 25.

The foliation or leafing of the firft four named trees, 1, 2, 3, 4, varies very much as to the time, and the day on which they break bud; for as the winter goes off fooner or later, fo they are in leaf fooner or later. But this does not hold of the reft, e. g. in the year 1750, in which there was fcarcely any winter-weather, but the whole was almoft a perpetual fpring, i obferved towards the latter end of March, that the *currant* and *goofeberry* were in blow about Gripenberg; whereas the laft year they did not blow till the middle of April. The *oak*, and the *afh* feldom fhew their leaves before the night frofts are over[v]. For which reafon gardeners do not venture to truft their houfe plants to the open air, till the leaves of the laft trees give fign of a mild winter.

[v] This agrees with lord Bacon's obfervations, Nat. Hift. p. 146. that a long winter makes the earlier and later flowers come together. This i obferved was the cafe in the year 1755, when the fpring was very backward. The author fays in a note, that it has been obferved for above ten years paft, that the oak has been always in leaf before the end of May, in Upland.

3   §. 41

§. 4.

The prudent hufbandman will above all things watch with the greateft care the proper time for fowing; becaufe this with the Divine affiftance produces plenty of provifions, and lays the foundation of the public welfare of the kingdom, and of the private happinefs of the people. The ignorant farmer being more te-nacious of the ways, and cuftoms of his an-ceftors, fixes his fowing feafon generally to a month, and to a day; whether or no the earth be prepared to receive the feed he little cares. From whence it frequently happens, that the fields do not return what might be expected, and that what the fower fowed with fweat, the reaper reaps with forrow. Wife œconomifts therefore in all ages have endeavored to their utmoft to fix a certain time for fowing; but hitherto their labor has proved fruitlefs. There have been fome, who have tryed to difcover the qualities of the land neceffary for this pur-pofe, by tafte and fmell; nor have there been wanting to others, who were perfuaded, that the fmell of the earth, and the *fila divæ vir-ginis* *, were infallible figns of feed-time. All

* I do not underftand the meaning of thefe words.

which,

which, although perhaps they are not wholly
without foundation, are yet infufficient for ob-
taining the end we aim at. For the experience
of many years has taught us, that the feeds of
one and the fame fpecies fown in the fame
ground at different times do not produce equal
crops. We have feen even a great difference
between what was fown in the morning, and
the afternoon. Thus alfo while one plant is
vigorous and florifhes, another of the fame
nature, and raifed in the fame foil withers, and
dyes. The farmer often throws the caufe of
fcarcity upon Providence, that means to punifh
an ungratefull people, by ordering the fields
to mourn in weeds, and the corn to mock the
the threfhers toil with empty hufks; but it may
be with truth afferted, that this furmife is
often without foundation. He ought rather to
complain of his own imprudence, and accufe
himfelf that his granary is not better ftored.

We look up to the ftars ", and without reafon fuppofe that the changes on earth will anfwer

---

" This looking up to the ftars for this purpofe, was tranf-
mitted down to us by the Greeks and Romans from Ægypt,
where the feafons being much more regular than in thefe northern parts, might be as fure a guide in that countrey, as any
they could follow. But an aftronomical calendar perhaps may

fwer to the heavenly bodies; entirely neglect-
ing the things that grow round about us.
We

be not fo good a guide to us as the vegetation of certain plants;
fuppofing we could once fix on the proper one for fowing
each kind of feed. I have been told by a common hufbandman in Norfolk, that when the oak catkins begin to fhed
their feed, it is a proper time to fow barley; and why might
not fome other tree ferve to direct the farmer as to other
feeds? The prudent gardener never ventures to put his houfe
plants out, till the mulberry leaf is of a certain growth.

It appears from Geminus in his elements of aftronomy,
that the coincidence of the feafons as to heat, cold, rain, &c.
with the rifings and fettings of the ftars, had caufed a notion
to prevail among the antients, that thefe celeftial phænomena
were not merely the figns, but the caufes of the different
feafons. This notion, which he takes fome pains to overturn, would never have begun in fuch uncertain climates, as
are found in thefe parts of the world. But in Ægypt, where
the Nile begins to rife regularly upon the appearance of Si-
rius, or the dog-ftar, where the Etefian winds begin, and
ceafe to blow conftantly about the fame time of the year;
and in general the variation of the weather is nearly uniform, fuch a notion might eafily prevail in the minds of an
unenlightened, and fuperftitious people. From them it was
propagated into Greece, where, tho' it muft have been frequently thwarted by a much lefs conftant uniformity, yet it
might ftill be upheld by that blind veneration, which generally
attends antiquity, efpecially amongft the ignorant, and unlearned. As for the Romans, they went ftill farther, for
without even adapting an almanack to their own climate
and time, they fixed the feafons for hufbandry-work of all
kinds by the rifings and fettings of the ftars, fuch as they
found

We fee trees open their buds, and expand
their leaves; from hence we conclude that
fpring

found them in the Greek calendars. To this cuftom Geminus
certainly alludes when he obferves, that an almanack, which
may pretty well foretell the weather in one countrey is good for
nothing in another, as one would think fhould be obvious at firft
fight. Yet this he thought neceffary to explain, and dilate
upon, in order to convince the Romans of their error; for
tho', as Petavius obferves, the later aftronomers went more
accurately to work, the prejudice ftill remained in the minds
of the countrey people, and the vulgar. Whether Geminus thought thofe predictions concerning heat, cold, rain,
drought, &c. which are found in the Alexardrian, Greek,
and Roman calendars, juft in fome of our modern ones, were
univerfally precarious, or whether he only thought they were
fo in fuch climates, as that of Rome, where he is fuppofed
to have lived, he commends Aratus for making ufe of the
natural figns, taken from the afpects of the fun, and fome of
the ftars, as alfo of the figns taken from brutes, inftead of
the rifing and fetting of the ftars, and gives this reafon of
his preference, that thofe predictions, which have fome natural caufe, have a neceffary effect; adding, by way of confirmation of his opinion, that Ariftotle, Eudoxus, and many
other aftronomers, made ufe of them. Thefe predictions
are copied by Virgil, but i do not recollect any place in his
Georgics, where the feafons for ploughing, fowing, &c. are
fixed by the appearance of birds of paffage, or of infects, or
by the flowering of plants, which method was begun by
Hefiod, but never afterwards attended to, that i know, till
Linnæus wrote. Hefiod fays, that if it fhould happen to
rain three days together when the *cuckow* fings, then late
fowing will be as good as early fowing. That when *fnails*

begin

fpring approaches, and experience fupports us
in this conclufion; but no body hitherto has
been

begin to creep out of their holes, and climb up the plants,
you muft leave off digging about vines and take to pruning.
That when the *artichoak* begins to blow, and the *grafhop-
per* chirps upon trees, which, as Theophraftus obferves, was
about the fummer folftice, then goats are in full feafon, &c.
That when the *fig leaf* is about as big as a crow's foot, the
time for failing comes on. That when the voice of the
crane is heard overhead, then is the time for ploughing. It
is true, the poet frequently marks the feafons by the rifings
and fettings of the ftars, and as aftronomy, befides its many
important ufes, is connected with finer fciences, has fomething in it very ftriking to the imagination, and has been
cultivated by men, who had leifure to make calendars for general ufe, it was natural that it fhould get the afcendant over
rules furer perhaps in themfelves, and more adapted to the
purpofe of the hufbandman, but which were deftitute of the
advantages abovementioned, and were moft probably looked
on only as poetical embellifhments.

It is wonderfull to obferve the conformity between vegetation, and the arrival of certain birds of paffage. I will
give one inftance as marked down in a diary kept by me in
Norfolk in the year 1755. April the 16th *young figs* appear, the 17th of the fame month the *cuckow* fings. Now
the word κοκκυξ fignifies a *cuckow*, and likewife the *young
fig*, and the reafon given for it is that in Greece they appeared together. I will juft add that the fame year i firft
found the *cuckow flower* in blow the 19th of April.

To the inftance of coincidence of the appearance of the
cuckow, and the fruit of the *fig-tree* in Greece and England,
i will

been able to ſhew what kind of tree Providence intended ſhould be our calendar, ſo that
we might know on what day the countreyman ought to ſow his grain.

The ſun acts on the earth by looſening,
warming, and preparing it, as the culinary fire
does on our meat, for which a certain degree
of heat is requiſite: For the ſun by its heat
drives the juices taken in by the roots thro' the
veſſels of the tree, which do not return by circulation, but become more copious by the
daily addition of freſh heat. It. Scan. 23.

I will here add ſome coincidences of the like nature, in
Sweden and England.

Linnæus ſays, that the *wood-anemone* blows from the arrival of the *ſwallow*. In my diary for the year 1755, I find
the *ſwallow* appeared April the 6th, and the *wood-auemone*
was in blow the 10th of the ſame month. He ſays, that
the *marſh-marygold* blows when the *cuckow* ſings. According to my diary the *marſh-marygold* was in blow April
the 7th, and the ſame day the *cuckow* ſung.

I have many other obſervations by me about the appear-
ances of birds and the flowering of plants, but as they were
made for one year only, and there are none of other authors
to compare them with, I ſhall not trouble the reader with
them. I have been induced to publiſh them for reaſons that
I have mentioned in the preface. Vid. the Calendar of Flora,

§. 5.

Nature always takes the eafieft, and fhorteft way in all her works. He therefore who would imitate her muft do the fame. No one, i think, can deny but that the fame force, which brings forth the leaves of trees, will alfo make the grain vegetate ; and no one can juftly affert that a premature fowing will always, and every where accelerate a ripe harveft. Perhaps therefore we cannot promife ourfelves a happy fuccefs by any means fo likely, as by taking our rule for fowing from the leafing of trees. We muft for this end obferve in what order every tree according to its fpecies, heat of the atmofphere, and quality of the foil, puts forth its leaves. Afterwards comparing together the obfervations of many years, it will not be difficult from the leafing of trees to define the time, if not certainly, yet probably, when not only *barley*, but *vernal rye*, *oats*, and other annual plants ought to be fown.

§. 6.

To attain this end there were many, who by the exhortation of our prefident noted, not only

only the time of the foliation of trees, but the day alfo on which *barley* was fown, and cut; and were fo kind as to communicate to me their obfervations [w]. I acknowledge myfelf much obliged to each of thefe worthy gentlemen for the benevolence fhewn me on this occafion, and more particularly to D. Torên, who for the fpace of three years made his obfervations on a tree of the fame fpecies with care and diligence; as alfo to D. Eric Ekelund, who did the fame with the like induftry for two years. Some perhaps had not always time, or opportunity to make their experiments with the fame attention; for thofe, who are detained in cities, often want a number of trees to obferve thefe things as they ought, and thofe, who live in the countrey, are often drawn by domeftic affairs from things of this nature. But if obfervations were made according to the following rules. 1ft, That they fhould be continued for *three years*, and thofe fpecified, as well as the *places* in every obfervation. 2d. That they fhould be made on the

[w] The author gives in a note a lift of eighteen perfons who had communicated their obfervations made in Sweden, Norway, Finland, and Lapland, fome for one, fome for two, others for three years from 1750 to 1752 both inclufive.

fame

fame *individuals*. And 3d. on trees which grow on the *fame foil*, and in the *fame expo-fition*, as the *field* that is to be fown. Were thefe circumftances, i fay, attended to, perhaps we might be able to form more certain rules for the ufe of the farmer; but fince thefe rules have been fometimes negleɛted, our bufinefs will not fucceed fo well; for who does not know that the *north wind, fhade*, and a *moift foil* hinder the leafing of trees as much as a *dry fituation* on the flope of a hill inclining to the fouth promotes it? Befides many errors have crept into thefe obfervations, e. g. fome trees between whofe leafing there ought not to intervene above two or three days, are often disjoyned from one another by the interval of a fortnight; not to mention the order of leafing § 3, which trees fcarcely, or rather never tranfgrefs, being tyed down to it by nature herfelf, but which often does not appear in thefe journals ˣ.

ˣ In the original there follows a feɛion which i have not tranflated. The intent of it is to explain a table giving an account of the different days of the foliation of fome trees and fhrubs in Sweden, Norway, &c. which i have omitted, as thinking it would afford little, or no entertainment to the reader.

§. 7.

§. 7.

If we confider the year 1750, we may remember, that the winter was milder than ordinary, and the fpring very early. Whence
fome in Upland fowed their lands about the
end of February; which they fcarcely ever do
in other years before April. I am not ignorant, that the lands in fome of the northern
provinces, efpecially thofe which abound in
clay, require early fowing, that the ground
may be broken with lefs trouble, and that
the firft fhoots of the barley may make their
way through it before it grows ftiff. But the
people of Schonen, and others, that dwell near
the fea, fow late whether the fpring be early
or not; and that fometimes to their great lofs,
for no other reafon but that they received
this cuftom from their anceftors. The moft
northern inhabitants of Sweden find it neceffary to fow, as foon as the froft breaks
up; that the fhort fummer may perfectly ripen
the grain before the winter approaches. For
as eggs require a fixed time for the exclufion
of the young, fo the barley does in different
provinces, to ripen the feed. To prove this
i will produce fome examples.

Sowing

		Sowing.	Harveſt.	Days.
Pithoa.	1740	June 4	Sept. 1	89
	1741	May 29	Aug. 31	94
	1742	27	29	94
	1743	27	26	91
	1744	31	26	87
	1745	24	27	95
	1746	26	25	91
	1747	28	23	87
	1748	June 4	22	79
	1749	May 21	22	93
	1750	19	14	87
	1751	21	11	92
			Medium	85
Upſal.	1747	April 28	Aug. 17	111
	1748	29	20	113
	1749	May 6	27	113
	1750	April 16	30	155
	1751	28	24	118
	1752	30	31	92
			Medium	105

Sowing

		Sowing.	Harveft.	Days.
Nafinge	1750	April 20	Aug. 12	113
toward		May 4	7	95
Norway		19	12	85
		21	14	85
		26	15	81
~		June 13	25	73
			Medium	93

Korn an	1731	May 28	Aug. 31	95
ifland of	1732	June 18	Sept. 14	88
Bahus.	1734	May 9	Aug. 18	101
	1735	25	15	82
	1736	29	27	90
	1738	June 3	Sept. 5	94
	1739	May 8	3	118
			Medium	100

From thefe obfervations, which i have produced, and many others, i can conclude nothing at prefent, unlefs that the *fowing of barley* nearly coincides with the *foliation of the
birch*, at leaft in Upland, and other places adjacent; and if this fign is not to be depended
upon every where, yet it would be eafy for us,
on a due examination, to find out fome other
tree,

tree, more fuited to this purpofe; and which fome provinces might ufe as a calendar; while the greateft part might confult the *birch*. It is a popular error, that lefs time paffes between the fowing, and ripening of wheat in our northern provinces, than here at Upfal, and that this happens becaufe the fummer days are longer in the north, and there is fcarcely any night to retard its growth. But this error is made evident by the grain ripening in as fhort a time in Schonen as in Lapland. For barley in the champain part of Schonen is fown about May the 29th, and reaped fooner than in Upland. But why *barley* ripens later in Upland and Weffmania, than in the other provinces of Sweden, is to me abfolutely a fecret.

§. 8.

If a number of future obfervations fhall confirm the doctrine, which i have been delivering, i do not doubt but that we may reap many advantages from it. For then we fhould not want a fure guide for the hufbandman to regulate himfelf by in fowing his grain, and for the gardener to fow his kitchen, and other feeds. What great benefit therefore would arife to the public,

public, if one in every province would yearly make obfervations in this way, and at laft com-municate them in the fame manner, as aftro-nomers do their meteorological ones to the royal fociety, or academy of fciences?

It will befides be neceffary to remark what fowing, made on different days in the fpring, produces the beft crop; that comparing thefe with the foliation of different trees, it might appear which is the moft proper time for this purpofe. In like manner it will not be amifs to note at what time certain plants, efpecially the moft remarkable in every province, blow; that it might appear whether the year made a flower or a quicker progrefs. For we fee, although obfervations of this kind have yet not come into ufe, that the mower can guefs at the time proper for cutting grafs, either from the flow-ers of the *parnaffia*, the *devil's bit*, the *marfh gen-tian*, or the *baftard afphodel* burfting forth, or from the flowers of the *purple meadow trefoil* withering, or from the ripening of the feeds of the *yellow rattle*, or in higher places from the yellow hue of the leaves of the *leopard's bane*. Would botanifts like aftronomers note the time of foliation, and flowering of trees and herbs, and the days on which the feed is fown, flowers

and

and ripens; and continue thefe obfervations for many years, there can be no doubt, but that we might find fomc rule, from which we might conclude at what time grains, and cu-linary plants, according to the nature of each foil, ought to be fown; nor fhould we be at a lofs to guefs at the approach of winter; nor be ignorant whether we ought to make our au-tumn-fowing later or earlier. Laftly, the gar-dener would have a more fure prophet to con-fult; whereas now he guides himfelf by no-thing but very fallacious conjectures.

§. 9.

This is all which i think fit to produce upon this copious fubject, and i hope the candid reader will not be furprifed, that i am fo fhort upon it, as it has hitherto not been handled; and is far from being hitherto perfectly un-derftood. It is much above my power to go to the bottom of this affair, but by touching upon it in a fummary way i mean to excite men of greater ability, who may treat it in the manner it deferves.

O F

OF THE

USE of CURIOSITY.

OF THE

USE of CURIOSITY.

BY

CHRISTOPHER GEDNER.

Upsal, 1752. October 21.

Amæn. Academ. vol. 3.

§. 1.

AS the three kingdoms of nature were created for the use of man, since to him alone is granted the prerogative of converting their inhabitants to his own advantage, so that part of knowledge which is conversant about the creatures throughout the terraqueous globe is the first, and chief by which men are enabled to provide themselves with what is necessary, both for the present, and future; and the more so because, besides these three kingdoms, and the elements there is nothing in

nature which can be of ufe to him. All thofe things by which man is fupported and grows, with which he is cloathed, and in which he prides himfelf, by which he is preferved, and becomes infolent; all the pomp, the fplendor, the richnefs, the luxury of drefs, as well as the neceffary covering from hence have their origin. Without thefe things man muft be as naked, as he was created, and came into the world. However obvious this truth may be, there is a common queftion propofed by the vulgar to men, who are bufied in examining the productions of nature, and that with fome fort of fneer; *To what end are all thefe inquiries?* By which they mean to infinuate, that thefe *vertuofi* are at the bottom but madmen, who fpend their time in a kind of knowledge, which promifes no advantage; and in this way of thinking they are the more convinced of being right, as they find natural hiftory no part of public inftitutions, not received into academies amongft the philofophical fciences, and as holding no rank either in church, or ftate. For this reafon they look on it as a *mere curiofity*, which only ferves as an amufement for the idle, and indolent. This objection has been made to myfelf, and almoft all others who give them-

felves

felves up - to the ftudy of nature, and by its
frequent repetition has at laft quite worn out
my patience. For which reafon i think it will
not be amifs to confider the queftion, and prepare fuch an anfwer to thofe, who for the future fhall not be afhamed to urge over and
over the fame objections, as may convince
them, if they will take the pains to read the
few following pages, and confider them thoroughly. All i defire of the reader is a candid
hearing.

§. 2.

The kind of men, who moft frequently afk
this queftion; *To what end all thefe inquiries?*
are of a heavy, dull, and phlegmatic difpofition, of weak judgment, and low education.
Amongft ourfelves, in great cities, in large
towns, and at academies, the fearching into
nature ceafes now to be uncommon. Nor is
this queftion ever heard among men of folid
learning. It is chiefly, and frequently put in
the more remote provinces by the inferior order
of people; who think of nothing but indulging their low appetites, and look on every thing
as ufelefs, which does not ferve that purpofe.

When electrical experiments firft began to
make a noife in the world, Samuel Klingenfti-

erna

erna was fent for by his majefty Frederic the
firft to fhew him fome of the electrical phænomena. When all was over, a man of great
rank, who happened to be one of the fpectators on this occafion, faid with a fneer, " Mr.
" Klingenftierna of what ufe is all this?" Klingenftierna replyed with fome acutenefs ; ' Sir,
' this very objection was made to me by J. C.'
(this J. C. was a very rich dry falter). Upon
which the king faid fmiling, to the nobleman,
i think he has given it you. Such men as thefe
refemble more the brute creation, than rational
creatures. They do not confider, that the all-
wife Creator made every thing for man's ufe.
They forget that every thing, which was created at the beginning, was declared to be good.
To thefe men whatever is curious is difguft-
full, and inquiries into nature are deemed
mere folly.

Ternftôm (Chrift.) when he went with the
Oftend fleet to the Eaft Indies, was treated
with contempt by fome of the company for his
curiofity *. They thought nothing of confequence, but what belonged to the winds, and
waves.

---

* Bellonius in his Obfervations, p. 3. fays the fame hap-
'pened to him.

Bart-

Bartſcius (John) when he arrived at Surinam, where he went in order to make obſervations in natural hiſtory, was deſpiſed for looking after plants, and infects. The inhabitants
there thought nothing worth minding, but
what belonged to *ſugar* and *coffé* plantations.
Vid. his letters to Linnæus.

Profeſſor Kalm dared not at the hazard of
his life let the ſavages of Canada, amongſt
whom he reſided, know that he deſcribed any
plant or other natural object, but was forced
to carry on all his reſearches in private.

When our preſident was gathering, and deſcribing the *rhen-deer-fly* on the Lapland mountains, the inhabitants wondered, and laughed
at him for troubling his head about catching
infects. Vid. Act. Stockhol. vol. 1. p. 121.
And we find that he, and his companions were
ſtared at as a ſpectacle in his journey through
Oeland. It. Oeland. p. 85. 109.

Dr. Haſſelquiſt was forced to have a guard
whenever he went out of Cairo in order to de-
ſcribe any natural object; and even then he was
not quite ſafe from the vulgar on account of
his curioſity. Theſe examples may ſuffice without producing any more.

§. 3.

§. 3.

We were created for the glory of the Creator, which cannot be brought about unlefs we
know him, either by revelation, or the works
of the creation. As to the latter i fufpeƈt, that
many come into the world, and remain here
even to old age, who never faw the creation,
but from afar; juft like the brute beafts,
which cannot fail of feeing the verdure, and
various colors, that cloath the earth, but go
not one ftep farther. This feems to me as if
any one, who fhould be carried into a botanic
garden to fee the immenfe variety of plants
brought together from all parts with incredible
trouble, care and expence, fhould only obferve that the leaves were green, and the flowers of various colors, juft as they are every
where elfe. Could fuch an one be truly, and
juftly faid to have feen the garden? Or if any
one fhould go into a mufeum, filled with natural objeƈts of the rareft kind preferved in
fpirit of wine, and fhould only attend to the
clearnefs of the liquor, and, though he faw a
body hanging in it, fhould not inquire what
body it was; would not he, who took the
trouble of fhewing thefe fights to fo curious a
                                    perfon,

perfon, think his time thrown away? Would fuch a fpectator deferve to be let into fuch a place?

I cannot help on this occafion calling to mind the manner, in which our prefident ufed fometimes to excite attention in his audience by an apt fimilitude, when he was reading upon *infects* to his pupils. The fimilitude or rather fable was as follows. ' Once upon a time
' the feven wife men of Greece were met toge-
' ther at Athens, and it was propofed that every
' one of them fhould mention what he thought
' the greateft wonder in the creation. One of
' them, of higher conceptions than the reft,
' propofed the opinion of fome of the aftrono-
' mers about the fixed ftars, which they believed
' to be fo many funs, that had each their pla-
' nets rolling about them, and were ftored with
' plants and animals like this earth. Fired with
' this thought they agreed to fupplicate Jupiter,
' that he would at leaft permit them to take a
' journey to the moon, and ftay there three days
' in order to fee the wonders of that place, and
' give an account of them at their return. Ju-
' piter confented, and ordered them to affemble
' on a high mountain, where there fhould be a
' cloud ready to convey them to the place they

M 4   ' defired

' defired to fee. They picked out fome chofen
' companions, who might affift them in defcrib-
' ing, and painting the objects they fhould meet
' with.   At length they arrived at the moon,
' and found a palace there well fitted up for
' their reception.   The next day, being very
' much fatigued with their journey, they kept
' quiet at home till noon ; and being ftill faint
' they refrefhed themfelves with a moft delici-
' ous entertainment, which they relifhed fo well,
' that it overcame their curiofity. This day they
' only faw through the windows that delightfull
' fpot, adorned with the moft beautiful flowers,
' to which the beams of the fun gave an uncom-
' mon luftre, and heard the finging of moft me-
' lodious birds till evening came on. The next
' day they rofe very early in order to begin their
' obfervations ; but fome very beautifull young
' ladies of the countrey, coming to make them a
' vifit, advifed them firft to recruit their ftrength
' before they expofed themfelves to the labori-
' ous tafk they were about to undertake.

    ' The delicate meats, the rich wines, the
' beauty of the damfels prevailed over the re-
' folution of thefe ftrangers. A fine concert of
' mufic is introduced, the young ones begin to
' dance, and all is turned to jollity; fo that this

    I   ' whole

' whole day was fpent in gallantry, till fome of
' the neighbouring inhabitants, growing envi-
' ous at their mirth, rufhed in with drawn
' fwords. The elder part of the company tryed
' to appeafe the younger, promifing the very
' next day they would bring the rioters to
' juftice. This they performed, and the third
' day the caufe was heard, and what with accu-
' fations, pleadings, exceptions, and the judg-
' ment itfelf the whole day was taken up, on
' which the term fet by Jupiter expired. On
' their return to Greece all the countrey flocked
' in upon them to hear the wonders of the moon
' defcribed, but all they could tell was ; for
' that was all they knew; that the ground was
' covered with green, intermixed with flowers,
' and that the birds fung amongft the branches
' of the trees ; but what kinds of flowers they
' faw, or what kinds of birds they heard, they
' were totally ignorant. Upon which they were
' treated every where with contempt.' If we apply this fable to men of the prefent age, we
fhall perceive a very juft fimilitude. By thefe
three days the fable denotes the *three ages*
of man. Firft *youth*, in which we are too
feeble in every refpect to look into the works
of the Creator. All that feafon is given up to
idle-

idleness, luxury and paftime. 2dly. *manhood*, in which men are employed in fettling, marrying, educating children, providing fortunes for them, and raifing a family. 3dly. *old age*, in which, after having made their fortunes, they are overwhelmed with lawfuits, and proceedings relating to their eftates. Thus it frequently happens that men never confider to what end they were deftined, and why they were brought into the world.

§. 4.

As to bodies, the vulgar are ready enough to admire them in the larger kinds of animals, plants, minerals and metals. But when they perceive any one examining into the minute parts of nature, fuch as *infects* and *shells*, *graffes*, and *moffes*, *earthy particles*, and *petrifactions*, they look upon it as idle curiofity. And when they fee us fearching after fuch natural productions of forreign countries, as are not found with us, their wonder increafes, and they think then they attack us with double advantage. Since we not only fpend our time in examining prefent objects, that are wholly ufelefs, but even fuch diftant ones, as we have fcarcely any means of coming at. They

have

have no notion that thefe can be of any manner of ufe but to thofe amongft whom they
are found. To the end therefore that we may
gain a clearer conception of the harmony, and
ufe of thefe things, it will be neceffary to run
thro' fome of the moft obvious particulars, re-
lative to this fubject, that every one from
hence may better comprehend the advantage
of natural hiftory in general.

§. 5.

The antients were of opinion, that the bodies about us concerned us no farther than as
they were good for *food* or *phyfic.* Hence
their inquiries all tended to find out what were
fit to eat, and what would cure fome diftemper, and whatever plant or animal could not
be referred to one of thefe claffes was neglected ʸ. It is true that the immediate ufe of
many

ʸ I muft take the liberty to contradict the ingenious author on this occafion. For any one who has ever looked
into Ariftotle's hiftory of animals, and Theophraftus's of
plants, muft at once be convinced of the contrary. This
juftice i thought due to thofe two firft fketches of natural
hiftory, in which the fagacious, and extenfive genius of the
mafter, and the difciple fully fhine forth. It is true this fpirit was not long kept up, nor is it to be wondered at, that
extravagant fpeculations, and fyftems concerning things out
of

many bodies is hitherto unknown to us, yet we
have great reafon to believe, that all the bodies in the univerfe, fome way or other, contribute to our advantage. *Hay*, which men
take fuch pains to collect in the fummer, is
of no ufe to man immediately, but it is a com-
modity of the utmoft confequence to him mediately, as being the food of cattle of all forts,
without which we could not well fubfift. Thofe
minute infects called *tree lice*, that live upon
the branches of trees, and plants, are looked
upon as of no ufe to us.   Thefe are devoured
by *flies*, *cochineals*, *golden eyes*, &c. in their firft
ftate; which alfo feem to be of no ufe to us,
but then many of the *fmall birds* feed upon

of mens reach, which are purfued in the clofet with eafe,
and when ingenious are apt to ftrike the imaginations of
mankind, fhould take place of the fober, and painful refearches into nature, little minded by the generality of people, and therefore lying out of the paths of reputation.
Thus what was fo well begun by Ariftotle and Theophraftus dropped at once for want of encouragement, and never
raifed its head again, till after the reftoration of learning;
when Gefner, Bauhin, Cæfalpinus, &c. in imitation of
thofe firft mafters, began to revive this part of knowledge;
and kindled up a fpark, which has never been totally ex-
tinguifhed fince, and has been raifed into a diffufive light
by feveral naturalifts of the laft age, and particularly by the
excellent Linnæus.

them,

them, and thefe not only delight us with their
fine fongs but afford us moft delicate food.
The *nettle* is a plant which is fcarcely eat by any
domeftic animal (Iter. Scand. p. 15.) but the
Author of nature has allotted to it more feed-
ers than to almoft any other plant, v. gr. *butterflies, moths, wevils, chermes*, &c. which devour it almoft entirely, and thefe infects are a
prey to many birds, which could by no means
live on the plant immediately. *Minute aquatic
worms*, and thofe in no fmall number are eat
by the larger, and thefe are eat by the fifhes,
and aquatic birds, and thefe by us ; and befides
food thefe birds fupply us with moft delicate
foft down to warm and repofe ourfelves upon.
It would be tedious to enumerate all the mediate advantages, which we obtain from the
moft contemptible; as they are deemed; both
plants and animals.

§. 6.

Many look upon *fhells*, and *corals* of various
kinds, which are collected and ranged in mu-
feums by the diligent inquirers into nature, as
an idle curiofity ; fince they neither ferve for
food or phyfic; but if thefe are neglected, how
many of the wonderfull works of the Creator
would

would be unknown? What man of fenfe is not
ftruck with wonder, when he beholds the innumerable objects, which the Author of nature
has buried, as it were, in the great abyfs. Objects for color, fhape, and mechanifm fo admirable, that they furpafs the imagination of
man to conceive without feeing them. If we
vifit a royal palace, and there behold the walls
covered with tapeftry, pictures, fculpture, and
other ornaments, are we not delighted, and
even in rapture? We ought therefore to feel the
fame pleafure, when we behold the beauties of
this our globe. To defcribe every fhell on this
occafion would far exceed the bounds of my
defign. At prefent i will only mention one, viz.
the *knotted marginated Cypræa.* Rump. t. 39.
f. C. Argenvnill. t. 21. f. K. Petiv. Faz. 97. t.
8. This is a fmall fhell, about the bignefs of
a hazel nut, and is gathered in the Maldivee
iflands by the women along the fea fhore in
fuch quantities, that 30 or 40 fhips are loaded with them yearly for Africa, Bengal and
Siam; fo that in thofe parts there are large
palaces filled with them, where they are preferved as treafures of the greateft value.

    Thefe fhells ferve there as gold, and filver
with us, for all kinds of commerce. In other
coun-

countries other fhells are made ufe of for various purpofes; fome inftead of horns to blow
with at their religious ceremonies; fome for
veffels for wafhing; fome for cups; fome for
boxes; fome for inlaying; all of them far exceeding the beft artificial works.

Nor are thofe innumerable *petrifactions*, fo
various in fpecies, and ftructure, to be looked
upon as vain curiofities. We find in our mountains, and even in the middle of ftones, as it
were embaumed, *animals*, *fhells*, *corals*, which
are not to be found alive in any part of Europe. Thefe alone, were there no other reafon, might put us upon looking back into antiquity, and confidering the primitive form of
the earth, its increafe, and metamorphofis.
This is a fubject, that would require a whole
volume to treat it amply as it deferves.

Wild beafts, and *ravenous birds*, though
they feem to difturb our private œconomy,,
are not without their ufes; which we fhould
be fenfible of, if they were extirpated [z]:
When

---

[z] Thus in Suffolk, and in fome parts of Norfolk, the
farmers find it their intereft to encourage the breed of rooks,
as the only means to free their grounds from the grub,
from which the tree or blind beetle comes, Vid. Lifter's
Goedact. p. 265. pl. III. Scarabæus. Melolontha. S. N. 10.
p. 351. which in its grub ftate deftroys the roots of corn
and

When the *little crow* was driven out of Virginia, and that at the expence of feveral tuns
of gold, the inhabitants would willingly have
brought them back again at double the price,
as we find by profeffor Kalm. The *vultures*
in Cairo are invited yearly, and daily to remain there, as doctor Haffelquift relates in
Act. Sac. reg. Scient. Stockhol. 1751. p. 196.
et fequ. Thefe creatures of prey cleanfe the
ground from carcafes, and make it wholefome,
and pure, and befides they ferve to keep up a
due proportion between animals, fo that one
fort may not ftarve the reft.

The vulgar think, and thofe who think
themfelves wifer than the vulgar, make no
fcruple to fay ; *let him who has nothing to do
employ himfelf in hunting after moffes and flies.*
By which they would infinuate, that fearching after the minute plants, and animals is
unbecoming, or at leaft unneceffary for a ra-

and grafs to fuch a degree, that i myfelf have feen a piece of
pafture land, where you might turn up the turf with your
foot.

Mr. Matthews a very obferving and excellent farmer, of
Wargrove in Berkfhire, told me that the rooks one year,
while his men were houghing a turnep field, fat down in
part of it, where they were not at work, and that the crop
was very fine in that part; whereas in the other part there
were no turneps that year.

tional

tional creature. As for *moffes*, i grant we have not authority on our fide; for till the end of the laft century, they were almoft wholly neglected; but now within thefe fifty years their hiftory is very near compleat by the diligence of Dillenius. C. Bauhin knew very few *moffes*; Dillenius has defcribed near 600. With unwearied pains he went through this very difficult, and extenfive branch of natural hiftory. But to what end? it is afked. I will not take upon me to anfwer this queftion by fhewing the particular ufe of every *mofs*, that grows; although i am certain the Lord of nature has made nothing in vain. But i will venture to affert, that pofterity will, one time or other, find as many advantages arifing from *moffes*, as from other vegetables. I affert this with the greater confidence, becaufe fince our acquaintance with *moffes*, we have many experiments, which fhew their ufefulnefs, a few inftances of which i fhall fubjoyn. The *bog mofs* covers deep bogs with its fpongy fubftance, and thus by degrees turns them into fertile meadows; not to mention its repelling virtue in medicine; at prefent alfo its turf is ufed inftead of wood in many provinces, and it is a cuftom eftablifhed among the workers in metals to burn it in-

N   to

to cinders in their forges. The Laplanders, who lay their children upon it in the cradle, find that it abates the acrimony of the urine. Act. Stock. 1740. p. 421.

The *fontinalis antipyretica*, a kind of *mofs*, contrary to the nature of all other *moffes*, guards the walls of houfes in cafe of fire. It. Scand. p. 20.

The *maiden-hair* furnifhes a very convenient bed to the Laplander, and the *bear* with this prepares his winter habitation. Moft of our *tumps* confift of this kind of *mofs*.

The *club-mofs* is ufed for making mats.

The *cyprefs-mofs* furnifhes a yellow dye.

The upright *fir-mofs* frees cattle from vermin, and purges ftrongly. It. Oel. p. 28.

The *fountain-mofs* points out cool fprings.

The *hypnum proliferum*, a kind of *mofs*, covers the ground in fhady places, where no other plant will grow. Iter. Oeland. p. 28.

The *hypnum parietinum* ferves for ftoppiag crevifes in walls.

All the kinds of *hypna* and *brya* [z] cover the earth with green, and keep it from being quite naked, as in beech groves and in the woods of both the Indies. They preferve the minute feeds of plants during the winter, fhelter their

[z] Names of *moffes*.

roots

roots and keep them from freezing; and gardeners gather *moffes* in the autumn, in order to preferve their plants from the froft; they are gathered by the birds to build their nefts; they grow in the moft barren foil; by degrees they rot towards the bottom, and thus lay a foundation for fertility.

The *bryum hypnoides* covers the rocks in the coldeft mountains.

The *mnium hygrometricum* fhews the drinefs, and moifture of the atmofphere.

Some kinds of *brya* cover the mountains, others the marfhes, fome are ufefull in moift meadow ground, fome fpread over the naked fields, fome are found upon ftones, and rocks, others on trunks of trees; and all of them bear the moft fevere winter, when the generality of other plants grow fickly.

§. 7.

As to the *lichens* or *liverworts*, they are not of lefs ufe; for many of them afford a beautifull dye. e. g. the *roccella* yields a moft valuable red colo, Act. Soc. reg. Scien. 1742. p. 21. to which purpofe the *lichen tartareus* ferves as a fuccedaneum. The *lichenes ftygius, onuphalodes,* &c. afford alfo a red dye, and the

N 2 *lichenes*

lichenes croceus, vulpinus a good yellow. There is no doubt, but that many colors in procefs of time may be obtained from this kind of plants.

If we confider the vertues of the *lichenes* or *liverworts* upon animate bodies taken internally, they are not inconfiderable. The *lichen vulpinus* is a deadly poifon to wolves. It. Scan. p. 40. The *lichen pyxidatus*, or *cup-mofs*, is efficacious in the hooping cough. The *lichen jubatus*, or *rock-hair* in exulcerations of the fkin. The *lichen omphalodes* in ftopping hæmorrhages. The *lichen aphthofus* in thrufhes, and againft worms. The *lichen caninus* or *afh-colored ground liverwort*, in the hydrophia and madnefs. The *lichen pulmonarius*, or *lungwort*, is found to be good in confumptions. The œconomical ufe of the *lichens* is of no fmall confequence. e. g. the *lichen rangiferinus* affords the moft delicious pafture to the rhen-deer. Upon this the whole œconomy of the Laplander turns, and by the help of this many millions of men are fupported. This *lichen* is alfo given to other cattle by the people of Norland. Act. Soc. reg. 1742. p. 153. Some of the kinds of *lichens* are the delight of *goats*. The moft barren woods, where no other plants grow, afford us the

lichen

lichen iflandicus, which in times of fcarcity ferves inftead of bread. Act. Soc. reg. Sc. 1742. p. 154.

The *lichen prunaftri*, or *plumb-liverwort*, is ground to powder for the hair.

The *lichen puftulatus* may be converted into a very black pigment. The very *fmall lichens* called *leprofus*, cover barren rocks, and makes them look pleafant; it gives birth to black mould, and confequently affords the firft degree of vegetative power. After all this can any one juftly fay that the knowledge of thefe plants is ufelefs?

The *mufhroom* kind alfo make a clafs of vegetables by no means to be defpifed. One fpecies is ufed in amputations and hæmorrhages, and another is lately come into reputation for ftopping the bleeding of arteries; infomuch that the inventor of this ufe of it was amply rewarded for the difcovery.

The *trufle* and *phalli* contribute to make our foups more delicate, and are commonly ufed at the tables of the great. Many *mufhrooms* are eat by the Mufcovites and the inhabitants of other countries, but fome of them are a moft deadly poifon; fo that it is of the utmoft confequence not to commit miftakes in this part of knowledge.

N 3   There

There is a *muſhroom* called *agaricus muſca-*
rius, on account of its driving away flies, and
the ſame plant is the ſafeſt remedy hitherto
diſcovered to deſtroy the *bug.* Thus the knowledge of theſe plants is of great uſe to man.

§. 8.

* The *graſſes* alſo are a kind of plants of great
value, as affording food for cattle.

The *reed canary graſs* ſerves for thatching
houſes.

The *meadow fox-tail graſs* is an excellent
graſs, which may be ſown to advantage in low
meadows. It. Oel. p. 156.

The *turfy-hair* cauſes the meadows in the
regio cuprimontana to be ſo extremely fertile,
Act. Soc. R.S. 1742. p. 30,

The *water meadow* is a large and very uſefull *graſs,* which grows by the ſides of moſt
ditches and rivers. It. W. Goth. p. 41.

The *narrow-leaved meadow* is the moſt common paſture in our parts.

The *ſeed of the flote* or *manna graſs,* affords
a very pleaſing and wholeſome nouriſhment
to man.

* Who is curious to know more of theſe graſſes may con-
ſult the laſt piece in the book, intitled, *Obſervations on graſſes.*

The

The *sheep's fefcue* makes our sheep very fat.

The *perennial darnel* is the beft *grafs* for *hay* on chalky hills.

The *fea lyme-grafs* and *fea mat-grafs* keep the fands on barren maritime tracts from being blown away.

The moft minute feeds of *grafs* afford nourifhment to fmall birds. The *graffes* befides give a moft agreeable color to the earth, and fill up the intervals between plants of other kinds; fo that they ferve both for pleafure, and utility. The Creator has affigned certain fpecies of *grafs* to every different fpecies of foil, which the hufbandman is obliged to know in order to make the moft advantage of his lands. Befides certain *graffes* are eat by fome animals, and left untouched by others; fo that without the knowledge of thefe he cannot avoid falling into error. It. Scand.

§. 9.

He that would exercife the art of hufbandry with the greateft advantage, ought to endeavor to get acquainted with all kinds of vegetables, and find out what fort of foil fuits each of them beft. He ought to know, that fome delight in open and expofed fituations, others in fhady; fome in moift ground, others

N 4 in

in dry; that fome plants thrive moft in fandy foils, others in claiey, others in black mould, others in fpungy ground, others in watry; fome ought to be fown in pools, others on the tops of hills.

Thofe barren defarts called Alvacu on the mountains of Oeland, It. Oel. p. 206. had long ago been covered with the *crocus*, from whence the inhabitants might have reaped great benefit, if the nature of that plant had been known to them. Our alps, that are more than a hundred miles long, had not remained to this day a mere wafte, if our induftrious hufbandmen, who not long fince began to improve the œconomical arts, had known how to cultivate fuch plants as might have been ufefull in food, or phyfic; and if they had known what ufefull trees, and herbs grow on the forreign alps, viz. the Swifs, the Sibirian, the Pyrenean, the Valefian, &c. from whence they ought to have got feed.

The banks of our lakes produce fcarcely any thing but *rufhes, horfetail, water lilly, pondweeds, reeds*, &c. where neverthelefs a great number of plants fit for food might be fown, fuch as *zizany* of Canada, *water caltrops*, &c.

Every province has its plants, which choak the

the grain, and render the fields foul, and poor. It. Scand. p. 421. Books of hufbandry are full of inventions how to break the earth by inftruments, and fit it to receive the feed; this kind of knowledge is infufficient, as long as the hufbandman is unacquainted with the nature of thofe various herbs, to which agriculture ought to be adapted. From hence the neceffity of natural hiftory appears.

§. 10.

It is alfo neceffary for the hufbandman to know the duration of every plant he fows in his fields, and meadows, viz. whether it be perennial, biennial, or annual. He who wants to know the ufe of our plants in œconomy, and how few there are, whofe ufe is hitherto difcovered, let him look over the *Flora œconomica.* Amæn. Academ. vol. 1 [a].

We fee how many in a time of dearth fuffer for want, fall into difeafes, and even perifh,

[a] The piece here referred to is full of new obfervations on the ufes of plants hitherto not attended to. I wifh i could have made fuch a tranflation of it, as could have been inftructive or entertaining to the public ; but a long lift of the names of plants, which could have conveyed no ideas to fuch readers, as this work is intended for, muft have been very tedious, and very ufelefs.

for

for no other reafon but becaufe they do not
know what plants are eatable, and how great
a plenty there is of them in our countrey, of
which D. Hiorth in this volume has given
an account, which the moft illuftrious fenator
Baron Lowenheilm has tranflated into Swedifh. Many people wonder, why the curious
enquirers into nature will give themfelves fo
much trouble about exotic plants ; but they
do not fufficiently confider, that many kinds
of *grain*, many *roots*, *legumes*, *fruits*, *fallads*,
and *trees* in common ufe with us for nourifhment, houfehold utenfils, cloathing, and
ornament are originally exotics. Here follows a lift of fome, which have lately been
brought into our countrey from the farther-
moft parts of Sibiria, that contribute to adorn
our gardens, and change our œconomy.

*Larkfpur, monks-hood, adonis, vetch, cow parf-
nep,* French *honey-fuckle, aftragalus, othonna,
baftard-faffron, greater centory, colombine, dra-
cocephalon, fpeedwell, claytonica, flax, hyacinth,
lilly, lychnis, poppy, cat-mint, yellow-flowered
fage, hooded willow herb, hyffop, wild navew, St.
John's wort, fow-thiftle, faw-wort,* &c.   From
that diftant countrey we have the *robinia's* and a
honey-fuckle, that make excellent quick-hedges;
                                                        from

from thence we have the Sibirian *nettle*, that ferves for making facks. If we had a more compleat knowledge of plants, that grow in the fouthern parts of Afia, and America, we fhould be able to make more ample, and ufe-full experiments,

To preferve our woods we want to be provided with quick-hedges, for which purpofe many kinds of trees are ferviceable, fuch as the *goofeberry bufh*, the *black-thorn*, the *white-thorn*, the *berberry*, the *fea buck-thorn*, the *alder*, the *fallow*, &c. provided each be planted in a proper foil.

§. II.

We have fome of our moft efficacious medicines, and beft fpices from the fouthern parts of the world; and were it not for the curious in botany they had been neglected; as the *lignum colubrinum* was for a long time. What end would it ferve to know, that the *fenega root* was good againft the bite of ferpents, unlefs botanifts had alfo known the plant? And who would ever have dreamed, that our *milk-wort* would anfwer the fame intent? What end would it have ferved, that profeffor Kalm was

witnefs

witnefs to the efficacy of the Virginia *avens*
and the *monacda* in intermitting fevers, and
of the root of the *ceanothus*, and *diervilla* in
venereal cafes; if we had not learned how to
raife thefe plants? Or to what end would it
have ferved to crofs the ocean, and attain the
American *water gladiole*, if we had not found
out that it was of the genus of our *water gladiole?* The Europeans at vaft expence went
on buying the *moxa* from China, the *figwort*
from Brazil, and the *jachafchapuch* from North
America, till it was known that they grew in
our own countrey.

§. 1 2.

There is, as it were, a certain chain of created beings, according to which they feem all
to have been formed, and one thing differs fo
little from fome other, that if we fall into the
right method we fhall fcarcely find any limits
between them. This no one can fo well obferve, as he who is acquainted with the greateft
number of fpecies. Does not every one perceive, that there is a vaft difference between
a ftone and a monkey? but if all the intermediate beings were fet to view in order, it
would

would be difficult to find the limits between them. The *polypus* and the *mofs* joyn the vegetable, and the animal kingdom together, for the plants called *confervæ* and the animals called *coralline*, are not eafy to diftinguifh, and the *corals* conneċt the animal, vegetable and foffil world.

Hence the botanifts of this age have been bufied about fettling natural-claffes, which is an affair of the greateft importance, and difficulty; but fince the vegetables hitherto difcovered are not fuffïcient for that purpofe, this part of knowledge is not compleat. It is therefore incumbent on botanifts to get acquainted with exotic plants, that they may arrive at the end defired. If all the *columniferous* plants except the *mufk-mallow* were known, the *turnera* never could be referred to this order, but that, as foon as it was examined, conneċted the *turnera* with the *columniferous* plants.

Where the natural claffes are fettled we find the vegetables fo near akin to one another, that we can fcarcely diftinguifh them, as in the *umbellated*, the *filiquofe*, the *leguminofe*, the *compofite*, &c. moft of thefe orders grow in Europe,

Europe, and therefore could be eafily known, and ranged.

He that knows but a few plants gives cha-racters, which are eafy to find out, but are in-fufficient to fettle any thing; and therefore tend to confound, rather than to advance know-ledge ; fo that the natural method is the ultimate end of our fyftematical inquiries. Without this all is a mere chaos, and if the knowledge of vegetables fails, all that ufe of them is gone, which the learned in this way might difcover to the great benefit of man-kind.

It is true indeed that vegetables act upon the human body by fmell, and tafte ; but thefe marks are not fufficient unlefs we know the natural orders of plants.

Thefe being known, and the vertues of fome vegetables being difcovered, we may go on fafely in the practice of phyfic, otherwife not. It follows from hence, that he who defires to make any confiderable improvement in this branch of knowledge, muft endeavor to get acquainted with thofe plants, whofe ufe he does not know ; and thus he is obliged not to ne-glect the moft contemptible. e. g. no body

was

2

was able to form a right judgment of the *caf-carilla*, who did not know, its natural order. No phyfician would have even fufpected, that our *milkwort* would be ufefull in the bite of ferpents, and inflammatory fevers, unlefs the principles of botany had led him to it. No one has even thought of trying the *mitreola Americana* againft the bite of ferpents, which yet without ever feeing it, we may certainly conclude to be efficacious in thofe cafes from the *ophiorrhiza Afiatica* or *true lignum colubrinum* [b]. When botanifts knew the above-mentioned *turnera*, but were ignorant to what natural clafs it ought to be referred, no man could guefs

[b] This root is known in the Eaft-Indies to be a fpecific againft the poifon of that moft dreadful animal called the *hooded-ferpent*. There is a treatife in Amæn. Acad. vol. 2. upon this fubject, wherein the author Joh. And. Darelius undertakes, from the defcription of fuch authors as had feen it upon the fpot, to afcertain the plant from which the genuine root is taken. It appears in this account that it had puzzled the European phyficians, and what had been fold in the fhops for it is the root of a very different plant and of a poifonous nature.

The true root is called *mungos* for the following reafon. There is a kind of *weefel* in the Eaft-Indies called *mungutia* by the natives, *mungo* by Portuguefe, and *muncas* by the Dutch. This animal purfues the *hooded-ferpent*, as the *cat* does

guefs its vertues. But now that we know, that it is of the *columniferous* order, we may without experience be affured that it is of the emollient kind.

Without this knowledge of the natural orders, the *materia medica* would be ftill as uncertain, as amongft the antients, which is of the utmoft importance to us if life and health be fo.

§. 1 3.

We are ready enough to put a due value on the larger animals, but many look on the minute tribe of infects, rather created to torment, than to be ufefull to mankind. We

does the *moufe* with us. As foon as this *ferpent* appears the *weefel* attacks him, and if fhe chances to be bit by him, fhe immediately runs to find a certain vegetable; upon eating which fhe returns, and renews the fight. The Indians are of opinion, that this plant is the *mungos*.

That celebrated traveller Kæmpfer, who kept one of thefe *weefels* tame, that eat with him, lived with him, and was his companion, wherever he went, fays he faw one of thefe battles between her and the *ferpent*, but could not certainly find out what root the *weefel* looked out for. But whether the *weefel* firft difcovered this antidote, or not, yet it is certain, adds Darelius, that there is a root, which is an infallible remedy againft the bite of the *hooded ferpent*. And this he undertakes to afcertain.

grant

grant that they are very troublefome to us. But is therefore all care about them to be given up? by no means. On the contrary we ought to contrive means to get rid of them, that they may not deftroy both us and our poffeffions. This cannot be brought about unlefs we know their nature; when that is known we fhall more eafily find out remedies againft them[c]. The ufe of infects has been fufficiently explained by the noble Carolus de Geer, lord of the bed-chamber to his majefty, in an oration which he made in the academy of fciences at Stockholm. Another of my fellow-ftudents has undertaken to explain what damages infects of various kinds do us, and another now is actually employed in fhewing what kind of infects live

[c] We have lately had a proof that the knowledge of the nature of infects may fometimes be ferviceable to us. The fagacious Dr. Wall of Worcefter, upon feeing the cafe of the Norfolk boy, who was cured of worms by taking down a large quantity of white lead, and oyl, gueffed that the cure was performed by the oyl, knowing that oyl is fatal to worms and other infects. Upon this he has fince tryed oyl in worm-cafes with a great appearance of fuccefs, an account of which i faw in a letter from him to be communicated to the Royal Society. That oyl is deftructive to worms was known to the antients, as appears by Arift. Vid. Hift. Anim. lib. 8. c. 27.

O   upon

upon every plant [d]. This makes it unneceſ-
ſary for me to enlarge at preſent upon the
almoſt incredible miſchief inſects do us. I
will only in a very few words mention, that
we ſhall never be able to guard ourſelves
againſt them, but by their means. For as
we make uſe of *dogs*, and other beaſts, in hunting down *ſtags*, *boars*, *hares* and other animals, which do us much damage in our fields
and meadows; or as *hawks* may be bred up
to as ſo aſſiſt us in taking *herons*, *larks* and
other birds, ſo alſo we might make uſe of
the fiercer kinds of inſects, in order to get
the better of the reſt of theſe troubleſome
animals.

We ſhall never be able to drive *bugs* out
of our houſes, before we introduce other inſects that will devour them, v. g. the wild
bugs, &c.

We have no eaſier method of deſtroying
knats and *flies* which cauſe us ſo much diſturb-

[d] The two laſt-mentioned perſons hinted at are, i imagine
J. G. Foſkahl, and M. Backner, the firſt of whom has written
a treatiſe ſhewing the plants which different inſects live upon,
the laſt a treatiſe on the miſchiefs done by inſects. Both
theſe are publiſhed in Amœn. Acad. v. 3.

ance,

ance, than by providing ourfelves with the *libellula*, which devours them, as the *kite* does poultry. We oftentimes find our largeft trees entirely ftripped of their leaves by the *cater-pillars* of the *moth* kind, &c. but when we fearch after them we find they are all eat up by the larger kind of *carabi* called *fycophantæ*; from whence we may learn, that there is no remedy more efficacious in our gardens, where leaves, flowers, and fruits are almoft every year deftroyed by thofe *caterpillars*, than ga-thering and preferving the above-mentioned *carabi* till they lay their eggs, and then placing them at the roots of trees in rotten wood, till they are hatched. And thus we fhould effectually guard our trees from thefe inhof-pitable guefts.

§. 14.

But if we do not think it worth our while for any other reafon to turn our attention to the works of nature, yet furely for the glory of the great Creator we ought to do it, fince in every plant, in every infect we may obferve fome fingular artifice, which is not to be found in any other bodies; and upon comparing

O 2   thefe

thefe together, we may be convinced, that this does not happen by chance, but was contrived for fome certain end, viz. either the propagation, or prefervation of the plant or animal with refpect to thofe other bodies. We find how many plants are fenced againft the inclemencies of the elements, and the devaftations of animals; and how every animal is furnifhed with fome means, by which it may defend itfelf againft the depredations of the reft; fo that no fpecies can ever totally perifh, which has been created.

Laftly, from the contemplation of nature we may fee, that all created things fome way or other ferve for ufe; if not immediately, yet by fecond or third means. Nay we may fee, that what we imagine, to be moft noxious to us is not feldom highly ufefull. Without fome of thefe things our œconomy would fuffer extremely. Thus were there no *thiftles* or *briars*, the earth would be more barren. We ought not to overlook the minuteft objects, but examine them with the glafs; for we fhall then perceive how much art the Creator has beftowed upon them.

He who beholds one of the *jungermanuia*, a kind of *wrack* with a microfcope, muft be forced

forced to confefs, that he beholds a moft ftupendous, and wonderful phænomenon. Many thoufands of people are fupported by ryebread, not one of them perhaps ever faw, in how furprifing a manner its hufks are armed; which any one, who is defirous, may fee by the help of a glafs.

The day would fooner fail me than matter, were i to take notice of every thing, which this fubject affords. Let this then be looked upon as the end of created beings; that fome may be ufefull to man as phyfic, others as aliment; fome in œconomy immediately, others mediately; fome vegetables prepare the ground, fome protect thofe which are more tender, others cover the earth with a green, and moft beautifull tapeftry, and that perennial; fome form thofe groves to which we fly for coolnefs, others adorn our globe with their moft elegant flowers, and regale our noftrils with their moft delicious odors. Laftly, all things demonftrate abundantly the omnifcience of the wife Creator, who created nothing in vain, but contrived every thing with fo much artifice, that human art, however great it may be, cannot imitate the leaft of his productions. If we neglect therefore to confider thefe ob-

jects,

jects, they would be like pearl thrown before
fwine. I befeech you then, who afk me with
a fneer to what end this or that ftone, plant
or animal ferves; i befeech you to awake,
and open your eyes while you live in this
world. All thefe things are not the work
of man, but of wifdom itfelf, which created
both thee and me. He has fettled an œconomy in this globe, that is truly admirable
by means of an infinite number of bodies,
and all neceffary, which bear fome refemblance
to one another ; fo that they are linked together
like a chain. For as in our œconomy neither
the plough, nor the hedges, nor the dunghill
are fit for food, or phyfic, yet are abfolutely
neceffary, fo in the œconomy of nature there
are many things, that are as neceffary, but
not immediately. Men reckon their œconomy amongft the chief of human inventions,
confider then the fublimity of the divine œconomy. You fee therefore that it muft at laft
be granted me according to the opinion of
divines and philofophers, that every thing was
created for the ufe of man, and man for the
glory of the Creator. Can you then believe,
that any thing can be ufelefs that ferves not
for food, or phyfic ? The Creator has fo framed

the

the world, that man fhould every where behold the miraculous work of his hands, and
that the earth fhould afford an endlefs variety,
feemingly with intent that the novelty of the
objects fhould excite his curiofity, and hinder
him from being difgufted by too much uniformity, as it has happened to fome wretches,
whofe ftation in life placed them above labor,
and who wanted curiofity to look into thefe
things. Some objects were made to pleafe the
fmell, the tafte, the fight, the hearing, or other
fenfes, fo that nothing can be faid to be without its ufe. That branch of knowledge which
ferves to difcover the characters of natural
things and teaches us to call them by their
names, feems perhaps by no means neceffary.
But let it be confidered that the firft degree
of wifdom is to know things when we fee
them, i. e. to know them by their names; and
without this knowledge fcarce any progrefs
can be made. To know the letters of the
alphabet, to joyn them into fyllables, to underftand words is not folid erudition; yet it
is abfolutely neceffary for him, who would
become learned. Thus the characters, and
names of things muft be thoroughly learned
in order to obtain any ufe from natural hiftory.

We

We find in the journals of travellers, many things mentioned, partly curious, partly ufe-full concerning animals, plants, and ftones ; but thofe obfervations can be of no ufe to us, till we are able to refer each to its genus ; that we may-make them a part of the fyftem, and know that this curiofity, or ufe belongs to this, or that object, when it happens to come in our way.

§. 15.

If man was created to give praife to his Cre-ator ; if the Creator has made himfelf known to man by creation, and revelation ; if all cre-ated things are formed with wonderfull me-chanifm ; laftly, if all things were created for the ufe of man, and nothing but natural things, and the elements can be of ufe to him ; then it may be inquired with the fame reafon, to what end any other thing was cre-ated, as well as man ; the fupreme Being having created nothing but for a certain end, and for fome valuable purpofe, We are often ignorant what that purpofe is, but it would therefore be impious to fay, that any thing was created in vain, fince he declared that *every thing which he had created was good*. Gen. i. 31.

O R-

OBSTACLES

TO THE

Improvement of PHYSIC.

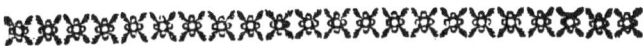

XXXXXXXXXXXXXXXXXXXXXXXXXX

OBSTACLES

TO THE

Improvement of PHYSIC.

BY

JOH. GEORG. BEYERSTEIN.

Amæn. Acad. vol. iii.

PREFACE.

Although phyſic in its whole extent has received great improvements in this age, as moſt of its parts have been diligently looked into and reformed; yet its chief ſtrength ſeems to conſiſt in accurate knowledge of diſeaſes, and medicines, and when we turn our eyes on the preſent times, we find that many ſimple medicines have been neglected; which ſo little deſerve it, that they rather ought to be re-
vived,

vived, and brought into pra&ife. Which being the cafe i have frequently endeavored to
find out the caufe of this common ignorance.
The refult of my inquiries i fubmit to the
judgment of the candid reader in this aca-
demical exercife, which, though far from
compleat, is the beft i could produce, and i
hope it may prove of fome ufe, and meet with
a favorable reception.

Various caufes have concurred to bring
many medicines into negle&.

1.

*Fafhion which prevails in phyfic, as it does in
every other earthly thing.* Hence phyficians prefcribe according to certain received forms, not
fufficiently confidering, whether the fuccefs anfwers. To this muft be referred the frequent
change of remedies.

*Brooklime, borrage, buglofs, plantain, faxi-
frage,* are properly only kitchen plants.
Larkfpur is fcarcely of any ufe, but to
adulterate fyrup of violets, for which purpofe it ought not to be ufed. *Bugle, motherwort, eye-bright, poley-mountain* of
Crete, are kept in fhops more from
cuftom, than for any good, and fufficient
reafons. The *knot-grafs* is retained ; while

on

on the other hand the *bear-berry* has been neglected, though an efficacious aftringent. The *grafs of Parnaffus*, and *fun-dew*, have crept into the fhop by chance. The *carline thiftle*, an excellent remedy in hyfteric complaints, is neglected. Thofe poor wretched plants the *vervains* increafe the number of officinals without any merit of their own, and only fupported by the teftimony of antiquity.

2.

The many theories and hypothefes of phyficians that vary in every age. For men have been vain enough to imagine that they knew the immediate caufes of difeafes, the manner in which medicines operate, and from their principles have undertaken to deduce the vertues of medicines.

Formerly *hot* and *volatile* medicines were ufed in acute diftempers. At prefent the *acid, cooling,* and *diluting* with *bleeding* are recommended. *Mufk*, *ambergris, civet* were looked upon as moft efficacious in *eruptive fevers*, now juft the contrary. And thus *meadow-fweet, woodruff, mufk cranés bill,* may in their turn come into credit, which now are feldom ufed for

driv-

driving out thefe eruptions; though we may be affured of their vertues by undoubted experiments long fince made.

3.

The neglect of fpecifying diftempers. Hence remedies, which are excellent for fome difeafes in one man ; nay even thofe very remedies that get the name of fpecifics on account of fome very remarkable vertue, when adminiftered to another, are either of no fervice, or even do mifchief; whereas they would perhaps never fail of a good effect, if the fpecies of the diftemper were the fame. Therefore till phyficians regulate the doctrine of difeafes in the fame manner, that botanifts have done that of plants, medicines muft be neceffarily precarious *.

Were any one to fet about curing the *hæmor-rhoidal colic* in a *plethoritic conftitution* by *fpirituous and hot carminatives,* which are proper for the *flatulent colic* in a *cold,* and *phlegmatic conftitution,* he would foon find moft fatal proofs of his error. Of this a very remarkable inftance may be feen in

---

* As well as i remember this obfervation is taken from Sydenham. But whoever is author of it, moft certainly phyfic muft ever be very imperfect, till this grand defideratum be performed.

diff.

diff. med. dni. Arch. Bæck. de medicam.
domeft.

4.

*An hafty and imprudent judgment about poi-
fons, and their difference from medicines which in
reality differ only in degrees of ftrength.* Hence
our anceftors fcarcely ever dared to prefcribe
the ufe of plants, which they imagined to be
poifonous.

The *laurel* is neither ufed in confumptions,
nor venereal complaints, though an excellent remedy; becaufe it is fufpected to be
poifonous. The *pafque flower,* whofe root
is very efficacious in hyfteric complaints,
is gone out of vogue; becaufe Helvigius
knew a perfon who dyed upon ufing a fyrup made of it; as if all inebriating drinks
were to be difcarded, becaufe fome have
loft their fenfes, and lives by an inordi-
dinate ufe of them. The *lignum colubrinum* ᵉ, that is famous in venomous
bites, and the quartan ague, is neglected
for the fame reafon. Scarce any one dares

* In vol. 2. Amæn. academ. there is a treatife on the *lignum colubrinum*, in which the author undertakes to determine from what plant this root is taken, and obferves that
druggifts, for want of a proper defcription, have confound-
ed it with two other plants, one of which, and that generally in the fhops, is of a poifonous nature.

recom-

recommend the use of the *mandragora*, although Schopperus has shewn its vertues
in the gout. The *deadly night-shade* is not
yet brought into practise, though we have
great reason to expect much from it in
disperfing tumours of the breast [f].

5.

The abufes of quacks, and their bold, and dan-

[f] I cannot omit faying a word or two on the fubject of the
deadly night-shade on this occafion, as the trial of it caufed
fo much noife in this town fome time ago. I know the
generality of people look on its fate as decided; and that it
is deftined never to revive again; but that is not clear to me.
Some of the faculty ftill entertain a good opinion of it, and
have feen fome benefit done by it. *Antimony* was once entirely difcarded out of phyfic, yet we have feen it fince become one of the moft fafhionable remedies in many difeafes.
New medicines, and particularly of fo ftrong a nature as the
night-shade, do not come at once into vogue. The not being able to afcertain the proper manner of giving it, the
uncertainty in what cafes it ought to be ufed, and how to
obviate the inconvenience attending its ufe, not to mention
many other reafons; thefe, i fay, joined together, are fully
fufficient to overturn a medicine of the moft promifing appearance for a time. But whatever may be the fate of the
night-shade itfelf, the difinterefted zeal of my worthy friend
Mr. Gataker to find out fome remedy for the moft dreadfull
and defperate of all difeafes; and the candid manner, in
which every circumftance, relating to that affair was communicated to the public, muft entitle him to the efteem of
every humane perfon.

gerous

gerous experiments. Thefe have made many patients averfe to fome of the moft celebrated medicines, infomuch that a phyfician dares not prefcribe them. - For fome timid injudicious friend is always at hand to impofe, upon their weaknefs, and let them know, that they are going to take a remedy, which had proved fatal to others; not confidering that it was owing to the wrong application, and not to the nature of the remedy.

The *hellebore* formerly cured many deplorable diftempers, but by the errors of quacks, and their immoderate dofes, it has fo happened, that it is fallen into difufe; but the *wild cucumber* and *bitter apple* are beginning to revive again. The bark of the *berry-bearing alder* is a very excellent purge, yet phyficians have been almoft afraid to prefcribe it, perhaps terrifyed by the ill fuccefs of thofe daring men above-mentioned, who gave too large dofes of it. Many of the moderns for a long while dared not make ufe of opium even externally.

6.

The timidity, and caution of phyficians left they fhould hurt their patients by violent remedies.

P   For

For which reafon they give rather mild, than efficacious ones, and act the part of fpectators, rather than phyficians.

For this reafon perhaps the difciples of Stahl reject the *bark*; though from ignorance of botany they ufe the *cafcarilla*, which is certainly a very good medicine in fhiverings, but not totally void of malignity. Phyficians did not for a long while prefume to prefcribe the *wild cucumber*; which is indeed pretty violent, but by no means fo terrible, that it ought not to be ufed even in the dropfy. For the fame reafon they did not venture to ufe the *fquill*, whofe vertue is very great in thining vifcidities; viz. becaufe they did not know the proper dofe of either of them. The *gamboge* is neglected, though the Turks have taught us its efficacy in a quartan; and the experiments of our prefident in the hofpital at Stockholm have confirmed their practice.

7.

Small dofes of phyfic. For while phyficians have been over-cautious in their prefcriptions, they have fallen into the inconvenience of doing the patient no fervice; and to confefs

the

the truth, i fufpect they more generally err this way at prefent; while they order drachms of plants for an infufion, where ounces would be more proper. On the other hand mounte-banks, and quacks, men of an intrepid mind, and invincible impudence, oftentimes make a cure, when the phyfician of probity fails.

If any one were to prefcribe only two grains of *rhubarb* for a purge, he might as well do nothing at all. The *honey-fuckle* is ufed in decoctions, but not in the quantity neceffary; for which reafon its vertue in purifying the blood is known but to few. The dofe of the *china root* ought to be large, or no good can be expected from it in venereal cafes. Thofe remedies which are fought for amongft vegetables for curing the venereal difeafe are perhaps given more fparingly, than they ought.

8.

The ignorance of apothecaries in botany, who often fell one plant for another; by which means, when the defired effect is not obtained, the phyfician is deterred from the ufe of them for the future.

For *rad. hermodact,* which is recommended

in the rheumatifm, the apothecary fometimes gives the root of the *meadow faffron*; fometimes of one of the *irifes*, which
differ from it in vertue. Hence the
effect of the phyfician's prefcription being
uncertain, he is at laft obliged to give
it up entirely. For the *fcabious* they give
the *centaury*, Fl. Suec. 708. For the *bran-
kurfine*, the *cow-parfnep*, 231; the root
of the *toothwort*, which is excellent in
the tooth-ach, is neglected, becaufe the
apothecary does not know, whether it
ought to be taken from the *toothwort*
565, or 518, or fome other plant. Inftead of the root of the *burnet faxifrage*,
which is a good aftringent in the hæmor-
rhage, the root of the *burnet* is wrongly
fubftituted. To this may be referred the
miftake of felling the *St. John's wort* 624
for the *St. John's-wort* 625, which is vulnerary and good in worm cafes.

9.

*The ignorance of phyficians in botany, or their
want of care to reject ufelefs, fpurious and improper fuccedaneums.*

We fufpect that this formerly was the cafe;
but now, that the knowledge of botany is

carried fo far, we have reafon to hope, that things will go better. The *acmella* which is very ferviceable in the ftone, fince it is extremely rare, and dear, is to be fupplyed out of thofe plants which are really akin to it. This choice belongs to the botanift: for which reafon our prefident has obliged the world by informing it, that the *fieges beckia*, as neareft allyed to the *acmella*, may be rightly fubftituted in its room [z]; which Dr. Haffelquift has confirmed by an experiment made here at Upfal upon a young man afflicted with the ftone. The fkilfull in botany will eafily judge that the *German leopard's bane*, as well as the *common*, carries fufpicion of poifon; yet the former has been looked on as harmlefs by thofe, who were ignorant of botany, and the latter dangerous. The *daify* is cried up in vain on account of the excellent vertue it is fuppofed to poffefs. Practitioners, unlefs they be fkilfull in botany, will fcarcely allow the *wild rofemary*

[z] Vid. Amænit. Academ. vol. 2. p. 151. where fome fuccedaneums to the Senega root are mentioned, founded on the fame principles.

to be a moft efficacious remedy againft the hooping cough; which yet is commonly ufed in this difeafe by the Weftrogoths. The *Turkey baum* is kept in our fhops, altho' much weaker than the *Canarian*, which is excluded. The *white faxifrage* and *dropwort*, tho' neither of them has any extraordinary quality, yet hold a place amongft our officinals. The *mechoacana* is feldom ufed, as being of no great ftrength, yet it is a very proper purge for infants. The *oak of Jerufalem* is gathered from the *European* plant, whereas both tafte and fmell inftruct us, that we ought to get it from the *American*, as a moft powerful remedy in confumptions. The plant, and ftalk of *black currants*, no contemptible medicine in the *hydrophobia*, in *feverifh dyfenteries*, and other contagious diftempers, are now neglected, as the antients have faid nothing about their vertues; which yet are difcoverable by the fmell, tho' not by the tafte.

10.

The ufe of compound medicines. Simples are

fo

fo very rarely ufed, that the vertues of plants are not known for want of experience.

It is fcarcely neceffary to produce inftances of this affertion. Whoever turns over the writings of the antients will be afto-nifhed at the prefcriptions, or rather in-dexes, in which numberlefs things are mingled together. This affair ought to be looked into, and regulated; that we might not fall under the lafh of fome future Serenus Sammonicus, who might addrefs himfelf thus to fome phyficians:

Ye jumble in one mafs fuch coftly juices,
So various in their natures, in their ufes;
That the poor patient, who relies upon you,
At once is cheated of his health, and money.

11.

The mixing things together of a different na-ture. For oftentimes many things are con-founded together, which feparately adminif-tered might affift the patient, and give cre-dit to the phyfician; whereas mixed they become ufelefs, one deftroying the effect of the other.

Thus *watery* mixed with *dry*, *vifcous* with *faline*, *glutinous* with *ftiptical*, *fweet* with

P 4 *acrid,*

acrid, acid with *bitter*, *fapid* with *naufeous*, mutually weaken each other [h].

12.

The ignorance of the natural claffes. From hence it happens that we cannot form any judgment, conformable to botanic principles, of one plant from the knowledge of another. And thus we are afraid of propofing any uncommon plant, being doubtful what we ought to expect from it.

Dogs mercury has been given internally, for want of knowing the natural claffes ; whereas he, who is qualifyed to reafon about the vertues of plants, will allow only the external ufe of this plant, and in glyfters. The *cow parfnep* has been

---

[h] I cannot help applying to this and the foregoing fection two verfes of that fenfible old poet, œconomift, and hufbandman Hefiod, tho' in a different fenfe from what he ufes them.

Νηπιοι ϰϰ ισασιν οσῳ πλεον ημισυ παντος,

Ουδ' οσον εν μαλαχη τε ϰ͜ ασφοδελῳ μεγ' ονειαρ.

Which i fhall tranflate for the fake of the unlearned reader. The meaning is as follows. " Foolifh man does not know " how much the half is more than the whole, and what " great benefit may be found from the plants, that grow " every where about us.

ranked

ranked amongſt the *emollients*, although
not one among all the *umbilliferous kind*
that i know of, is famous for this quality.
The people of America ought to give
the *mitreola*, Hort. Cliff. for the bite of
ſerpents inſtead of the *ophiorrhiza*; which
if they were to do, they would hardly
ever fail of ſucçefs, if botaniſts be not
greatly miſtaken.

13.

*The negleE of vulgar medicines eaſily to be pro-
cured.* For we owe the very beſt of our medicines to the vulgar, who have been taught
the uſe. of them by neceſſity, and conceal
them as ſecrets.

We learned the uſe of the *mezereon* in the
cancer from the countrey people. The
noble liverwort is reckoned a ſpecific in
hypochondriac affections by the Gothlanders. The *linnæa* is commonly uſed
by the Oſtrobothnians in gouty pains.
The common people uſe *pepper* oftentimes very injudiciouſly in acute diſtem-
pers; in eruptive fevers under certain
circumſtances very rightly. The countrey people taught us the vertues of the
thruſh-moſs for ſore throats; of the *hop*
in

in diflocations ; and of the *tremella*, Flor. Suec. 1017. for fixed pains in the joynts. They alfo chew, and blow the fumes of *garlic* into infants to affwage their gripes; or bruife, and apply it to the navel by way of poultice [i].

14.

The neglect of travelling out of Europe. Which would afford us an opportunity of knowing plants, familiar to forreign nations. And I fee not why we fhould be afhamed of learning any thing ufeful from Barbarians.

It is not long ago that fome botanifts, who went to America, difcovered to us thofe excellent medicines, the *great water-dock* in the worft fcorbutic cafes ; the *monarda* in intermittents ; the *collinfonia* in the colics of lying-in women ; the *lobelia*, the *ceanothus*, the *diervilla* in venereal cafes ; the *fenega root* and *ophiorrhiza* againft the bite of ferpents and burning fevers. The celebrated Kalm very lately let us know,

---

[i] Ulluoa obferves that fome difeafes at Carthagena are become fatal, which formerly were not fo. Which he attributes to the neglect of the Indian remedies. For he fays the old women even now fometimes cure the *chapetonade*, which is one of the diftempers he mentions, and formerly never failed to cure it.

that

that the *water avens* is looked on as a fuccedaneum to the *bark* by the people of Canada. The *water figwort* that corrects *fenna*; the *bark*, &c. were communicated by the Barbarians.

15.

The neglect of reading botanical writers, especially thofe, who in thefe latter times have faithfully fet forth what they knew, by certain experiments concerning the vertues of plants.

Of this kind are Rheede, Sloane, Feuilleè, &c. The ufe of the *coris* is unknown to moft people, who have not feen what Shaw fays on that fubject. The vertues of the ftalks of the *bitter-fweet* purifying the blood were a fecret, till our prefident brought them to light. Before him the apothecaries gave only the *garden night-fhade*, or the leaves of the *bitter-fweet*, yet few here have found any good effect from them; as we have rarely given this remedy hitherto in fufficient dofes. The *reft-harrow* is feldom prefcribed, becaufe phyficians have not learned its vertues in the Hungarian fever from Scyller. The antients recommended the *cot-*

ton-thiftle in cancerous cafes; but from neglect of reading the antients, this fpe-cific is almoft forgot.

16.

Neglect of a method in exhibiting medicines. For inftance, phyficians expect thofe vertues from a dryed plant, or in a decoction, which is not to be found but in the frefh plant, or from its expreffed juice. Hence it may juftly be expected from apothecaries, that they fet about cultivating plants; that fuch, as ought to be ufed frefh, may be had daily from their gardens.

The *hedge hyffop*, when frefh, purges very fmartly and vomits; when old it produces no effect at all. The diuretic vertue of our *water flag*, which is very confiderable, when the plant is frefh, intirely goes off, when it is kept long. Therefore we ought to expect this vertue from the expreffed juice, and not from a decoction of it. The *ftone crop*, when dry, has none of that efficacy in the fcurvy, which is found in it, when frefh. The fame may be faid of the *houfe-leek*, the juice of which is celebrated by the Hottentots. The *radifh*, the *fcurvy-grafs*, the *horfe radifh*, the *garden*, *water*, and

, and *Indian crefs*, and the *all-fawce*, ought to be fold in the fhops frefh, and not dryed; in order to be of any fervice in the fcurvy. The *recent* root of the *rofe-wort* is vaftly fuperior to the *dry* in head-achs. Befides it ought carefully to be confidered in what part of a plant its vertue refides. Thus it is the *juice* of the *poppy*, that fpreads over the brain, as it were, a Lethean drowfinefs; and not the *feeds*, for thefe are eatable. The fagacity of the moderns has reduced the immenfe number of diftilled waters to a very fmall lift.

17.

Neglect in cultivating plants. Hence apothecaries are neceffitated to fell plants which they have had by them many years, and which have loft all their vertues.

The *fpikenard* is more durable, perhaps than any other plant; for it will keep its fragrance above an age, as appears by Burferus's Herbary. But other plants are very different in this refpect. e. g. the root of *ginfeng*, tho' a great reftorative, being fo very coftly, is feldom prefcribed; and when it is, it generally has loft its properties thro' age. For which reafon we ought to con-

contrive methods of cultivating it ourfelves. Inftead of the leaves of the true
marum, which has not its equal in art, or
nature, the mouldy ftalks of it are generally found in apothecaries fhops. But we
would not be underftood as if in all cafes
we prefer the cultivated plants to the wild
ones. On the contrary the *vipers grafs,* the
goats beard, the *fuccory* from the fields are
fuperior to thofe which the induftry of the
gardener has rendered more delicate ; on
account of the medicinal bitter, which is
wanting in their cultivated ftate. See a
catalogue of fuch plants as may be raifed
with us in Linn. Mat. Med. p. 212.

18.

*The ignorance of phyficians and apothecaries in
relation to our own plants.* From whence it happens that they are obliged to procure plants
from abroad, which may be had at home.
Thus our people buy the root of the *rofewort*
.and root and feeds of the *garden angelica*
collected by the Norwegians on our alps,
and fold by them to forreigners. For the
reft fee a catalogue of fuch plants, as are
natives of our countrey, in Mat. Med.
above cited, p. 210. If a purge or any
other

other flight medicine is prefcribed to a poor countrey fellow, it muft be the produce of the Indies, fo that they cannot afford to purchafe it. Hence people abhor the thoughts of employing a phyfician or an apothecary.

19.

The ignorance of many forreign plants. Hence we are uncertain whether thofe which are brought to us be genuine or fpurious; and hence alfo their genera being unknown, we are uncertain about their vertues.

To this head may be referred the *fea lavender*, the *myrobalan*, the *ftarry annifeed*, the *balfam* of *Copaiva*, the *balfam* of *Peru*, the *gum animæ, caraunæ, elemi*, the *gum rofins* of *myrrh, bdellium, fagapenum*, the *aloes wood, calambac* [k].

20.

The ufual cuftom in apothecaries fhops of providing only drugs of quick fale. Thus they will not procure fome whofe vertues are now-a-days well known, for fear they fhould lye up-

[k] Hence appears one of the advantages amongft many others that may arife from the voyages of the difciples of Linnæus into the remoteft parts of America, and Afia, from whence many of our drugs come.

on their hands. It is the bufinefs therefore of the phyfician who has any regard for his own reputation, and the patient's welfare, to require the apothecary to procure fuch plants, as he thinks may be ufefull.

Simorouba an excellent remedy in the dyfentery, the *fenega root* in venomous bites, the *profluvii cortex* in the diarrhæa, the *camphorata* in the green ficknefs, the *auricularia* in deafnefs, the *Peragua* in the diabetes, the *fouth-fea tea* in the fmall-pox, the *ferpentum radix* againft venomous bites, the *wild flax*, a very ufefull purge, are neglected. The juice of the *hypociftis*, and *fungus melitenfis*, altho' powerful medicines in hæmorrhages, and the *herba dyfenterica*[1], which is named fo from its peculiar vertues, have not yet got a place amongft our officinals.

21.

Want of care in gathering fimples at a proper time, and keeping them, when gathered, in a proper manner.

[1] I fuppofe the Inula diffenterica L. Conyza Media. R. 174. is here meant; as i find this note upon it in Fl. Suec. edit. 2. 'General Keith told me that the Ruffians, when 'extremely reduced by the bloody flux, in their expedition 'into Perfia, were reftored to health by this plant.'

The

The root of the *avens,* unlefs gathered in the beginning of the fpring, before the fap by nourifhing, and pufhing out the leaves has wafted its aromatic vertue, will by no means anfwer what may be juftly expected from it. *Rhubarb* ought not to be brought into an apothecary's fhop under ten years from the time of its gathering. The flowers of the St. *John's wort* ought to be gathered before they are full blown, that their balfamic vertue may be preferved. The root of the *angelica* is good for nothing unlefs it be gathered in the winter. *Sloes* ought to be gathered before they are ripe, and the juice preffed out of them in this ftate, i. e. before the harfhnefs is foftened by the froft, if it be defigned for an aftringent. *Marum* ought to be kept in veffels well clofed, left the volatile part, in which its vertue refides, fhould evaporate.

—— Still an ample field remains,
But not for me, to others i give way,
Who choofe a longer courfe.

Q   As

A S i do not pretend to underftand the fubject of this piece, and therefore cannot
fay how far the obftacles to the advancement
of phyfic charged upon the Swedes fubfift in
this countrey, or whether all thofe obftacles,
which the author has mentioned, be real or not,
my fole motive for tranflating it was to draw it
out of that obfcurity in which it was buried
amongft many other pieces, relating to curiofities of natural hiftory. I think i may be allowed to fay a piece is buried in obfcurity,
which is only known to a few, who happen to
be in the way where fuch curiofities are talked
of; and an attempt to fpread it over the nation cannot but be right, if the doctrine be folid, and affects our practitioners.

Tho' as i faid i do not pretend to underftand
the fubject of this piece; yet i hope the learned reader will excufe me, if i add one obftacle
more to the foregoing lift : it is *the notion
which has and i believe ftill does prevail a-
mongft fome phyficians, that the doctrine of
fpecifics is groundlefs, and took its rife merely
from ignorance in natural philofophy.* I will
not undertake to treat this fubject, as the importance of it deferves; and therefore fhall
refer

refer thofe who choofe to look farther into this affair, to a very curious and ingenious book publifhed not many years ago by doctor Martyn, entitled, *Effaies Philofophical and Medical.* The reader may perhaps find there fufficient reafons to incline him to lay fome ftrefs on the old-fafhioned doctrine concerning the peculiar vertues of fome medicines preferably to others, feemingly of the fame intention. I will add that the phænomena of chemiftry give continual proofs of the reality of this doctrine, and afford fo many inftances of it, that were i fo inclined, i could eafily fill fome pages with them out of Mr. Boyle and other authors of credit. Ray in his hiftory of plants, p. 49. cites fome very curious obfervations of this tendency from Grew, which are well worth the confideration of phyficians. Upon the whole i cannot help thinking that the want of true and genuine philofophy ought rather to be imputed to thofe who deny, than to thofe who maintain the doctrine of fpecifics; and that we might as well undertake to open all locks with one key, as purge all humors with one medicine.

Q 2   THE

THE
CALENDAR
OF
FLORA,
SWEDISH and ENGLISH.

Made in the YEAR 1755.

Φραζεαϛ δ' ευτ'αν φωνην γερανϑ επακϑσηϛ, &c.
Ημοϛ κοκκυξ κοκκυζͅͅͅͅ, &c.
Ημοϛ δε σκολυμοϛ τ'ανθͅ κͅ ηχετα τετͅιξ, &c.
Ημοϛ.δͅη το ϖρωτον, οσοντ' εϖιβασα κορωνη·

Heſiod.

ABSOLVENT POSTERI.

Q 3

TO THE

RIGHT HONOURABLE

THE

Lord Vifcount BARRINGTON,

SECRETARY AT WAR.

My Lord,

I Embrace with great pleafure the liberty you allow me of dedicating the follow-ing pieces to your Lordfhip. For tho' i muft not prefume to fpeak all i feel on this occafion ; yet i hope i may without offence, take notice of that moft amiable and bene-volent difpofition, which makes you de-light in affifting thofe, who are incapable of making any return. This is the leaft that can be faid by one, who is himfelf of that number, and who is defirous to ex-prefs in a public manner his fincere grati-tude and refpect. I am,

MY LORD,

YOUR LORDSHIP's MUCH OBLIGED

AND VERY HUMBLE SERVANT,

BENJ. STILLINGFLEET.

PREFACE.

IN my notes on thofe treatifes felected out of the Amænitates Academicæ, which i publifhed not long ago, i marked the day of the month on which certain trees leafed in the year 1755; and likewife mentioned fome co-incidences of the coming of birds, and the flowering of plants in this and other countries. The inftances i there gave were but few, as i could then find no more parallel obfervations made in other countries to compare mine with. Since that time another volume of the Amæn. Academ. is come out, in which is a fmall treatife entitled, the Calendar of Flora. This treatife contains an account of the leafing, flowering, &c. of a great number of plants, as alfo of the departure and return of birds. As thefe obfervations happen to be made the very fame year in which mine were, and as they are the firft of the kind perhaps that ever were made, i was induced to look over my papers again, which i had thrown by as of no confequence; thinking that in thefe circumftances fome ufe ought to be made of them, as they might prove entertaining at leaft, if not inftructive to thofe whofe genius leads them to curiofities of this kind. I am very fenfible how fmall the number of fuch perfons is, but i am contented to write for thofe few, nay, indeed i write becaufe they are fo few, being willing as far as lies in my power to increafe their number.

But it may be afked perhaps by fome, even after they have confidered all that is faid on this fubject in the introduction to the following Swe-difh Calendar, and in the piece De Vernatione Arbo-

Arborum, why endeavor to increase their number? Are there not idle people enough already? What signifies whether such a plant be in blow or in leaf at the same time with some others; or when such a bird comes or goes; sings or is silent? If we hear the bird sing, and know for what purposes the plant is useful, we know all that is necessary; every thing beyond that is but the wish, or rather dream of enthusiasm, which wants to give an air of importance to its favorite subject. This perhaps may be said by some; but the same way of reasoning applied to other things will shew, that it may possibly be wrong. For instance, the sea swells twice in 24 hours, and the moon passes thro' the meridian circle as often in the same time. Now should it be said, that if we know each of these truths separately it is enough; and that to know farther what relation in point of time one of these phænomena has to the other, is nothing to the purpose; i believe such an assertion would at this time appear absurd, however it might have passed in ignorant ages. I think we may assert universally, that whenever two things, however disparate in their nature, constantly accompany one another, they are both actuated and influenced by the same cause. Now that cause may probably operate on other things that lye within the reach of our powers, and depend on our determination. Thus that constitution of the air, which causes the cuckow to appear about the time, when the fig-tree puts forth its fruit, may indicate the properest season to sow some of our most useful seeds, or do some other work which it imports us to do at a right time; and that time may not be according

cording to certain calendar days, but according
to a hitherto unobferved calendar, which varies
feveral weeks in different years. I do not abfolutely affert, that we can come to make ufe of
fuch a calendar, but i defire that others will not
affert the contrary at prefent, but leave this affair to be decided by the only proper way, which
certainly muft be experience.

We know from Hefiod, that hufbandry was in
part regulated by the blowing of plants, and the
coming or going of birds; and moft probably it
had been in ufe long before his time, as aftronomy was then in its infancy *; but when artificial
calendars came into vogue the natural calendar
feems to have been totally neglected, for i find
no traces of it after his time, whether for good
and fufficient reafons i pretend not to determine.
That it was laid afide before the time of Ariftophanes we have a pofitive proof in his *Aves*, where
he makes Pifthetairus fay, ' Formerly the kite
' governed the Græcians, which according to the
' explication of the fcholiaft means, that formerly
' the appearance of the kite was looked on as a fign
' of fpring. He fays afterwards, that the cuckow
' formerly governed all Ægyt and Phœnicia, be-
' caufe when that bird appeared they judged it
' was time for wheat and barley harveft.'

I fhall make no farther mention at prefent of
the ufe of plants in directing the hufbandman,
but take this opportunity of making a digreffion

---

* Hefiod himfelf was one of the earlieft of the Greek aftronomers. He lived, according to Sir Ifaac Newton, about 70
years after Chiron, who formed the conftellations for the ufe
of the Argonauts; and from Hefiod the grofs and coarfe method of aftronomy was called the Hefiodean method.

about

about birds in relation to their prognoftic nature. Henceforward then, i. e. from the time
of Hefiod, they feem to have been looked upon
as no longer capable of directing the hufbandman in his rural affairs, but they did not however lofe their influence and dignity ; nay, on
the contrary, they feem to have gained daily a
more than ordinary, and even wonderful authority, till at laft no affair of confequence, either
of private or public concern, was undertaken
without confulting them. They were looked upon
as the interpreters of the gods, and thofe who
were qualified to underftand their oracles were
held among the chief men in the Greek and Roman ftates, and became the affeffors of kings, and
even of Jupiter himfelf *. However abfurd fuch
an inftitution as a college of augurs may appear
in our eyes, yet like all other extravagant inftitutions, it had in part its origin from nature.
When men confidered the wonderful migration
of birds, how they difappeared at once, and appeared again at ftated times, and could give no
guefs where they went, it was almoft natural to
fuppofe, that they retired fomewhere out of the
fphere of this earth, and perhaps approached the
ætherial regions, where they might converfe with
the gods, and thence be enabled to predict
events. This i fay was almoft natural for a fu-
perftiticus people to imagine, at leaft to believe,

---

* Jovi optimo maximo fe confiliarum atque adminiftrum da-
tum meminerit augur. Cicero.
  Lacedæmonii reges augurem affefforem habuerunt. Id.
  Aves internunciæ Jovis. Id.
  Sacerdotum collegium vel nomine folenne. Plin. Nat. Hift,
fpeaking of the augurs.

as

as foon as fome impoftor was impudent enough
to affert it. Add to this, that the difpofition in
fome birds to imitate the human voice muft contribute much to the confirmation of fuch a doctrine. This inftitution of augury feems to have
been much more antient than that of arufpicy; for
we find many inftances of the former in Homer,
but not a fingle one of the latter that i know of;
though frequent mention is made of facrifices in
that author. From the whole of what i have obferved, i fhould be apt to think that natural augury gave rife to religious augury, and this to
arufpicy, as the mind of man makes a very eafy
tranfition from a little truth to a great deal of
error.

A paffage in Ariftophanes gave me the hint for
what i have been faying. In the comedy of the
Birds he makes one of them fay thus : ' The
' greateft bleffings which can happen to you
' mortals are derived from us; firft we fhew you
' the feafons, viz. fpring, winter, autumn. The
' *crane* points out the time for fowing, when fhe
' flies with her warning notes into Ægypt; fhe
' bids the failer hang up his rudder and take his
' reft, and every prudent man provide himfelf
' with winter garments. Next the *kite* appear-
' ing, proclaims another feafon, viz. when it is
' time to fhear your fheep. After that the *fwal-*
' *low* informs you when it is time to put on fum-
' mer cloaths. We are to you, adds the chorus,
' Ammon, Dodona, Apollo; for after confult-
' ing us you undertake every thing; merchandize,
' purchafes, marriages, &c. Are we not then to
' you on the footing of Apollo, &c.'. Now it
feems not improbable, that the fame tranfition

was

was made in the speculations of men, which appears in the poet's words, and that they were ea-
sily induced to think, that the surprising fore-
sight of birds, as to the time of migration, in-
dicated something of a divine nature in them;
which opinion Virgil, as an Epicurean, thinks fit
to enter his protest against; when he says,

Haud equidem credo quia sit divinitus illis
Ingenium.

But to return to Aristophanes. The first part
of the chorus from whence the afore-cited paffage is taken, seems with all its wildness to contain the fabulous cant, which the augurs made
use of in order to account for their impudent
impositions on mankind. It sets out with a cof-
mogony, and says, that in the begining were
Chaos, and Night, and Erebus, and Tartarus.
That there was neither water, nor air, nor sky;
that Night laid an egg, from whence, after a
time, Love arose. That Love, in conjunction
with Erebus, produced the bird kind, and that
they were the first of the immortal race, &c.

With this passage in Aristophanes, the account
of the oracle of Dodona seems to agree. This
oracle was the oldest in Greece, and there a *dove*
prophesied, according to the concurrent testimony of history; but according to the explication of Herodotus, this strange opinion arose from
hence, that the Theban priestess, who was stolen
by the Phœnicians, and carried into Greece, was
called a *dove*, because being a barbarian, she
seemed to the Dodoneans to chatter like a bird,
till she had learned the Greek language, and then
she was said to speak with a human voice. This
expli-

explication feems to me extremely forced, and
every thing is much better accounted for by fuppofing, that at Dodona natural augury was firft
changed into religious augury; for there the oaks
alfo prophefied; which plainly fhews the firft
ftate of religious augury, when it had not wholly
put off its antient form, but like the monfters in
Ovid's Metamorphofes, ftill retained enough of it
to convince us what it had once been. That
Dodona was one of the firft places where augury
was practifed, is highly probable; for it is
mentioned by Homer as an oracle of eftablifhed
reputation at the time of the Trojan war: now
Pliny tells us, that Tirefias invented augury and
arufpicy; and that he was reputed an augur appears by Sophocles in the Œdipus Tyrannus,
where he is introduced faying thus to Tirefias,
' If you have received any information concern-
' ing the death of Laius from the birds, or by
' other means, do not envy it us.' Tirefias therefore, according to Sophocles, lived in the time of
Laius; and Laius, according to Sir Ifaac Newton, lived not 80 years before the taking of
Troy.

I will here fubjoin an account of what has
been obferved about the difappearance of birds,
which will ferve to confirm what i faid above concerning the effect, which that phænomenon might
not improbably have on the minds of men; and
give room for the fuperftitious impoftures that
arofe from thence. Ariftotle has a chapter on
that fubject; wherein he fays, ' that many birds,
' and not a few, as fome imagine, hide themfelves
' in holes;' he then enumerates the *fwallow*, the
kite, the *thrufh*, the *ftarling*, the *owl*, the *crane*,

the

the *turtle*, the *blackbird*, and the *lark*, as certainly hiding themſelves; which ſhews how little was known of their real ſtate in his days; nay, ſo much was he puzzled about this ſubject, that in another place he ſuppoſes ſome of the birds to be changed in their form and voice at different ſeaſons. Thus he ſays, that the *redſtart* changes into the *robin redbreaſt*; and Geſner gives this reaſon for Ariſtotle's falling into this opinion, that during the ſummer the *robin redbreaſt* lives in deſert places, and comes towards towns and houſes in the autumn, when the *redſtart* diſappears. Again Ariſtotle ſays, that the *black cap* changes into a *beccafigo*, which laſt appears, as Geſner obſerves, about autumn, when the figs are ripe, and the former after the autumn. It is true Ariſtotle mentions ſome kinds of birds which go to warmer climates when they diſappear, which is a proof that their migrations were not wholly unknown in thoſe days; and indeed the poems of Homer prove that they were in part known much earlier. Nor could it happen otherwiſe, when the inquiſitive genius of Greece began to work, and carry men into Phœnicia and Ægypt, with a view of improving themſelves in all parts of learning; where they could not avoid obſerving, that ſome birds which left Greece in the winter were found at that time in thoſe warmer climates. But the ſuperſtition was already confirmed before this happened. Dodona was eſtabliſhed on a foundation not to be ſhaken by the weak attempt of reaſon and experience. The birds had given good advice time out of mind, and brought many a general and a magiſtrate, as well as private men without number,

out

out of difficulties; and therefore, whether they wintered in Ægypt or not, fignified little; and indeed it was only fuppofing them to go a little further, viz. into Æthiopia, and there they might meet Jupiter at his annual vifit, μεθ' αμυμονας Aιθιοπνας, and have the gift of prophecy conferred upon them, or confirmed. Agreeably to thefe notions we find feveral birds were looked upon as facred to particular gods; thus the owl to Minerva, the peacock to Juno, the eagle to Jupiter, the crow to Apollo whofe meffenger he was called as appears by Hefiod.

Some will be apt to think that i have dwelt much longer upon this fubject that it deferved; but i cannot help thinking, that even the infirmities of the human mind, efpecially fuch as have like this prevailed amongft the moft ingenious and fagacious people we read of, and for a long courfe of time influenced their moft ferious concerns, ought to be looked upon as not below our notice.

It may feem wonderful to fome, that naturalifts have been fo long without being able to determine any thing certain about the ftate of feveral birds when they difappear. The beft writers have given it as their opinion, that *fwallows* lye under water all winter; one of the lateft ornithologifts, a writer of great character, falls into this opinion, and the author of the following Calendar adopts it; and indeed till Monf. Adanfon cleared up this point, it muft appear a problematical point to any man. But though the migration of this bird is at laft determined, yet what becomes of the *nightingale*, the *cuckow*, the *goat-fucker*, and feveral others, is ftill undecided.

R　　　　Nor.

Nor is this wonderful, though it may feem fo; for the generality of mankind, and efpecially thofe who travel merely for the fake of a liveli-hood, or a fortune, are fo little folicitous about things of this kind, that the air might be filled with *fwallows* in winter without their obferving it, as was plainly the cafe at Senegal.

The number of birds that difappear in this kingdom is much greater than is generally ima-gined; efpecially if we reckon amongft them the birds which fhift quarters at different feafons, but do not crofs the feas. I fhall not attempt to give a lift of them, but recommend it to the curious, who live in the countrey the year round to watch them more narrowly, than they have hitherto been. Linnæus fays, that moft of that genus of birds, which he calls *motacillæ*, i. e. *thofe fmall birds, which have a beak fubulated aud ftrait, with chaps nearly equal, noftrils of a pointed oval form, and tongue jaggedly indented*, live upon infects and not grain; and therefore mi-grate from the northern to the fouthern parts to-wards winter; but it appears, that many birds migrate not only in Sweden, but in Greece and other climates, that live with us all the year round.

It is poffible, that after all i have faid, tending to revive natural augury, and after all the ne-ceffary obfervations fhall have been regiftred, that no ufe can be made of it; but i am certain, that as long as men have ears and eyes, they muft think that one of the greateft delights of the countrey, efpecially during the fpring months, is owing to the lively motions, beautiful fhapes and colours, and melodious notes of birds, which will

will afford more pleafure, as they are more obferved; and therefore, i am not furprifed, that
Peter the Great of Mufcovy did not think it beneath his attention to endeavor to enliven his
new feat of empire, by fending for colonies of
them from other parts, as they were fcarce where
he refided.

I will finifh this digreffion with a refle&tion that
occurs to me on the different fates of natural and
religious augury. The firft was fimple, unattend-
ed with any of thofe circumftances that are apt
to roufe the paffions of man; and therefore, tho'
likely to prove ufeful, if purfued with proper diligence, fell into negle&t. The latter was com-
plicated, applying itfelf to fome of the ftrongeft
paffions in man, and therefore, though unlikely
to a ferious mind, to have the leaft foundation in
truth, or ever to be ufeful, was encouraged and
adorned with all the pomp that a fuperftitious
people could invent in honor of a flattering, and
therefore favorite art.

I fhall now come to fome points that more
immediately relate to the following Calendars.

1. I have retained the Linnæan names of every
plant, and animal in the Swedifh Calendar; and
have added the Englifh names to the plants taken
from Ray's Synopfis, and his hiftory, with no
fmall trouble, as any one will eafily believe who
has done the like *. The numbers which follow
the Englifh names refer to the above-mentioned
books with an H. to diftinguifh the hiftory. The

---

* This trouble we fhall for the future be relieved from,
when that accurate and fkilful botanift, Mr. Hudfon, has publifhed his Flora Anglica, which is now in the prefs.

num-

numbers after the Englifh names of animals refer either to his Hiftoria Avium, or Pifcium, according to the fubject†. I chofe to refer to Ray,
as well as barely give the Englifh names, for the
eafe and fatisfaction of fuch as put a due value
on that ineftimable writer, whofe works do honor
to our nation, as a late difciple of the great Swedifh naturalift juftly obferves. I cannot help faying farther upon this occafion, that no writer till
his time ever advanced all the branches of natural hiftory fo much as that fagacious, accurate,
and diligent Englifh obferver, whofe fyftematical
fpirit threw a light on every thing he undertook,
and contributed not a little to thofe great and
wonderful improvements, which have been fince
introduced.

2. I have omitted moft of the plants which are
not natives of England; both becaufe it is not
eafy to find Englifh names for them which have
any authority, and becaufe i had fcarcely any obfervations in my own Calendar, but on fuch plants
as are native. Some foreign ones however i have
retained, particularly fuch as are common in almoft every garden; and fuch as are marked in
the Calendar, as more than ordinary prognoftic.
Thefe laft are printed in large characters.

3. I have retained the divifion of months according to budding, leafing, flowering, &c. tho'
i could not imitate this method in my own Calendar for want of more experience; but i am

† Some perhaps may think that i need not have referred to
Ray for birds fo well known as feveral mentioned in the Calendars; but the want of this caution in many authors, has
produced great confufion and doubt about the things meant in
every branch of natural hiftory.

convinced

convinced that this method marks more precifely when we may expect the flowering of any plant, or the return of any bird, &c. than the bare mention of the day of a common calendar month, and at the fame time marks it more univerfally. Thus, when Ariftotle fays *, That the nightingale fings continually day and night for fifteen days about the time when the young leaves begin to expand and thicken the woods, he not only marks a time, when they might expect to hear the nightingale in Greece, but in every other countrey; for thus it happens in Sweden and England, as may be feen in the following Calendars; whereas if he had faid, it appeared in fuch a day of the month, it would bear true perhaps for that year only; and in fact we find in the old almanacks the fame author marking days very diftant from one another, for the appearance of the fame birds, and thus it muft be likewife in relation to plants.

Thus far for the Swedifh Calendar. As to my own, 1ft. i have marked every circumftance down as i found it in my journal, and hope the learned reader will pardon any miftakes which might happen, either from want of judgment or attention. It is poffible, that i might put down fome plants as firft being in bud, or flower, or

---

* His words are οἷαν τὸ ορος ἡδὴ δασυνῆται. i. e. when the mountain is thickening, where it is certain the word *mountain* is ufed for the trees which generally grow upon it. Thus Homer applies the word σκιοενῆα to ορεα for that reafon, Iliad, A. 157. and Euftathius upon the place fays, ἰςεον δὲ ὅτι, σκιοενῆα μεν, ὑπο τὲ παρςκολυθεντος, λεγει. τα δασεα κỳ σκιας αποτελεσικα δια το της υλης λασιον.

Pliny tranflates this paffage, *denfante fe frondium germine.*

R 3   eaf,

leaf, becaufe i happened then firft to obferve them, or they might be in thofe ftates fome time before in fome place where i happened not to go.

2. I wanted fuch a guide as the ingenious author of the Swedifh Calendar. My obfervations then perhaps might have been lefs unworthy of the public, as they would have been better directed to a particular purpofe; but now the reader muft expect to find in it all the imperfections that generally accompany firft attempts of any kind.

3. I have caufed all the prognoftic plants, which are mentioned in my Calendar, to be printed in large letters as in the Swedifh. The other marks i fhall explain in a page by itfelf, for the more eafy recurring to it.

4. Thefe two Calendars would perhaps upon comparifon have furnifhed me with fome obfervations, had i been able to find time fufficient for that purpofe; but a ftrong defire to communicate them to the public early in the year, that others might be induced to keep journals of the fame kind, determined me to fend them out in this naked condition; and the more fo, as i am affured on very good authority, that fuch journals will be kept in Sweden, Germany, Italy, and France, the next year; and i think it would be pity, that an opportunity fhould be loft of making fo curious a comparifon between thefe different climates, and which perhaps may not occur again, or at leaft not for many years.

5. The obfervations on heat and cold were made with a thermometer, marked in a way peculiar to myfelf. The degrees are thofe of Farenheit, which i chofe as being in common ufe, but

but inftead of 32 i have made o the freezing point. This method is more fimple, natural, and uniform, and conveys a more diftinct idea to the mind. To this fcale i have reduced the Swedifh author's obfervations, as well as thofe of Dr. Hales, taken from his Vegetable Statics; who i am pleafed to find has made ufe of the method above-mentioned, in his late works, and i wonder it is not univerfally adopted. The degrees below o i have marked thus,—1.—2.—3, &c.

6. My botanical obfervations were made on plants growing in the fields chiefly; the Swedifh plants growing in the Upfal garden; which method is beft, where either is in our power, i cannot determine. There are conveniences and inconveniences attending each; but there is one great convenience vifibly on the fide of the garden; which is, that the plants lye within a fmall compafs, and therefore may be looked over more furely and regularly every day.

7. I once defigned to place the two Calendars over-againft one another, in oppofite pages, part by part, according to the days of the month, but upon confideration i found, the climates being fo different, that there would be great vacancies in many of the pages; at the fame time that the fame plants would be in different pages, and the bulk of the book would be increafed without any advantage to the reader; i therefore thought it would be better to make an index, which will furnifh an eafy method to the curious of comparing the two climates.

8. If ever any ufe be made of Calendars of this kind, it muft be by finding out, after a long feries of obfervations, and publifhing by itfelf a

R 4
lift

lift of a few regularly prognoftic plants, either common in every field, if native; or, if not native, common in every garden. For it muft be noted, that many plants will blow even in the depth of winter, if the weather be mild. This is the cafe of *dandelion*, *chickweed*, *fhepherd's purfe*, *daify*, &c. As for other precautions, I will refer the reader to the piece concerning the leafing of trees in the Amæn. Academ.

This Calendar was made at the hofpitable feat of my very worthy and ingenious friend Mr. Marfham, who has likewife made obfervations of this kind, and lately communicated to the world his curious obfervations on the growth of trees. All the countrey about is a dead flat; on one fide is a barren black heath, on the other a light fandy loam; partly tilled, partly pafture land fheltered with very fine groves.

T H E

INTRODUCTION.

BEFORE i fet forth the Calendar of Flora, or the delights of the year, arifing from mere fublunary things according to its progrefs, and that from obfervations made in the climate of Upfal, ann. 1755. i think it neceffary to fay fomething by way of introduction. Time moves on flowly; every thing is in progreffion and motion, and has its allotted time, as the wifeft of men Solomon obferves; to which purpofe Virgil fays, *Stat fua cuique dies.*

Aftronomers have exerted all their power to meafure time. To them we owe the accurate divifions of it; for they by obferving the courfe and motion of the celeftial bodies, have been at laft enabled to reduce it to ftated periods, and to divide it in fuch a manner into years, months, weeks and days, that we have calendars conftructed for common ufe, as a rule by which to obferve and number its equal parts.

As the ftars radiate, fhine, and adorn the celeftial regions of the fummer months, fo flowers beautify and illuminate the earth with a wonderful variety of bright and delightful colors. Thus, according to the ftile of the chymifts, that which is above is as that which is below.

How much time foever and labor botanifts have beftowed for many ages back, in order to know the names, nature and vertues of plants, they have not hitherto arrived at that degree of perfection, as to be able to equal the fuccefs of aftronomers, in noting the properties and phænomena of each of them.

Every

Every flower has its appointed feafon. It would therefore be in vain for us to feek the fpring plants in autumn, and the autumn plants in the fpring. We fee them at ftated times emerging, ftalking, flowering, fruiting, decaying. Again in another feafon we fee others rifing in their room, and that in fo fhort a time, by fo regular and conftant a law, according to the direction of their natures, that it feems impoffible for any one to behold this feries and variety, without the higheft admiration.

The fun at the fame time that it raifes, as it were, to life thefe beings, that are deftitute of animal functions, brings them forth alfo fooner, or later, according to the nature and difpofition of each, i. e. as this or that plant requires a leffer or a greater degree of heat, before it can obtain its juft maturity. For as eggs, differing in fpecies, when fit on by a hen, will not all be hatched the fame day, but fome fooner, fome later, fo neither do flowers come forth together, but at ftated times, as they fhall have received the degree of heat proper to their natures.

Altho' the year was formed by the Creator in fuch a manner, as to be divided into diftinct parts, by the fun fending forth its rays equally on the furface of the earth, yet we are not therefore from thence to define and meafure the fummer, the quantity of ice and fnow and Northern ·colds hindering the air from being equally foon warmed in different years; and according to the heat of the air, the feafons are advanced or retarded, and this is beft known and meafured by the various kinds of flowers.

Since therefore the fummer feafon depends
upon

upon the greater or leffer degree of heat, fo that flowers come forth proportionably to thofe different degrees, but yet in fuch a manner, that one fpecies follows another in a regular order; fince this is the cafe, i fay, the feafons of the year, and particularly the fummer, may eafily from thence be meafured; which hitherto has been a defideratum, on account of œconomical ufes, in fpite of all the affiftance from aftronomers.

Hence plants in different years often flower a month fooner or later, although, as i obferved before, they ftill follow one another in their natural order, as far as the fummer folftice; at which time they hardly ever differ in any year; and in the fame manner they proceed, haften on, or are retarded, the nearer they approach towards autumn, and the winter is farther off or nearer at hand. Now in order to determine accurately the acceleration or retardation of the winter, we muft obferve all the different kinds of flowers in every place, at what time they firft appear, and this daily, that the order which they obferve may be better afcertained.

By way of fpecimen i have exhibited the flowers in the fame order in which they appeared the laft year, 1755, in the Upfal garden. I muft obferve, that almoft all the plants mentioned in the following calendar grew in the open air, and in the fame kind of foil, which is rather low and loamy, excepting about half a fcore, which were gathered in the woods not far diftant; and which are with difficulty raifed in the garden.

I have marked the month and day all along

on

on the fide of the page, not meaning that any one fhould thence imagine that the flowers will return every year on the fame day and month, but with intent to fet forth the calendar of that individual year, and that it might appear with what diligence and circumfpection it was made.

In order to diftinguifh the cultivated plants from the wild, i have ufed italics for the firft, and have marked the plants which appear to be moft prognoftic by an afterifk *.

I have befides thought fit to difpofe them all into months, according to a divifion the apteft i could contrive; but i did not think it neceffary to form equal months, as my defign was not to determine days, but chiefly and indeed only the greater or leffer acceleration of fummer.

Having fo accurately obferved the flowers, i thought fit to add the times at which the animal kingdom undergoes certain alterations, fuch as when birds of paffage come and go, when birds of every kind lay, or hatch, or moult, when feveral kinds of fifhes celebrate their nuptials near the fea fhore, when it is fowing time, when grain flowers, ripens, &c.

By the help of fuch obfervations we may at laft come to know what is to be done, or obferved, every day, by the flowering of plants. But much time is required to bring this to perfection; and he who obferves, muft, if he means to do any thing to the purpofe, live in the countrey, where it is much eafier to fee every thing that prefents itfelf.

---

* Inftead of an afterifk i have ufed great letters.

If

If the gentlemen of our own, or other countries, took delight in such observations, they might amuse themselves very agreeably, by giving up some of their time to things of this kind; and i am most certainly persuaded, that this so slight a sketch, gaining continually new additions, would at last produce a work of great use; as it might furnish materials for directing private œconomy, and the more so as the times for sowing of seeds, for reaping, and mowing, and for gathering fruits of various kinds, might from thence be best settled.

Gardeners might thence learn at what time of the spring, they ought to lay the roots of plants bare, when to sow their seeds, when to expose to the open air, and when to put under shelter their tender plants, and how to furnish the garden with flowering plants; so that there might be a perpetual blow all possible months of the year; thus the *lilac* follows the *cherry*, the *mock orange* follows the *lilac*, and the *late roses* follow the *mock orange*.

THE ORDER OF BLOWING OF THE BULBOUS PLANTS IN BORDERS, AND THEIR DURATION. N. B. The plants are numbered from the first day of budding, by the figures bered on the left hand, the other figures on the right hand shew the duration of their blow *.

---

* The meaning is this, as explained to me by Mr. Solander; suppose the *snow-drop* buds on any given day, then the *crocus* will bud the second day after it, the *hyacinth* the 12th day after it, &c.

1. Snow-

1. Snow-drops, 1144. H. Galanthus *nivalis*, 26.
Violet, *bulbous* 1144. H. Leucoium *vernale*, 26.
2. Crocus, *spring*, 1174. H. Crocus *vernus*, 17.
12. Hyacinth, *oriental*, 1159. H. Hyacinthus *orientalis*, 18.
20. Fumitory, *bulbous*, 975. H. 4. Fumaria *bulbofa folida*, 20.
23. Hollow-root, 975. H. 5. Fumaria *bulbofa cava*, 20.
28. Hyacinth, *grape*, 1161. 28. H. Hyacinthus *botryoides*, 19.
34. Daffodil, *English*, 371. 2. Narciffus *pfeudonarciffus*, 19.
Daffodil, *sweet*, Narciffus *odorus*, S. N. 19.
37. Crown, imperial, 1105. H. Fritillaria *imperialis*, 10.
Fritillary, *Pyrenean*, 1107. H. Fritillaria *Pyrenaica*, 14.
38. Lilly, *chequer'd*, 1106. H. Fritillaria *meleagris*, 10.
44. Tulip, 1146. H. Tulipa *Gefneriana*, 13.
47. Primrofe, *peerlefs*, 1133. H. Narciffus *poeticus*.
50. Hyacinth, *summer*, 1160. H. Hyacinthus *amethyftinus*.
15. Hyacinth, *Spanish*, 1160. 21. H. Hyacinthus *cernuus*.
59. Star of Bethlehem, 1153.9. H. Ornithogalum *umbellatum*.
68. Lilly, *fiery*, 1110. 3, 4, 5, 7. H. Lilium *viviparum*.
69. Moly, *yellow*, 1123. 4. H. Allium *moly*.
76. Martagon *of Pompony*, 1114.7. H. Lilium *Pomponium*.
79. Star of Bethlehem, *spiked*, 1151.1. H. Ornithogalum *Pyrenaicum*.   69. Moly,

80. Corn flag. 1168. H. Gladiolus *communis*.
81. Martagon, *common*; 1112. H. Martagon *vulgare*; 15.
86. Martagon, *white*, 1112. Martagon *album*, 13.
100. Lilly, *white*, 1109. H. Lilium *album*.
111. Hyacinth, *dun-coloured*, 1160. 22. H. Hyacinthus *serotinus*.
113. Saffron, *meadow*; 373. Colchicum *autumnale*.

When many calendars of this kind shall be made in different places and nations in the same year, it will be eafy to collect from the blowing of thefe forts of flowers, and from the leafing of trees, how one climate differs from another, and why plants brought from the Southern parts feldom produce fruit with us, whereas the Northern plants fucceed very well. Thus at Montpelier the fpring is forwarder than at Upfal by 31 days, at London by 28, at Falconia by 6; and the winter comes on as much later in thofe places.

Botanifts and apothecaries, whofe bufinefs it is to gather plants juft when they are in blow, may by this means learn at what time that may be done, and need not feek in vain at an improper feafon, and may farther know by their garden plants, what wild ones are to be found in the fields precifely at the fame time; and on the contrary.

The night frofts which fo often deftroy our plants, and which i imagine come to us from Lapland, may be known in the fame way.

Thus the LEAD cold arifing from the thaws in Lapmarck, happens at the end of the leafing feafon.

S   The

The BRASS cold from the fnow melting in Lapland in the beginning of the fruiting feafon.

The IRON cold from the freezing on the Lapland alps in the middle of the fowing feafon.

Thefe colds do not happen with us the fame night as in Lapland, but arrive in about 8 days.

On thefe and fuch like calendars vulgar practical hufbandry ought to be eftablifhed; but the foundation hitherto not having been fufficiently well laid, this method is become fo much out of ufe, that it is even looked upon as abfurd and chimerical; neverthelefs it may and ought to be carried fo far, that no prudent œconomift will choofe to be without fuch a guide, and the hufbandman fhall find it the fureft way to regulate his affairs by, not to mention other particulars.

THE
CALENDAR

OF

FLORA,

SWEDISH and ENGLISH.

Made in the YEAR 1755.

S 2

THE MONTHS.

I.   Reviving winter month from Dec. 22. to March 19.
II.   Thawing month from Mar. 19. to Apr. 12.

1.   SPRING.

III.   Budding month from April 12 to May 9.
IV.   Leafing month from May 9 to May 25.
V.   Flowering month from May 25 to June 20.

2.   SUMMER.

VI.   Fruiting month from June 20 to July 12.
VII.   Ripening month from July 12 to Aug. 4.
VIII.   Reaping month from Aug. 4 to Aug. 28.

3.   AUTUMN.

IX.   Sowing month from Aug. 28 to Sept. 22.
X.   Shedding month from Sept. 22 to Oct. 28.
XI.   Freezing month from Oct. 28 to Nov. 5.

4.   WINTER.

XII.   Dead winter month from Nov. 5 to Dec. 22.

THE
CALENDAR of FLORA.

I. REVIVING WINTER MONTH.
From the winter folstice to the vernal æquinox.

Dec. XII.
xxii. *Butter shrinks and separates from the sides of the tub.*
xxiii. Asp flower buds begin to open.
Jan. I. i. *Ice on lakes begins to crack.*
ii. *Wooden walls snap in the night.*
Cold frequently extreme at this time, the greatest observed was 55.7.
iv. **Horse dung spirts.*
viii. *Epiphany rains.*
xxvi. St. *Paul's rains.*
Feb. II.
xxii. *Very cold nights often between Feb.* 20 *and* 28, *called* STEEL NIGHTS.

---

* Note. This was explained to me by Mr. Solander, an ingenious and learned disciple of Linnæus, now in England, who says, that horse dung, in very severe frosts, throws out particles near a foot high, and that no other dung does the like.

S 3   II. THAW-

II. THAWING MONTH.

From the firſt melting of the ſnow to the floating of ice down the rivers.

Vere novo gelidus canis cum montibus humor
Liquitur, et zephyro putris ſe gleba reſoivit.

VIRG.

Mar. III.
  xix. *Eves drop towards the noontide ſun.*
    Sallow, *round leaved*, flower-buds, 449.
    15. Salix *caprea*, open.
  xx. *Snow melts againſt walls.*
    LARK *begins to ſing.*
  xxii. *Water flows by the walls.*
  xxv. *Roads very dirty and full of water.*
April IV.
  i. *Horſe dung melts the ice.*
    Moſs, *upright fir.* Lycopodium *ſelago*,
    106. ſheds its duſt.
  iii. STONES *are looſened from the ice.*
  vi. *Hills begin to appear, the ſnow being melted.*
    Serpents come out of their holes.
    SPIDER, *water, friſks about. The* FLY *creeps forth.*
    GAME, *black*, 53. *Tetrao tetrix.*
    LAPWING, 110. *Tringa vanellus, returns.*
  vii. BUTTERFLY, *nettle, Papilio urticæ, appears in abundance.*
Some people, ſays Pliny, think the appearance of the butterfly the ſureſt ſign of ſpring, on account of the delicacy of the animal.

DUCK,

April IV.
  vii. DUCK, *tame*, 145. *Anas bofchas, fits.*
  Wild DUCK *returns.*
  x. *An inundation of fnow water.*
  SWAN, 37. *Anas cygnus, and* DAKER-
  HEN, 58. 8. *Rallus crex, by their appearance proclaim the fpring.*
  RIVERS *are unbound, and ice floats down.*
N. B. *The river at Upfal, for* 70 *years, has never
been frozen beyond the* 19th *of April, according to
the obfervation of O. Celfius, fen.*
  PIKE, 112. *Efox lucius, fpawns. This
  fifh gives over fpawning when the frog
  begins.*
  xi. *Snow water foaks into the earth.
  Subterraneous places are inundated.*
  FROG *comes forth.*
  *Winter fhelters ought to be removed from
  garden plants, that they may not be too
  much drawn up.
  Hot-beds for melons fhould be fown,*

Solvitur acris hyems grata vice veris et Favonii.
HOR.

III. BUDDING MONTH.
From the return of the WHITE-WAGTAIL,
Motacilla alba, 75. 1. *to the coming of the fwallow ; or from the firft flower to the leafing of the
firft tree, during the whole time of the flowering of
the bulbous violet.*

A Favonio veris initium notant. CICERO.

April IV.
  xii. Hafel-nut tree, 439. Corylus *avellana.*
  S 4   COLTS-

April IV.

xii. COLTSFOOT, 173. Tuffilago *farfara.*

xiii. Saffron, 374. Crocus *fativus.*

VIOLET, *bulbous,* 1144. H. Leucoium
vernale, 26.

Snow drops, 1144. H. Galanthus *nivalis,* 26.

WAGTAIL, *white,* 75. 1. *Motacilla
alba, returns.*

KESTREL, 16. 16. *Falco tinunculus, returns.*

FROG, 247. *Rana temporaria, croaks.*

Saffron, 374. Crocus *fativus,* 17.

xv. Pilewort, 246. Ranunculus *ficaria.*

Star of Bethlehem, *yellow,* 372. Ornithogalum *luteum.*

Grafs, *whitlow,* 292. Draba *verna.*

Mezereon, 1587. H. Daphne *mezereon.*

TURKEY *hen,* 51. 3. *Meleagris gallo-
pavo, fits.*

Honeyfuckle, *double,* 1490. H. Lonicera
perfoliata.

xvi. Liverwort, *noble,* 580. H. Anemone *he-
patica,* 34.
The time for fowing barley at Upfal.

xvii. Lilly, *yellow water,* 368.1. Nymphæa
lutea, leaves emerge.

xix. Afp, or *trembling* poplar, 446.3. Populus *tremula,* 13.

Abele, 446.2. Populus *alba,* 13.
*Hot-beds to be fown from the budding of
the poplar to the leafing month.*

xxi. SMELT, 66.14. *Salmo eperlanus, fpawns,
at which time generally tempefts and
fnowy weather at* Upfal, *and intermitting fevers very common.*

April IV.

xxi. Hellebore, *black*, 271.1. Helleborus *viridis*.

Willow, *round leaved*, 449. 15. Salix *caprea*.

xxx. Crake *berries*, 444. Empetrum *nigrum*.

Poplar, *black*, 446. Populus *nigra*.

Bur *butter*, 179. Tuffilago *petafitis*, 25.

May V.

i. Mercury *dogs*, 138. 1. Mercurialis *perennis*.

Polyanthus, 1083. Primula veris *hortenfis*.

iii. ANEMONE, *wood*, 259.1. Anemone *nemorofa*, 21.

Saxifrage, *golden*, 158. 2. Chryfofplenium *alternifolium*.

Violet *with throat-wort leaves*, 365. 8. Viola *hirta*.

Affarabacca, 158.1. Afarum *Europæum*.

Violet, *fweet*, 364.8. Viola *odorata*, 24.

Pepperwort, 304. Lepidium *petræum*.

Fields are covered with verdure.

After the return of the WHEAT EAR*, 75.1. *Motacilla Oenanthe, there is feldom any fevere froft, and therefore the peafants in Upland have this proverb; When you fee the* WHITE WAGTAIL *you may turn your fheep into the* † *fields ; and when you fee the* WHEAT EAR, *you may fow your grain.*

---

* If this bird does not quit England, it certainly fhifts places. For i have obferved, that about harveft time they were not to be found where there were before great plenty of them.

† The fheep are houfed all winter in Sweden, as Mr. Solander informs me, who gave me the tranflation of the Swedifh proverb in the very words here printed.

Ofier,

May V.

   vii. „Ofier, 450.21. Salix *viminalis.*

       Bramble, 467.1. Rubus *fruticofus*, leafs.

       STARLING, 67.1. *Sturnus vulgaris,*
       returns.

   viii. Mofcatel, *tuberous*, 267. Adoxa *mofca-*
       tellina.

       Seeds of kitchen plants to be sown. Ten-
       der plants to be taken out of the green
       houfe.

       ELM TREE, 469. Ulmus *campeftris.*
       Snow melts even in the fhade.

Diffugere nives, redeunt jam gramina campis.
Arboribufque comæ.   HOR.

IV. LEAFING MONTH.

The compleat leafing of trees from the bird cherry to
the afh; from the coming of the fwallow to the
tulip.

Nunc herbæ rupta tellure cacumina tollunt ;
Nunc tumido gemmas cortice palmes agit. OVID.

May V.

   ix. SWALLOW *and* STORK *return.*

       CHERRY, BIRD, 463. Prunus *padus**. L.

       Filberd, 439. Corylus *avellana.* L.

   xi. Afp, 446.3. Populus *tremula, out of blow.*

   xii. CUCKOW, 23. *Cuculus canorus, fings.*

---

* The letter L. at the end of the lines fignifies that thofe plants
came into leaf on the days marked. All the plants befides thrcugh-
out this Calendar are fuppofed to have flowered on the days marked,
unlefs the contrary is expreffed.

I   Sorrel

May V.

xiii. Sorrel *wood*, *281. Oxalis *acetofella*.
BIRCH TREE, 443. Betula *alba*. L.
Barberry bufh, 465. Berberis *vulgaris*.L.
The beft time for fowing barley, and the feeds of of garden plants.
Ofier, 450.21. Salix *viminalis*. L.

xiv. Spindle tree, 468.Euonymus*Europæus*.L.
Bear's ear, 1083. H.Primula *auricula*, 12.
Goule, or Dutch myrtle, 443.Myrica *gale*.
Orange, *mock*, 1763. H. Philadelphus *coronarius*. L.
Elder, *water*, 460. Viburnum *opulus*. L.
Lilac, 1763. H. Syringa *vulgaris*. L.
Privet, 463. Liguftrum *vulgare*. L.
Buckthorn, *fea*, 445. Hippophae *rhamnoid*. L.
Alder tree, 442. Betula *alnus*. L.

xv. Daffodil, *wild Englifh*, 371.1. Narciffus *pfeudonarciffus*, 19.
Rofes *garden*.
Elm tree, 469. Ulmus *campeftris*. L.
NIGHTINGALE, 78. *Motacilla lufcinia, returns.*
Thorn, *white*, 453.3. Cratægus *oxyacantha*. L.
Apple tree, 451. Pyrus *malus*. L.
Primrofe, 284. Primula *veris*, 16.
Cherry tree, 463. Prunus *cerafus*. L.
Thorn *buck*, 466. Rhamnus *catharticus*. L.
Cinquefoil, *fmall rough*, 323. Potentilla *verna*, 16.

xvi. Sallow, *round leaved*, 449.15.Salix *caprea*. L.

Beam

May V.

xvi. Beam tree, *white*, 453. Cratægus *aria*.L.
Chefnut tree, *horfe*, 1683. Æfculus *hip-pocaftanum*. L.
Beech tree, 439. Fagus *fylvatica*. L.
Hornbeam, 451. Carpinus *betulus*. L.
Poplar, *black*, 446. Populus *nigra*. L.

xx. Afp, 446. Populus *tremula*. L.

xxi. Marygold, *marfh*, 272. Caltha *paluftris*.
Lime tree, 473. Tilia *Europæa*. L.
Alder, *berry bearing*, 465. Rhamnus *frangula*. L.
*Fly, dragon, Moufet, p.*67. *Libellula.*
Salmon, 63.2. *Salmo, falar.*
Oak tree, 440. Quercus, *robur*. L.
ASH TREE, 469. Fraxinus *excelfior*. L.

xxiv. *While the afh is leafing there is fcarcely any more froft : therefore green houfe plants ought to be brought into the open air.*
THE LEADEN NIGHTS *happen before the leafing of the afh ; from that time the fummer is fettled.*
There are very few flowers in this month ; for nature being intent on the young offspring of the bird kind, prepares abundance of flowers, againft the hatching feafon.

V. FLOWERING MONTH.

From the firft ear of rye to its blow.
From the tulip, 1146. *Tulipa Gefneriana, to the wall pepper*, 270. 5. *Sedum acre.*

It ver, et Venus, et Veneris prænuncius ante
Pinnatus graditur zephyrus veftigia propter.

LUCRET.

---

* CHERRY,

May V.

xxv. * Cherry, bird, 463. Prunus *padus.*
Currants, *black,* 456. Ribes *nigrum.*
Jack by the hedge,293.Eryſimum *alliaria.*
Cicely, *wild,* 207.Chærophyllum *ſylveſtre.*
Tulip, 1146. H. Tulipa *Geſneriana,* 13.
Milkwort, *287. Polygala *vulgaris.*
Lady's mantle, 158. Alchemilla *vulgaris.*
ROCHE, 122. *Cyprinus rutilus, ſpawns.*
Firſt ear of rye.

xxvi. Saxifrage, *white,* 364. 6. Saxifraga gra-
nulata.
Ivy, *ground,* 243. Glechoma *hederacea.*
Goldilocks, 248. Ranunculus *auricomus.*
Pear tree, 452. Pyrus *communis,* 14.

xxvii. Celandine, *greater,* 309. Chelidonium
majus.
Cloud berries, 260. Rubus *chamæmorum.*
Cat's foot, 181. Gnaphalium *dioicum.*
Crane's bill, 361. 18. Geranium *ſyl-
vaticum.*
Globe flower, 272. Trollius *Europæus.*

xxviii. Cuckow flower, 299. Cardamine *pratenſis.*
*While the cuckow flower blows, the ſalmon goes up
the rivers, and dragon fly comes forth.*
Thorn, *black,* 462. Prunus *ſpinoſa,* 10.
Cherry tree 463. Prunus *ceraſus,* 10.
Plumb tree, 462.2,3. Prunus *domeſtica.*
Peaſe, *wood,* 124.2. Orobus *tuberoſus.*
Plantain, *hoary,* 314.3. Plantago *media.*

---

* While the bird cherry flowers, happens what iscalled the grey
weather, between the old and new moon. I am indebted to Mr.So-
lander for the interpretation of this paſſage: it is in the original called the plenilunium cornicum, but ought to be read interlunium.

Butter-

May V.
xxx. Butterwort, *281. Pinguicola *vulgaris*.
Lilly in the valley, 264. Convallaria *Mai-alis*, 21.
Bugle, *mountain*, 245.2. Ajuga *pyramidalis*.
Rufh, *hare's tail*, 436. Eriphorum *vagi-natum*.
Grafs, *cotton*, 435. Eriophorum *polyfta-chyon*.
Honeyfuckle, *dwarf*, 261. Cornus *Suecica*.
Whorts, *red*, 457. Vaccinium *vitis idæa*.
CROWFOOT, CRANE'S BILL, 361.18. Ge-ranium *fylvaticum*, 120.
Catchfly, *red German*, 340.14. Lychnis *vifcaria*.
Germander, *wild*, 282. 11. Veronica *cha-mædrys*.
BREAM, 116.5. *Cyprinus brama, fpawns*.
The bream fports while the bird cherry fades, and the juniper begins to blow, and when this fades the dragon fly comes out.

Nunc frondent fylvæ, nunc formofiffimus annus.

June VI.
i. Fir, *fpruce*, 441. Pinus *abies*, drops its male flower.
ii. PEIONY, 694. H. Pæonia fl. *fimplici*, 10.
AVENS, PURPLE MOUNTAIN, 253. Geum *rivale*.
Tormentil *feptfoil*, 257.1. Tormentilla *erecta*.
APPLE TREE, 451. Pyrus *malus*.
Rye in ear.
iii. Juniper tree, 444. Juniperus *communis*.
Quicken tree, 452. Sorbus *aucuparia*.
Buck-

June VI.
  iii. Buckbean, 285. Menyanthes *trifoliat.* 18.
  iv. Grafs, *foxtail,* 396.1. Alopecurus *pratenfis.*
  v. Plantain, *ribwort,* 314.5. Plantago *lanceolata.*
  Crane's bill, *dufky,* 361. 21. Geranium *phæum.*
  vii. Orchis, *male handed,* 310. 19. Orchis *latifolia.*
  Goofeberry, bufh, 1484. H. Ribes *groffularia.*
  Paris, *herb,* 264. Paris *quadrifolia.*
  Trefoil, *bird's foot,* 334. 1. Lotus *corniculata.*
  Bilberry bufh, *great,* 457. Vaccinium *uliginofum.*
  Comfrey, 230. Symphytum *officinale.*
  Flax, *purging,* 362.6. Linum *catharticum.*
  Columbines, 273. Aquilegia *vulgaris.*
  Violet, *dame's,* 790. H. Hefperis *matronalis.*
  Flora unrobed. The pear, plumb, Scotch fir and fpruce out of blow.
The fummer is then in its higheft beauty, when Pomona, dreffed as it were in her fnow-white garment, celebrates her nuptials ; while the tulip, narciffus and peiony adorn the garden, the frefh fhoots of the fir illuminate the woods, and the juniper fheds its impregnating vapour.
  Chriftopher, *herb,* 661. Aétæa *fpicata.*
  Grafs, *melic,* 403.6. Melica *nutans.*
  Bramble, *ftone,* 261. Rubus *faxatilis.*
  Crowfoot, *bulbous,* 247.2. Ranunculus *bulbofus.*

                Hawk-

June VI.

 vii. Hawkweed, *dandelion*, 245. Leontodon
  hifpidum.

 viii. Barberry, 465. Berberis *vulgaris*.
  Lilac, 176. H. Syringa *vulgaris*.
  The meadows glow with crowfoots.

 ix. Crane's bill, *dovefoot*, 359.11. Geranium
  molle.

 x. Flower de luce, *yellow water*, 374. Iris
  pfeud-acorus.

 xi. Crane's bill, *crowfoot*, 360.17. Geranium
  pratenfe.
  Bell flower, *leffer round-leaved*, 277. 5.
  Campanula *rotundifolia*.
  Camomile, *Roman*, 189. Matricaria *cha-
  momilla*.
  Cinquefoil, *fhrubby*, 256. 4. Potentilla
  fruticofa.

 xii. Beam tree, *white*, 453. Cratægus *aria*.
  Vetch, *kidney*, 325. 1. Anthyllis *vulne-
  raria*.
  Henbane, 274. Hyofcyamus *niger*.

 xiii. Catchfly, *white*, 340.11. Silene *nutans*.
  Avens, 253.1,2. Geum *urbanum*.
  Adonis, *flower*, 251. Adonis *annua rubra*. •
*The fingle peiony fades before the double blows; as is
the cafe of rhubarb and rhapontic.*

 xiv. Lilly, *yellow water*, 368.1. Nymphæa *lutea*.
  Orchis, *female handed*, 381. 20. Orchis
  maculata.
  Robert, *herb*, 358.6. Geranium *rober-
  tianum*.
  Cinquefoil, *upright baftard*, 255. Poten-
  tilla *rupeftris*.
  Campion, *white*, 339. 8. Lychnis *dioica*.

             Elder,

June VI.

xiv. Elder, *water*, 460. Viburnum *opulus*.
xv. Rofe, *pimpernel*, 454.3. Rofa *fpinofiffima*.
Briar, *fweet*, 454.2. Rofa *eglanteria*.
Thorn, *buck*, 466. Rhamnus *catharticus*.
Orchis, *leffer butterfly*, 380.18. Orchis *bifolia*.
xvi. Grafs of Parnaffus, 355.1. Parnaffia *paluftris*.
Grafs, *marfh goofe*, 255.3. Galium *uliginofum*.
Lilly, *white water*, 368.3. Nymphæa *alba*.
Tanfey, *wild*, 256.5. Potentilla *anferina*.
Alder, *berry bearing*, 465.1. Rhamnus *frangula*.
PEIONY, DOUBLE, 693. H. Pæonia *plena*, 13.
Rampions, 274.4. Campanula *patula*.
Rhapontic, 170. H.Rheum *rhaphonticum*.
xvii. Pink, *meadow*, 338. Lychnis *flos cuculi*.
Valerian, *great wild*, 200.1. Valeriana *officinalis*.
Vetch, *chichling*, 320.5. Lathyrus *paluftris*.
Daify, *great, or ox eye*, 184. Chryfanthemum *leucanthem*.
xvii. Eyebright, *284. Euphrafia *officinalis*.
Spear wort, *leffer*, 250.7. Ranunculus *flammula*.
Groundfel, 178.1. Senecio *vulgaris*.
Thorn, *white*, 453. Cratagus *oxyacantha*.
xviii. Lilly, *bulbous*, 1110. H. Lilium *bulbiferum* to VII. 4.
Saxifrage, *burnet*, 213.1,2. Pimpinella *faxifraga*.

T   Tor-

June VI.

xviii. Tormentil *cinquefoil*, 255.2. Potentilla *argentea*.

Grafs, *quaking*, 412. Briza *media*.

Nightfhade, *deadly*, 265. Atropa *bella-donna*.

RYE, *winter*, 388.1. Secale *hybernum*.

Winter rye flowers generally from the firſt blow of wall pepper, 270.5. *Sedum acre, to the firſt blow of the roſe bay willow herb,* 310.1. *Epilobium an-guſtifolium, with the bulbous lilly, beginning often-times four days before the ſolſtice.*

VI. FRUITING MONTH.

During the whole blow of the wall pepper. From *the yellow to the red day lilly.*

———Revoluta ruebat,

.Matura jam luce dies.   VIRG.

xx. PEPPER, WALL, 207.5. Sedum *acre.*

Orchis, *frog*, 381.22. Satyrium *viride.*

Ciſtus, *dwarf*, 341. Ciſtus *helianthem.*

LILLY, YELLOW DAY, 1191. H. He-merocallis *flava.*

Cinquefoil, *marſh*, 256.2. Comarum *pa-luſtre.*

xxi. *After the ſolſtice trees ſcarcely grow, and therefore hedges ſhould then be clipped. The high-eſt degree of heat with us is hardly above* 54.8. *within the tropics the heat is not much above* 57.6, *nor below* 40.8. *the heat of a hatching hen between* 63 *and* 68.4. *a heat above* 72 *deſtroys the embryo.*

BRASS

June VI.

xxi. BRASS NIGHTS *from the thaw of the high-est mountains.*

xxii. Orchis, *fly,* 379.13. Ophrys *infectifera myodes.*

Blue bottle, 198. Centaurea *cyanus.*

Vetch, *great tufted wood,* 322.4. Vicia *fylvatica.*

Dropwort, 259. Spiræa *filipendula.*

Thistle, *gentle,* 193.2. Carduus *heleniodes.*

Loofe strife, *yellow,* 283.3. Lyfimachia *thyrfiflora.*

Self heal, 283. Prunella *vulgaris.*

Gentian, *vernal dwarf,* 275.4. Gentiana *campeftris.*

xxiii. Mayweed, *stinking,* 185.4. Anthemis *cotula.*

Yarrow, 183.1. Achillea *millefolium.*

WILLOW HERB, *rofe bay,* 310. Epilobium *anguftifolium.*

Moonwort, 128.1. Ofmunda *lunaria.*

Liquorice, *wild,* 326.1. Aftragalus *alpinus.*

Knapweed, *great,* 198.1. Centaurea *fcabiofa.*

Vetch, *tufted,* 322.3. Vicia *cracca.*

Nightshade, *woody,* 265.1,2. Solanum *dulcamara.*

Golden rod, 176.1. Solidago *virgaurea.*

ORANGE, MOCK, 1763. H. Philadelphus *coronarius,* 14.

Sweet-william, 991.2. H. Dianthus *barbatus.*

POPPY, *Turkey,* Papaver *orientale,* 13.

Flax, *perennial blue,* 362.3. Linum *perenne.*   T 2   Dewberry

June VI.

xxiii. Dewberry bufh, 467.3. Rubus *cæfius*.
xxv. Nettle, *hedge*, 237. Stachys *fylvatica*.
Spiked willow of Theophraftus, 1699.
H. Spiræa *falicifolia*.
Lilac out of blow.
xxvi. Willow herb, *hooded*, 244.1. Scutellaria
galericulata.
Willow herb, *great fmooth leaved*, 311.4.
Epilobium *montanum*.
Twayblade, 385.1. Ophrys *ovata*.
Strawberries ripening.
xxvii. Hawkweed, *Hungarian*, 167.17. Hypo-
chæris *maculata*.
Medic, *yellow*, 333.1. Medicago *falcata*.
Parfley, *great baftard*, 219.2. Tordylium
latifolium.
xxviii. Toad flax, *yellow*, *281.1. Antirrhinum
linaria.
Grafs, *fea dog*, 390.1. Elymus *arenaria*.
Bryony, *white*, 261.1,2. Bryonia *alba*.
Campion, *wild purple*, 341.17. Silene
armeria.
xxix. Marygold, *corn*, 182.1. Chryfanthemum
fegetum.
Heath, *Dutch or befom*, 471.4. Erica
tetralix.
Bilberry bufh, 457.2. Vaccinium *myrtill*.
Berries ripe.
Peafe, *everlafting*, 319.1. Lathyrus *lati-
folius*.
Throatwort, *little*, 277.3. Campanula
glomerata.
Feverfew, 187.1. Matricaria *parthenium*.
PEACOCK *moults*.

Ox-eye,

June VI.
  xxix. Ox-eye, 183.1. Anthemis *tinctoria*.
    Sneezewort, 183. Achillea *ptarmica*.
    Rupturewort, 160.1. Herniaria *glabra*.
    Hawkweed, *fuccory-leaved*, 166.12. Crepis
      biennis.
    PINK, MAIDEN, 335.1. Dianthus *deltoides*.
    SCABIOUS, FIELD, 191.1. Scabiofa *arvenfis*.
    St. John's wort, *large flowered*, 1017.1.
      H. Hypericum *afcyron*.
    Elder tree, 461.1. Sambucus *nigra*.
    Woad, 367.1. Ifatis *tinctoria*, out of blow.
July VII.
  i. Willow herb, *purple fpiked*, 367.1. Ly-
      thrum *falicaria*.
    Parfnep, *cow*, 205.1,2. Heracleum *fphon-
      dylium*.
    Bindweed, *fmall*, 275.1. Convolvulus *ar-
      venfis*.
    Knapweed, 198.2. Centaurea *nigra*.
    Mullein, *white flowered*, 287.2. Verbafcum
      lychnit. alba.
    Rampions, 277.4. Campanula *ranunculus*.
  ii. Throatwort, *giant*, 276. Campanula *lati-
      folia*.
    Afphodel, *Lancafhire*, 375.1. Anthericum
      offifragum.
    Mullein, *black*, 288.4. Verbafcum *nigrum*.
    Rue, *meadow*, 203.1. Thalictrum *flavum*.
    Hellebore, *baftard*, 383.1. Serapias *hel-
      lebor. paluftr*.
    The hotteft days.
    Bindweed, *great*, 275. Convolvulus *fepium*.
    Willow herb, *yellow*, 282.1. Lyfimachia
      vulgaris.

               T 3   Moneywort,

July VII.
  iv. Moneywort, 283.1. Lyfimachia *nummu-laria*.
  FOXGLOVE, PURPLE, 283.1. Digitalis *rubra*.
  Meadow fweet, 259.1. Spiræa *ulmaria*.
  Cockle, 338. 5. Agroftema *githago*.
  Speedwell, *fpiked male*, 279.2. Veronica *fpicata*.
  Grafs, *foft tufted meadow*, 404.14. Hol-cus *lanatus*.
  Primrofe, *evening or tree*, 862. Oeno-thera *biennis*.
  vi. Yarrow, 183.1. Achillea *millefolium*.
  BEDSTRAW, YELLOW LADY'S, 224.1. Ga-lium *verum*.
  Agrimony, 202.1. Agrimonia *eupatoria*.
  Throatwort, *great*, 276. Campanula *tra-chelium*, 25.
  St. John's wort, 342.1. Hypericum *per-foratum*.
  St. John's wort, *tutfan*, 343.4,5. Hy-pericum *hirfutum*.
  Spearwort, *great*, 250.8. Ranunculus *lin-gua*.
  Carrot, 218. Daucus *carota*.
  Stone crop, *yellow* 269.1. Sedum *rupeftre*.
  Gladdon, *ftinking*, 375.3. Iris *fætidiffima*.
  Knapweed, 198.2. Centaurea *jacea*.
  Hops, 137.1. Humulus *lupulus*.
  Reft harrow, 332.1. Ononis *fpinofa*.
  Parfley, *Scotch fea*, 214. Ligufticum *Sco-ticum*.
  vii. BRIAR, or DOG ROSE, 454.1. Rofa *canina*.
  Rofe, *white*, 1373.23. H. Rofa *alba*.
  Rofe, *French*, Rofa *Gallica*.

July VII.

vii. *The late rofes now begin to blow.*
Hay harveft begins with the lime tree, clover
being out of blow, and yellow rattle or
coxcomb, *284. *fhedding its feeds.* ·
Burnet, 203.2. Sanguiforba *officinalis.*
Poppy, *wild,* 308.1. Papaver *fomniferum.*
Sneezewort, 183.1. Achillea *ptarmica.*
Lilly, *yellow day,* out *of blow.*
Chervil, *wild,* 207.1. Chærophyllum *fyl-*
veftre, out *of blow.*
Barley every where in ear.
Peafe ripe.
Cherries ripe.
Beginning of hay harveft.
Motherwort, 239.1. Leonurus *cardiaca.*

viii. Pink, *Deptford,* 337.1. Dianthus *armerius.*
Orange, *mock,* out *of blow.*
Bilberries ripe.

ix. Thiftle, *mufk,* 193.1. Carduus *nutans.*
Burdock, 196. Arctium *lappa.*
Horehound, *bafe,* 339.1. Stachys *Ger-*
manica.
Hemp, 138. Cannabis *fativa.*
351.13. Frankenia *pulverulenta.*
Red currants ripe.

x. Mugwort, 190.1. Artemifia *vulgaris.*
Thiftle, *ivy leaved fow,* 162.5. Prenanthes
muralis.
Marjoram, *wild,* 236.1. Origanum *vul-*
gare.
Horehound, *ftinking,* 244.1. Ballota *nigra.*
Bafil, *great wild,* 239. Clinopodium *vul-*
gare.
Pine, *ground,* 244. Teucrium *chamæpilys.*

T 4   Betony,

July VII.

 x. Betony, *water*, *283.1. Scrophularia a-
  quatica.
  Nightſhade, *enchanters*, 289. Circæa ca-
  nadenſis.
  Clover, 328.4. Trifolium *pratenſe*, *out of*
  blow.
 xi. Thiſtle, *tree ſow*, 163.7. Sonchus *arvenſis*.
  LIME TREE, 473.1,2,3. Tilia *Europea*,
  out of blow.
  Marjoram, *wild*, 236. Origanum *vulgare*.

Feſtinat decurrere velox floſculus æſtatis.

VII. RIPENING MONTH.

From the white ſtonecrop, 271.7. *Sedum album*, *or*
the red day lilly, *to the devil's bit*, 191.3. *Sca-*
bioſa ſucciſa.

---

 xii. SUCCORY, WILD, 172. Cichorium *intybus*.
  Willow herb, *great hairy*, 311.2. Epilobium *hirſutum*.
  Langue de bœuf. 166.13. Picris *echi-*
  oides.
  Woodbind, 456. Lonicera *periclymenum*.
  Mallow, *vervain*, 252. Malva *alcæa*.
  St. John's wort, *large flowered*, 1017. H.
  Hypericum *aſcyron*, *out of blow*.
 xiii. Fleabane, *ſmall*, 174.2. Inula pulicaria.
  Pepperwort, 304.1. Lepidium *latifolium*.
 xiv. STONECROP, WHITE,271.7. Sedum *album*,
  out of blow.
 xv. Agrimony, *hemp*, 179. Eupatorium *can-*
  nabinum.

           Tanſey,

July VII.

xv. Tanfey, 188. Tanacetum *vulgare*.

Golden rod, *white*, 175.1 Erigeron *canadenfe*.

Saw-wort, 196.1. Secratula *tinct. præalt.*

Mint, *red*, 232.5. Mentha *gentilis.*

Mint, *long leaved horfe*, 234.5. Mentha *fpicata.*

Pepper, *wall*, 270.5. Sedum *acre, out of blow.*

CUCKOW *is filent.*

xvi. Hawkweed, *bufhy*, 168.3. Hieracium *umbell.*

LILLY, RED DAY, 1191.2. H. Hemerocallis *fulva.*

All the marvels of Peru, 398. H. Mirabiles.

The height of hay harveft.

xvii. Thiftle, *fpear*, 194.8. Carduus *lanceolatus.*

ELDER, DWARF, 461.4. Sambucus *ebulus.*

xviii. Touch me not, 316.1. Impatiens *noli tangere.*

Saffron, *meadow*, 373.1. Colchicum *autumnale. Leaves fall.*

Teafel, *wild and manured*, 192.3. Dipfacus *fullonum.*

x. LILLY, WHITE, 1109. H. Lilium *candidum.*

Teafel, *fmall wild*, 192.3. Dipfacus *pilofus.*

xxi. Thiftle, *marfh tree fow*, 163.8. Sonchus *paluftris.*

xxii. Soapwort, 339.6,7. Saponaria *officinalis.*

Grafs, *Effex cocks foot*, 393.4. Dactylis *cynofuroides.*

Knapweed, great, 198.1. Centaurea *fcabiofa.*   Spikenard,

July VII.
  xxiii. Spikenard, *plowman's*, 179.1. Conyza
    fquarrofa.
  xxiv. Elecampane, 176.1. Inula *helenium.*
  xxv. Fleabane, *middle*, 174.1. Inula *dyfenter.*
  xxvi. Violet, *Calathian*, 274.1. Gentiana *pneu-
    monanthe.*
    Baum, 570. H. Meliffa *officinalis.*
  xxvii. Thiftle, *great foft or gentle*, 193.3. Ser-
    ratula *alpin. lat.*
Aug. VIII.
  i. Chickweed, *berry bearing*, 267.1. Cucu-
    balus *baccifer.*
    Orpine, 269.1. Sedum *telephium.*

Mirabar celerem fugitiva æftate rapinam,
Et dum nafcuntur confenuiffe rofas.

VIII. REAPING MONTH.

---

*From the devil's bit to the blow of the meadow
  faffron.*

---

  iv. DEVIL'S BIT, 191.3. Scabiofa *fuccifa.*
    Rye harveft.
    *Winter rye has for many years ripened with
    the firft blow of the devil's bit, in the
    garden at Upfal.*
    BIRDS OF PASSAGE, *after having ce-
    lebrated their nuptials in the vernal
    months, and feafted on the fummer fruits,
    now prepare for departing.*
  vii. Rofe, *French*, Rofa Gallica, *out of blow.*
  xiv. Wormwood, 188.1. Artemifia *campeftris.*
  xvi. *Barley harveft.*
  xxvi. Lilly, *red, out of blow.*

*IX. SOWING MONTH.

From the firſt blow of the meadow ſaffron to the departure of the ſwallow.

Pomifer autumnus fruges effudit et mox
Bruma, recurrit iners.

Aug. VIII.
xxviii. SAFFRON, MEADOW, 373.1. Colchicum
autumn.
*This plant ought to admoniſh gardeners to put Indian
plants under ſhelter, as the iron nights are near.
The* IRON NIGHTS, *as they are called with us, generally happen between Auguſt* 17 *and* 29, *and deſtroy tender plants.
After the blow of the meadow ſaffron, we have ſtorms
that ſhake off ripe ſeeds.*

Fern, female, 124.1. Pteris *aquilina, grows
yellow in the woods after the firſt cold
nights.*
xxxi. *A gentle froſt that ſcarcely did any damage.*
Sept. IX.
i. Adonis flower, 251.1. Adonis *annua ſer.*
Mulberry tree, 1429. H. Morus *nigra,
grows pale.*
iv. Fig tree, 1431. H. Ficus *carica, grows pale.*
vi. Wormwood, *ſea,* 188.2. Artemiſia *maritima.*
Travellers joy, 258.1. Clematis *vitalba.*
xi. *The froſt has deſtroyed ſouthern plants.*
xii. *The froſt milder.*
xiv. *Seeds to be gathered.*

---

* By ſowing, in this place, is meant not man's but nature's.

I   Sampire

Sept. IX.
xvii. Sampire, *golden flowered*, 174.1. Inula
crithmoid.
*SWALLOW *goes under water.**
WAGTAIL, *white, departs.*

Nos quoque floruimus, fed fios fuit ille caducus.

X. SHEDDING MONTH.

From the first fall of the leaves of trees to the laft.

xxii. Orach, *fea*, 152.8, Artiplex *maritima.*
Leaves of trees are changed, of the oak, maple, robi-
nia caragana, elm, lime, to a yellow ; of the fpin-
tree to a brown ; of the quicken tree and fumach,
to a red colour.
Leaves of the oak dry and yellow.
xxiv. || *Leaves of the maple begin to fall in the night.*
xxv. *Hoar frost.*
xxvi. *Leaves of the robinia caragana fall.*
Sycamore *ftripped of its leaves.*
Oct. X.
iv. Cherry, *bird, ftripped of its leaves.*
v. *A ftorm.*

* Adamfon in the account of his voyage to S. negal, p. 121. fays,
that October 1749, European fwal'ows lodged on the veffel in which
he went from Goree to Senegal, and that they are never feen there but
at this time of the year, along with quails, wagtails, kites, and fome
other birds of paffage, and do not build nefts there. This teftimony
feems to take away all doubts about this long contefted point.

|| Geminus, either from himfelf or Democritus, which is much the
fame, as Rome and Abdera were nearly in the fame latitude, fays
that the leaves of trees began to drop the fourth of Scorpio, which
anfwers to October 28.

Green

Oct. X.

vi. *Green leaves of the afh fall. When they fall fouthern plants ought to be put under fhelter.*

vii. Elm *is ftripped.*
   A ftorm.
   Froft.

xii. *The leaves of the lime tree fall.*
   Green houfes ought to be fhut.

xiii. *The afp tree ftill in leaf.*

xiv. *Ice.*

xvii. *Hafel nut tree ftripped.*

xxv. Abele, 446.2. Populus *albc, ftripped.*

xxvi. Saffron, *meadow, juft out of blow.*
   Poplar, *black, ftripped.*

xxvii. *Summer ended,*

xxviii. *Sallows only in leaf.*

Vernantefque comas triftis ademit hyems.

PETRON.

XI. FREEZING MONTH.

From the laft fhedding of leaves to the laft green plant.

Iva *annua.*

Nov. XI.

ii. *Alternate fnow and froft.*

v. Milleria *quinqueflora.*
   Thaw with rain.
   The earth ccvered with fnow.
   Rivers are frozen.
   Snow with a thaw.
   Firm fnow.
   Thaws again.

Ditches

Ditches filled with water.
Winter thoroughly settled.

Heu quam cuncta abeunt celeri mortalia curfu.

XII. DECLINING WINTER MONTH.

From the laft green plant to the winter folftice.

Nov. XI.

   v. *Moffes and lichens only flourifh.*
     Thermometer, gr. 34.2.
  vi. *Thaws.*
  xx. *Cold changeable weather.*

Quælibet orta cadunt, et finem cæpta videbunt.

THE

CALENDAR of FLORA.

By BENJÁMIN STILLINGFLEET.

Made at STRATTON in N O R F O L K,
Anno 1755. Latitude 52° 45′.

MARKS EXPLAINED.

b fignifies buds fwelled.

B - - - - buds beginning to open.

f - -- - - - flowers beginning to open

F - - - - - flowers full blown.

l - - - - - leaves beginning to open.

L - - - - leaves quite out.

r. p. - - - fruit nearly ripe.

R. P. - - fruit quite ripe.

E - - - - emerging out of the ground.

D - - - - flowers decayed.

THE
CALENDAR of FLORA.

I. MONTH.

Reviving nature feems again to breath,
As loofen'd from the cold embrace of death.

Jan. 5. Rofemary, 515. H. Rofmarinus *officinal.* f.
  11. Honeyfuckle, 458. Lonicera *pericly-
  menum*, l.
  23. Archangel, *red*, 240.2. Lamium *purpu-
  reum*, F.
  Hafel nut tree, 439. Corylus *avellana*, f.
  Honeyfuckle, 458. Lonicera *pericly-
  menum*, L.
  Lauruftinus. 1690. H. Viburnum *tinus*, F.
  Holly, 466. Ilex *aquifolium*, f.
  26. Snow drops, 1144. H. Galanthus *nivalis*,
  F.
  Chickweed, 347.6. Alfine *media*, F.
  Spurry, 351.7. Spergula *arvenfis*, F.
  Daify, 184. Bellis *perennis*, F.

II. MONTH.

Love's pleafing ferment gently now begins
To warm the flowing blood.

U   WOOD

Feb. 4. WOOD LARK, 69.2. *Alauda arborea,*
sings.
Elder tree, 461. Sambucus *nigra,* f.

12. ROOKS, 39.3. *Corvus frugilegus, begin to*
pair.
GEESE, 136.1. *Anas, anfer, begin to lay.*
* WAGTAIL WHITE, 75.1. *Motacilla*
alba, appears.

16. THRUSH, 64.2. *Turdus muficus, sings.*
† CHAFFINCH, 88. *Fringilla cælebs.*
sings.

20. *Thermometer,* 11. *Higheft this month.*
Thermometer, -2. *Loweft this month.*

22. PARTRIDGES, 57. *Tetrao perdix, begin*
to pair.
Hafel tree, 439. Corylus *avellana,* F.

25. Goofeberry bufh, 1484. H. ⎫
Ribes *groffularia,* 1. ⎬ both young
Currant, *red,* 456.1. Ribes ⎰ plants.
rubrum, 1. ⎭

Thermometer from the 19*th to the* 25*th, be-*
tween 0 *and* -1 *with fnow.*
Wind during the latter half of the month be-
tween E. and N.

---

* The wagtail is faid by Willughby to remain with us all the year
in the fevereft weather. It feems to me to fhift its quarters at leaft, if
it does not go out of England. However, it is certainly a bird of
paffage in fome countries, if we can believe Aldrovandus, the author
of the Swedifh Calendar, and the author of the treatife De Migrationibus Avium. Linnæus obferves, S. N. Art. Motacilla, that moft
birds which live upon infeɛts, and not grains, migrate.

† Linnæus fays, that the female chaffinch goes to Italy alone, thro'
Holland; and that the male in the fpring, changing its note, foretells
the fummer: and Gefner, ornithol. p. 388. fays that the female
chaffinch difappears in Switzerland in the winter, but not the male.

III.

III. MONTH.

Winter ftill ling'ring on the verge of fpring,
Retires reluctant, and from time to time
Looks back, while at his keen and chilling breath
Fair Flora fickens.

March
2. ROOKS, 39.3. *Corvus frugilegus*, begin to
build.
Thermometer, 10.
4. THRUSH, 64.2. *Turdus muficus*, *fings*.
Thermometer, 11.
5. DOVE, RING, 62.9. *Columba palumbus*,
cooes.
7. *Thermometer*, 0. *Loweft this month*.
11. Sallow,   Salix,   F.
Lauruftinus, 1690. H. Viburnum *tinus*, l.
*BEES, *Apis mellifera*, out of the hive.
Laurel, 1549. H. Prunus *laurocerafus*, l.
Bay, 1688. H. Laurus *nobilis*, l.
20. *Vernal equinox*.
21. Grafs, *fcurvy*, 302.1. Cochlearia *officinalis*,
F.
Afp, 446.3. Populus *tremula*, F.
26. Speedwell, *germander*, 279.4. Veronica
agreftis, F.
Alder, 442. Alnus *betula*, F.
28. Violet, *fweet*, 364.2. Viola *odorata*, F.
Parfnep, *cow*, 205. Heracleum *fphondy-*
lium, E.
Pilewort, 296. Ranunculus *ficaria*, F.

---

* Pliny, nat. hift. lib. 11. §. 5. fays, that bees do not come out of
their hives before May 11. and feems to blame Ariftotle for faying
that they come out in the beginning of fpring, i. e. March 12.

March

28. *Thermometer*, 25.50. *Higheſt this month.*
29. Cherry tree, 463. Prunus *ceraſus*, B.
    Currant buſh, 456.1.Ribes *rubrum*, B.
    Primroſe, 284.1. Primula *veris*, F.
    Yew tree, 445. Taxus *baccata*, F.
    Elder, *water*, 460. Viburnum *opulus*, B.
    Thorn, haw, 453.3. Cratægus *oxyacantha*,
    B.
    Larch tree, 1405. H. Pinus *larix*, B.
    Hornbeam, 451. Carpinus *oſtrya*, B.
    Tanſy, 188. Tanacetum *vulgare*, E.

IV. MONTH.

- - - - - - - - Airs, vernal airs,
Breathing the ſmell of grove and field, attune
The trembling leaves.   MILTON.

April 1. Cheſnut, *horſe*, 1683. Æſculus *hippocaſ-
tanum*, B.
    BIRCH, 443. Betula *alba*, L.
    Willow, *weeping*,   Salix *Babylo-
    nica*, L.
    ELM TREE, 468. Ulmus *campeſtris*, F.
    Quicken tree, 452.2. Sorbus *aucuparia*, f.
    Apricot, 1533. H. Prunus *Armeniaca*, F.
    Narciſſus, *pale*, 371.2. Narciſſus *pſeudo-
    nar*.
3. Holly, 466.1. Ilex *aquifolium*, f.
    Bramble, 467.1. Rubus *fruticoſus*, L.
    Raſberry buſh, 467.4. Rubus *idæus*, L.
    Currants, *red*, 456. Ribes *rubrum*, F.
    Dandelion, 179.1. Leontodon *taraxicum*,
    E.

    Cleavers,

April 3. Cleavers, 225. Galium *aparine,* E.
4. Lauruſtinus, 1690. H. Viburnum *tinus,* F.
APPLE TREE, 451.1,2. Pyrus *malus,* B.
Orpine, 269.1. Sedum *telephium,* B.
Briar, 454.1. Roſa *canina,* L.
6. Gooſeberry, 1489. H. Ribes *groſſularia,* f.
Maple, 470.2. Acer *campeſtre,* B.
Peach, 1515. H. Amygdalus *Perſica,* L.
et F.
Apricot, 1533. H. Malus *Armeniaca,* L.
Plumb tree, 462. Prunus *præcox,* L.
Pear tree, 452. Pyrus *communis,* B.
*SWALLOW, 71.2. Hirundo *urbica,*
returns.
7. Filberd, 439. Corylus *avellana,* L.
Sallow, Salix, L.
Alder, 442.1. Betula *alnus,* l.
Lilac, 1763. Syringa *vulgaris,* l.
Oak, 440.1. Quercus, *robur,* f.
Willow, *weeping,* Salix *Babylonica,* b.
8. Juniper, 444. Juniperus *communis,* b.
9. Lilac, 1763. Syringa *vulgaris,* b.
Sycamore, 470. Acer *pſeudoplatanus,* L.
Wormwood, 188.1. Artemiſia *abſinthium,*
E.
† NIGHTINGALE, 78. *Motacilla lu-*
ſcinia, ſings.

U 3   Auricula,

---

* According to Ptolemy, Swallows return to Ægypt about the latter end of January.

† From morn 'till eve, 'tis muſic all around ;
Nor doſt thou, Philomel, diſdain to join,
Even in the mid-day glare, and aid the quire.
But thy ſweet ſong calls for an hour apart,
When ſolemn Night beneath his canopy,
Enrich'd with ſtars, by Silence and by Sleep

Attended,

April

9. Auricula, 1082. H. Primula *auricula*, b,
10. Bay, 1688. H, Laurus *nobilis*, L.
Hornbeam, 451. Carpinus *betulus*, b.
Willow, *white*, 447.1. Salix *alba*, b.
BEES *about thè male fallows.*
Feverfew, 187.1. Matricaria *Parthenium*, E.
Dandelion, 170.1. Leontodon *taraxicum*, E,
Hound's tongue, 226.1. Cynogloffum *officinale*, E.
Elm, 468. Ulmus *campeftris*, l.
ANEMONE, *wood*, 259. Anemone *nemorofa*, F.
Jack in the hedge, 291, Eryfimum *alliaria*, E,
Quince tree, 1452. H. Pyrus *cydonia*, L,
11. Elder, *water*, 460. Viburnum *opulus*, L.
Alder, *berry bearing*, 465. Rhamnus *frangula*, L.
12. Acacia, 1719. H. Robinia *acacia*, l.
Mulberry tree, 1429, H. Morus *nigra*, l,
Lime tree, 473.1,2,3. Tilia *Europæa*, l.
Mercury, *dogs*, 138.1 Mercurialis *perennis*, F.
*Elm, *wych*, 469.4. L.
Ragweed, 177. Senecio *jacobæa*, E.

Attended, fits and nods, in awful ftate ;
Or when the Moon in her refulgent car,
Triumphant rides amidft the filver clouds,
Tinging them as fhe paffes, and with rays
Of mildeft luftre gilds the fcene below ;
While zephyrs bland breath thro' the thickening fhade,
With breath fo gentle, and fo foft, that e'en
The poplar's trembling leaf forgets to move,
And mimic with its found the vernal fhower ;
Then let me fit, and liften to thy ftrains, &c.

Linnæus does not feem to know this fpecies of elm,

April

13. Laburnum, 1721. Cytifus *laburnum*, f.
Strawberry, 254. Fragaria *vefca*, F.
Quicken tree, 452.2. Sorbus *aucuparia*, L.
Sycomore, 470. Acer *pfeudoplat*, L.
Laurel, 1549. H. Prunus *laurocerafus*, L.
Goofeberry bufh, 1484. H. Ribes *grof-fularia*, F.
Currant bufh, 456.1. Ribes *rubrum*, F.
Mallow, 251.1. Malva *fylveftris*, E.
Hornbeam, 451. Carpinus *betulus*, L.

14. Flixweed, 298.3. Sifymbrium *fophia*, E.
Apple tree, 451. Pyrus *malus*, L.
Hops, 137.1. Humulus *lupinus*, E.
Plane tree, 1706. H. Platanus *orientalis*, b.
Walnut tree, 438. Juglans *regia*, f.
BITTERN, 100.11. Ardea *ftellaris*, *makes a noife*.

15. Vine, 1613. Vitis *vinifera*, B.
Turneps, 204.1. Braffica *rapa*, F.

16. Abele, 446.2. Populus *alba*, B.
Chefnut, 138.2. H. Fagus *caftanea*, B.
Ivy, *ground*, 243. Glechoma *hederacea*, F.
Fig tree, 1431. Ficus *carica*, b.
Apricots and peaches out of blow.
RED START, 78.5. Motacilla *Phæni-curus*, *returns*.
Tulip tree, 1690. H. Liriodendron *tuli-pifera*, B.
Plumb tree, 462. Prunus *domeftica*, F.
Sorrel, *wood*, *281.1,2. Oxalis *acetofella*, F.
Marygold, *marfh*, 272. Caltha *paluftris*, F.
Laurel, *fpurge*, 465. Daphne *laureola*, F.

17. Jack in the hedge, 291.2. Eryfimum *alliaria*, F.

U 4   Willow,

April

17. Willow, *white*, 447.1. Salix *alba*, L. et F.
Cedar, 1404. H. Pinus *cedrus*, l.
Elder, *water*, 460.1. Viburnum *opulus*, f.
Abele, 446.2. Populus *alba*, L.
*CUCKOW, 23. Cuculus *canorus*, *fings*.
18. Oak, 440.1. Quercus, *robur*, l. F.
Thorn, *black*, 462.1. Prunus *spinosus*, B.
Pear tree, 452. Pyrus *communis*, f.
Mulberry tree, 1429. H. Morus *nigra*. B.
Violet, *dog*, 364.3. Viola *canina*, F.
Lime tree, 413.1,2,3. Tilia *Europæa*, L.
Nightshade, 265. Atropa *belladonna*, E.
Cherry tree, 463.1. Prunus *cerasus*, F.
Ash tree, 469. Fraxinus *excelsior*, f.
Maple, 470. Acer *campestre*, L,
Broom, 474. Spartium *scoparium*, b.
Chesnut, 138.2. Fagus *castanea*, L.
Fir, *Scotch*, 442. Pinus *sylvestris*, b.
Cuckow flower, 299. Cardamine *pratensis*,
20. *Thermometer*, 42. *the highest this month*.
21. Walnut-tree, 438. Juglans *regia*, L.
Plane tree, 1706. H. Platanus *orientalis*, L.
Fir, *Weymouth*, 8. dend. Pinus *tæda*, B.
Acacia, 1719. H. Robinia *pseudo-acacia*,
L.
Fig tree, 1431. H. Ficus *carica*, L.
Wall flower, 291. Cheiranthus *cheiri*, F.
Poplar, *black*, 446.1. Populus nigra, L.
Beech tree, 439.1. Fagus *sylvatica*, L.
22. Fir, *balm of Gilead*,   Pinus *balsamea*,
l. et f.

* Aristophanes says, that when the cuckow sung the Phœnicians eaped wheat and barley. Vid. Aves.

Young

April

22. *Young Apricots.*
Fir, *Scotch*, 442. Pinus *fylveſtris*, f.
Asн, 469. Fraxinus *excelſior*, F. et L.
Broom, 474. Spartium *fcoparium*, L.
Poplar, *Carolina*.   L.
Meadow fweet, 259. Spiræa *ulmcria*, E.
Fig tree, 1431. H. Ficus *carica, fruit formed.*
Tormentil, 257.1. Tormentilla *erecta*, E.
Phyllerea, 1585. H. Phyllerea *latifolia*, F.
Thorn, *evergreen*, 1459. H. Meſpilus *pyracantha*, F.
Rofemary, 515. H. Rofmarinus *officinalis*, F.
Campion, *white*, 339.8. Lychnis *dioica*, F.
Buckbean, 285.1. Menyanthes *trifol.* F.
Furze, *needle*, 476.1. Genifta *Anglica*, F.
Stitchwort, 346.1. Stellaria *holoſtea*, F.

23. Crab tree, 451.2. Pyrus *malus fylv.* F.
Apple tree, 451.1. Pyrus *malus*, f.
Robert, *herb*, 358. Geranium *Robertian.* F.
Fieldfares, 64.3. *Turdus pilaris, ſtill here.*

24. Broom, 474. Spartium *fcoparium*, F.
Mercury, 156.15. Chenopodium *bonus henr.* F.
Yew tree, 445. Taxus *baccifera*, L.
Holly, 466.1. Ilex *aquifolium*, B.
Furze, 475. Ulex *Europæus*, l.
Agrimony, 202. Agrimonia *eupctor.* E.

25. Sycomore, 470. Acer *pfeudoplat.* F.
Hornbeam, 451. Carpinus *betulus*, F.
Afp, 446. Populus *tremula*, l.
Spurge, *fun*, 313.8. Euphorbia *peplus*, F.
Elder tree, 461.1. Sambucus *nigra*, f.
Nettle, 139. Urtica *dicica*, F.

April

25. Bindweed, *small*, 275.2. Convolvulus *arvenf.* E.

Fir, *balm of Gilead*, Pinus *balfamea*, L.

Cicely, *wild*, 207.1. Chærophyllum *fylveftre*, F.

Young currants and goofeberries.

26. Plantain *ribwort*, 314.5. Plantago *lanceol.* F.

Germander, *wild*, 281.11. Veronica *chamæd.* F.

Cuckow pint, 266. Arum *maculatum*, *fpatha out.*

Holly, 466. Ilex *aquifolium*, F.

Harebells, 373.3. Hyacinthus *nonfcript.* F.

27. LILAC, 1763. H. Syringa *vulgaris*, F.

Crane's bill, *field*, 357.2. Geranium *cicutar.* F.

St. John's wort, 342.1. Hypericum *perforat.* E.

Betony *water*, 283.1. Scrophularia *aquat.* E.

Bryony, *white*, 261. Bryonia *alba*, E.

Birch tree, 443.1. Betula *alba*, F.

28. Jeffamine, 1599.1. H. Jafminum *officinale*, l.

Thorn, *white*, 453.3. Cratægus *oxyacantha*, f.

*BLACK CAP, 79.12. *Motacilla atracapilla, fings.*

* The black cap is a very fine finging bird, and is by fome in Norfolk called the mock nightingale. Whether it be a bird of paffage i cannot fay.

WHITE

April

28. * WHITE THROAT, 77. Motacilla
    fylvia,
    Juniper, 444.1. Juniperus *communis,* f.
    Rafberry bufh, 467.4. Rubus *idæus,* f.
    Quince tree, 1452. H. Malus *Cydon.* f.
    Crowfoot, *fweet wood,* 248.1. Ranunculus
    auric. F.
29. Bugle, 245. Ajuga, *reptans,* F.
    Bay, 1688. H. Laurus *nobilis,* f.
    Peas and beans, f.
    Snow.
    Chervil, *wild,* 207.1. Chærophyllum *te-
    mulent,* f.
    Parfnep, *cow,* 205.1. Heracleum *fphon-
    dyl.* f.
    Pine, *manured,* 1398.1. H. Pinus *pinea,* f.
30. *Snow.*
    † *Thermom.* 5, *The lowest this month.*

---

* I have fome doubt whether this bird be the Sylvia of Linnæus,
though the defcription feems to anfwer to Ray's, and to one of my
own, which I find among my papers.

† Vernal heat, according to Dr. Hales, at a medium, is 18.25.

V. MONTH.

All that is fweet to fmell, all that can charm
Or eye or ear, burfts forth on every fide,
And crouds upon the fenfes.

May 1. Crofswort, 223.1. Valantia *cruciata,* F.
     Avens, 253.1. Geum *urbanum,* F.
     Mugwort, 191.1. Artemifia *campeftris,* E.
     Bay, 1688. H. Laurus *nobilis,* L.
                                          Lilly

May 3. Lilly of the valley, 264. Convallaria *Maialis*, f.

Violet *water*, 285. Hottonia *palustris*, F.

4. Lettuce *lambs*, 201. Valeriana *locusta*, F.
Tulip tree, Liriodendron *tulipifera*, L.
Hound's tongue, 226.1. Cynoglossum *officinale*.
Cowslips, 284.3. Primula *veris*, F.
Valerian, *great wild*, 200.1. Valerian *officinalis*, F.
Rattle, *yellow*, 284.1. Rhinanthus *crista galli*, F.
Ice.

Thermom. 8. The lowest this month.
Fir, *silver, buds hurt by the frost.*

5. Twayblade, 385. Ophrys *ovata*, f.
Tormentil, 257. Tormentilla *erecta*, F.
Celandine, 309. Chelidonium *majus*, E.
Betony, 238.1. Betonica *officinalis*, E.

6. Oak, 440. Quercus, *robur*, F. et L.
Time for sowing barley.
Saxifrage, *white*, 354.6. Saxifraga *granulata*, F.
Ash, 469. Fraxinus *exelsior*, f.
Ramsons, 370.5. Allium *ursinum*, F.
Nettle, *white*, 240.1. Lamium *album*, F.
Quicken tree, 452.2. Sorbus *aucuparia*, F.

7. Fir, *Scotch*, 442. Pinus *sylvestris*, F.

8. Woodruffe, 224. Asperula *odorata*, F.

9. Chesnut tree, 1382. H. Fagus *castanea*, f.

10. Celandine, 309. Chelidonium *majus*, F.
Solomon's seal, 664. Convallaria *polygonat*. F.
Thorn,*white*,453.3.Cratægus *oxyacantha*, F.

3   Maple,

May

11. Maple, 470.2. Acer *campeſtre*, F.
Roſes, *garden*, f.
12. Barberry buſh, 465. Berberis *vulgaris*, F.
Cheſnut, *horſe*, 1683. H. Æſculus *hippocas*. F.
Bugloſs, *ſmall wild*, 227.1. Lycopſis *arvenſis*, F.
13. Graſs, *water ſcorpion*, 229.4. Myoſotis *ſcorpᶦoid*. F.
Quince tree, 1452. H. Pyrus *Cydonia*, F.
Cleavers, 225. Galium *aparine*, F.
14. Mulberry tree, 1429. H. Morus *nigra*, L.
Aſp, 446.3. Populus *tremula*, l.
Crowfoot, *bulbous*, 247.2. Ranunculus *bulbos*. F.
Butter cups, 247. Ranunculus *repens*, F.
15. *Young turkies*.
Lime tree, 473. Tilia *Europæa*, f.
Milkwort, *287.1,2. Polygala *vulgaris*, F.
Crane's bill, 359.10. Geranium *molle*, F.
Walnut, 1376. H. Juglans *regia*, F.
16. Muſtard, *hedge*, 298.4. Eryſimum *officinale*, F.
20. Bryony, *black*, 262.1. Tamus *communis*, F.
Many oaks, and more aſhes and beeches, ſtill without leaf.
Violet, *ſweet*, 364.1. Viola *odora*, D.
Stitchwort, 346. Stellaria *holoſtea*, D.
Anemone, *wood*, 259.1. Anemone *nemoroſa*, D.
Cuckow flower, 299.20. Cardamine *pratenſis*, D.
Earth nut, 209. Bunium, bulbocaſt. F.
Mulberry tree, 1429. H. Morus *nigra*, f.

Nightꜱ

May
21. Nightſhade, 265. Atropa *belladonna*, f.
Rye, 288. Secale *hybernum*, *in ear*.
23. Pellitory *of the wall*, 158.1. Parietaria
officin. F.
24. Bramble, 467. Rubus *fruticoſus*, f.
25. Moneywort, 283.1. Lyſimachia *nummul.*
F.
Columbines, 173.1. Aquilegia *vulgar.*
F. *in the woods.*
26. Tanſy, *wild*, 256.5. Potentilla *anſerina*, F.
Henbane, 274. Hyoſcyamus *niger*, F.
27. Campion, *white*, 339.8. Lychnis *dioica*, F.
Clover, 328.6 Trifolium *pratenſe*, F.
28. Avens, 262.1. Geum *urbanum*, F.
Chervil, *wild*, 207. Chærophyllum *te-
mulent.* F.
30. Bryony, *black*, 262.1. Tamus *communis*, F.
Brooklime, 280.8. Veronica *beccabunga*, F.
Cuckow flower, 338. Lychnis *flos cuculi*, F.
Creſſes, *water*, 300.1. Siſymbrium *naſturt.*
F.
Thermom. 32. Higheſt this month.
31. Spurrey, 351.7. Spergula *arvenſis*, F.
Alder, *berry bearing*, 465. Rhamnus *fran-
gula*, F.

VI. M O N T H.

Now the mower whets his ſcythe,
And every ſhepherd tells his tale
Under the hawthorn in the dale.   Milton.

June 2. Elder, *water*, 460.1. Viburnum *opulus*, F.
Lilly, *yellow water*, 368.1. Nymphæa
lutea, F.   Flower

June 2. Flower de luce, *yellow water*, 374. Iris *pfeudo-acor*. F.

Mayweed, *ftinking*, 185.3. Anthemis *cotula*, F.

Pimpernel, 282.1. Anagallis arvenfis, F.

3. Arfmart, 145.4. Polygonum *perficaria*, F.

* Thyme, 430.1. Thymus *ferpyllum*, F.

Parfnep, *cow*, 205. Heracleum *fphondylium*, F.

Quicken tree, 452. Sorbus *aucuparia*, D.

5. Radifh, *horfe*, 301.1. Cochlearia *armorac*. F.

Thorn, *evergreen*, 1459.3. H. Mefpilus *pyracantha*, F.

Bramble, 467. Rubus *fruticofus*, F.

†GOAT SUCKER, or FERN OWL, 27. Caprimulgus *Europæus*, *is heard in the evening*.

6. Vine, 1613. H. Vitis *vinifera*, b.

Flix weed, 298.3. Sifymbrium *fophia*, F.

Rafberry bufh, 467.4. Rubus *idæus*, F.

Mallow, *dwarf*, 251.2. Malva *rotundifolia*, F.

Elder, 461.1. Sambucus *nigra*, F.

Stitchwort, *leffer*, 346. Stellaria *graminea*, F.

Tare, *everlafting*, 320.3. Lathyrus *pratenfis*, F.

---

* Pliny, lib. 11. §. 14. fays, the chicf time for bees to make honey is about the folftice, when the vine and thyme are in blow. According to his account then thefe plants are as forward in England as in Italy.

† This bird is faid by Catefby, as quoted by the author of the treatife De Migrationibus Avium, to be a bird of paffage.

Gouf

June 6. Gout *weed*, 208.3. Ægopodium *podagrar.* F.

Bryony, *white*, 261.1,2. Bryonia *alba*, F.
Rose, dog, 454.1. Rofa *canina*, F.
Buglofs *vipers*, 227.1. Echium *vulgare*, F.
7. Grafs, *vernal*, 398.1. Anthoxanthum *odorat.* F.
Darnel, *red*, 395. Lolium *perenne*, F.
Poppy, *wild*, 308.1. Papaver *fomnifer*, F.
Buckwheat, 181. H. Polygonum *fago-pyrum*, F.
8. Pondweed, *narrow leaved*, 145.9. Polygonum *amphib.* F.
Sanicle, 221.1. Sanicula *Europæa.* F.
9. Eyebright, *284.1. Euphrafia *officinalis*, F.

Heath, *fine leaved*, 471.3. Erica *cinerea*, F.
Saxifrage, bugle, hyacinth, D.
Broom, 474.1. Spartium *fcoparium*, *podded.*
Nettle, *hedge*, 237. Stachys *fylvatica*, F.
12. Wheat, 386.1. Triticum *hybernum*, *in ear.*
Meadow fweet, 259.1. Spiræa *ulmaria*, f.
Scabious, field, 191.1. Scabiofa *arvenfis*, F.
Valerian, *great water*, 200.1. Valeriana *officinal.* f.
Cinquefoil, *marfh*, 256.1. Comarum *paluftre*, F.
Orchis, *leffer butterfly*, 380.18. Orchis *bifolia*, F.
13. Willow herb, *great hairy*, 311.2. Epilobium *hirfutum*, F.
Parfnep, *cow*, 205. Heracleum *fphondyl.*F.
Betony, *water*, 283.1. Scrophularia *aquat.* F.

Cockle,

June
13. Cockle, 338.3. Agroftemma *githago*, F.
    Sage, 510.7. H. Salvia *officinalis*, F.
15. Mallow, 251.1. Malva *fylveftris*, F.
    Nipplewort, 173.1. Lapfana *communis*, F.
    Woodbind, 458.1,2. Lonicera *pericly-
    men*. f.
    NIGHTINGALE, *fings*.
16. Fir, *Weymouth*, 8. dend. Pinus *tæda*, F.
    Hemlock, 215.1. Conium *maculatum*, F.
    Nightfhade, *woody*, 265. Solanum *dulca-
    mara*, F.
    Archangel, *white*, 240. Lamium *album*, F.
17. Vervain, 236. Verbena *officinalis*, F.
    Agrimony, 202. Agrimonia *eupator*, F.
    Hemlock, *water*, 215. Phellandrium
    aquatic. F.
    Acacia, 1719. H. Robinia *pfeudo-acacia*,
    F.
18. Yarrow, 183. Achillea *millefolium*, F.
19. *Thermom.* 44.25. *Higheft this month.*
21. Orache, *wild*, 154.1. Chenopodium *al-
    bum*, F.
    Solftice. About this time ROOKS *come not
    to their neft trees at night.*
    Wheat, 386.1. Triticum *hybernum*, F.
    Rye, 388.1. Secale *hybernum*, F.
    Self-heal, 238. Prunella *vulgaris*, f.
    Parfley, *hedge*, 219.4. Tordylium *anthrif-
    cus*, f.
    *Graffes of many kinds, as feftuca, aira, agrof-
    tis, phleum cynofurus, in ear.*
22. Horehound, *bafe*, 239. Stachys *Germa-
    nica*, F.

X   St.

June

22. St. John's wort, 342. Hypericum *perforatum*, F.

Parfnep, 206.1. Paftinaca *fativa*, F.

Mullein, *white*, 287. Verbafcum *thapfus*, F.

Poppy, *wild*, 308. Papaver *fomnifer*, F.

23. Larkfpur, 708.3. H. Delphinium *Ajacis*, F.

Marygold, *corn*, 182.1. Chryfanthemum *feget*. F.

24. Rofemary, 515. H. Rofmarinus *officinalis*, D.

25. Vine, 1613. H. Vitis *vinifera*, F.

Bindweed, *great*, 275.2. Convolvulus *arvenfis*, F.

Feverfew, 187. Matricaria *parthenium*, F.

Woad, *wild*, 366.2. Refeda *luteola*, F.

Rocket, *bafe*, 366.1. Refeda *lutea*, F.

Archangel, *yellow*, 240.5. Galeopfis *galeobdolon*, F.

Wheat, 386.1. Triticum *hybernum*, F.

Thermom. 20. The loweft this month.

27. *Clover mowed.*

Pennywort, *marfh*, 222. Hydrocotule *vulgaris*, F.

Meadow, *fweet*, 259. Spiræa *ulmaria*, F.

28. Oats *manured*, 389. Avena *fativa*, F.

Barley, 388. Hordeum *vulgare*, F.

Midfummer fhoots of apricot, oak, beech, elm.

Succory, wild, 172.1. Cichorium *intybus*, F.

Blue bottles, 198. Centaurea *cyanus*, F.

Knap-

3

June
  28. Knapweed, *great,* 198. Centaurea *fca-biofa*, F.
  30. *Currants ripe.*
  According to Dr. Hales, May and June heat is, at a medium, 28.5.

---

* The groves, the fields, the meadows, now no more
With melody refound. 'Tis filence all,
As if the lovely fongfters, overwhelm'd
By bounteous nature's plenty, lay intranc'd
In drowfy lethargy.

---

* I heard no birds after the end of this month, except the STONE CURLEW, 108.4. Charadrius Oedicnemus, whiftling late at night; the YELLOW HAMMER, 93.2. Emberiza flava; the GOLD-FINCH, 89.1. and GOLDEN CRESTED WREN, 79.9. Mota-cilla regulus, now and then chirping. I omitted to note down when the cuckow left off finging, but, as well as i remember, it was about this time. Ariftotle fays, that this bird difappears about the rifing of the dog ftar, i. e. towards the latter end of July.

VII. M O N T H.

Berries and pulpous fruits of various kinds,
The promife of the blooming fpring, now yield
Their rich and wholefome juices, meant t' allay
The ferment of the bilious blood.

July 2. Beech, 439. Fagus *fylvatica*, F.
  Pearlwort, 345.2. Fagina *procumbens*, F.
  Carrot, *wild,* 218. Daucus *carrota*, F.
  Grafs, *dog,* 390.1. Triticum *repens, in ear.*
  Violet, *Calathian,* 274. Gentiana *pneu-monan.* F.
  4. Silver weed, 256.5. Potentilla *anferina,* F.
  Betony, 238.1. Betonica *officinalis,* F.
  Nightfhade, *enchanters,* 289. Circæa *lute-tiana,* f.

          X 2   Lavender,

July 6. Lavender, 512. Lavendula *fpica*, F.
Parfley, *hedge*, Tordylium *anthrifcus*, F.
Gromill, 228.1. Lithofpermum *officinale*,
F.
Furze, 475. Ulex *genifta*, D.
Cow wheat, *eyebright*, 284.2. Euphrafia
odont. F.

7. Pinks, maiden, 335.1. Dianthus *deltoides*,
F.

8. Tanfey, 188.1. Tanacetum *vulgare*, f.
Bed-ftraw, *lady's yellow*, 224. Galium
verum, F.
Sage, *wood*, 245. Teucrium *fcorodonia*, F.
Spinach, 162. H. Spinacia *oleracia*, F.
Thermom. 22. Loweft this month.

9. Angelica, *wild*, 208.2. Angelica *fyl-
veftris*, F.
Strawberries ripe.
Fennel, 217. Anethum *fœniculum*, F.

10. Beans, *kidney*, 884. H. Phafeolus *vulgaris*,
podded.
Parfley, 884. H. Apium *petrofelinum*, F.
Sun dew, *round leaved*, 356.3. Drofera
rotundifol. F.
Sun dew, *long leaved*, 356.4. Drofera *lon-
gifol*. F.
Lilly, *white*, 1109. H. Lilium *candidum*, f.

11. Mullein, *hoary*, 288. Verbafcum *phlo-
moid*. F.
Plantain, *great*, 314.1,2. Plantago *major*,
F.
WILLOW, SPIKED, of Theophr.
1699. H. Spiræa *falicifol*. F.
Jeffamine, 1599. H. Jafminum *officinale*,
F.
Reft harrow, 332. Ononis *fpinofa*, F.
Hyffop,

July

11. Hyffop, 516. H. Hyffopus *officinalis*, F.
    Potatoes, 615.14. H. Solanum *tuberofum*,
    F.
    Second shoots of the maple.
    Bell flower, *round leaved*, 277.5. Campa-
    nula, F.
    LILLY, WHITE, 1109. H. Lilium *can-
    didum*, F.
    Rafberries ripe.
    Figs yellow.
13. LIME TREE, 473. Tilia *Europæa*, F.
    Knapweed, 198.2. Centaurea *jacea*, F.
    Stonecrop, 269. Sedum *rupeftre*, F.
    Grafs, *knot*, 146. Polygonum *aviculare*, F.
    Grafs, *bearded dog*, 390.2. Triticum *ca-
    ninum*, F.
15. *Thermom*. 39. *Higheft this month.*
16. Afparagus, 267.1. Afparagus *officinalis*,
    berries.
    Mugwort, 190.1. Artemifia *vulgaris*, F.
18. Willow herb, *purple fpiked*, 367.1. Ly-
    thrum *falicaria*, F.
    YOUNG PARTRIDGES.
    Agrimony, *water hemp*, 187.1. Bidens
    tripart. F
20. Flax, *purging*, 362.6. Linum *catharticum*,
    F.
    Arfmart, *fpotted*, 145.4. Polygonum *per-
    ficaria*, F.
    Lilly, *martagon*, 1112. H. Lilium *mar-
    tagon.*
    HENS *moult.*
22. Orpine, 269. Sedum *telephium*, f.
    Hart's tongue, 116. Afplenium *fcolc
    pendra*, F.   Penn.

July

22. Pennyroyal, 235. Mentha *pulegium*, F.
    Bramble, 461.1. Rubus *fruticofus*. *Fruit red.*
    Lauruſtinus, 1690. H. Viburnum *tinus*, f.
24. Elecampane, 176. Inula *helenium*, F.
    Amaranth, 202. H. Amaranthus *cau-datus*, F.
27. Bindweed, *great*, 275.1. Convolvulus *ſe-pium*, F.
28. Plantain, *great water*, 257.1. Aliſma *plan-tago*, F.
    Mint, *water*, 233.6. Mentha *aquatica*, F.
    Willow herb, 311.6. Epilobium *paluſtre*, F.
    Thiſtle tree ſow, 163.7. Sonchus *arvenſis*, F.
    Burdock, 197.2. Arctium *lappa*, f.
    Saxifrage, *burnet*, 213.1,2. Pimpinella *ſaxifraga*, F.
    DEVIL'S BIT, 191.3. Scabioſa *ſuccifa*, F.
30. Nightſhade, common, 288.4. Solanum *nigrum*, F.
    DOVE, RING, 62.9. Columba *palumbus*, cooes.

VIII. M O N T H.

Pour'd from the villages, a numerous train
Now ſpreads o'er all the fields. In form'd array
The reapers move, nor ſhrink for heat or toil,
By emulation urg'd. Others diſpers'd,
Or bind in ſheaves, or load or guide the wain
That tinkles as it paſſes. Far behind,
Old age and infancy with careful hand
Pick up each ſtraggling ear, &c.

Auguſt

1. Melilot, 331.1. Trifolium *officinale*, F.
   Rue, 874.1. Ruta *graveolens*, F.
   Soapwort, 339.6. Saponaria *officinalis*, F.
   Bedſtraw, *white, lady's*, 224.2. Galium *paluſtre*, F.
   Parſnep, *water*, 300. Siſymbrium *naſturt.* F.
   Oats almoſt fit to cut.

3. *Barley cut.*

5. Tanſy, 188.1. Tanacetum *vulgare*, F.
   Onion, 1115. H. Allium *cepa*, F.

7. Horehound, 239. Marrubium *vulgare*, F.
   Mint, *water*, 233.6. Mentha *aquat.* F.
   Nettle, 139. Urtica *dioica*, F.
   Orpine, 269.1. Sedum *telephium*, F.
   NUTHATCH, 47. Sitta *Europæa, chatters.*

8. *Thermom.* 20. *Loweſt to the 27th of this month.*

9. Mint, *red*, 232.5. Mentha *gentilis*, F.
   Wormwood, 188.1. Artemiſia *abſinthium*, F.

12. Horehound, *water*, 236.1. Lycopus *Europæus*, F.
    Thiſtle, *lady's*, 195.12. Carduus *marianus*, F.
    Burdock, 196. Arctium *lappa*, F.
    ROOKS *come to the neſt trees in the evening, but do not rooſt there.*

14. Clary, *wild*, 237.1. Salvia *verbenaca*, F.
    STONE CURLEW, 108. Charadrius *oedicnemus, whiſtles at night.*

15. Mallow, *vervain*, 252. Malva *alcea*, F.

X 4   GOAT

Auguſt

15. GOAT SUCKER, 26.1. Caprimulgus *Europæus, makes a noiſe in the evening, and young owls.*

16. *Thermom.* 35. *The higheſt to the 27th of this month.*

17. Orach, *wild,* 154.1. Chenopodium *album.* ROOKS *rooſt on their neſt trees.* GOAT SUCKER, *no longer heard.*

21. *Peas and wheat cut.* Devil's bit, *yellow,* 164.1. Leontodon *autumnal.* F.

26. ROBIN RED BREAST, 78.3. Mota-cilla *rubecula, ſings.* Goule, 443. Myrica *gale,* F. R. Golden rod, *marſh,* 176.2. Senecio *pa-ludoſus,* F.

29. Smallage, 214. Apium *graveolens,* F. Teaſel, 192.2. Dipſacus *fullonum,* F. *Vipers come out of their holes ſtill.*

IX. MONTH.

How ſweetly nature ſtrikes the raviſh'd eye
Thro' the fine veil with which ſhe oft conceals
Her charms in part, as conſcious of decay !

September

2. WILLOW HERB, *yellow,* 282.1. Lyſi-machia *vulgaris,* F. Traveller's joy, 258. Clematis *vitalba,* F.

---

* From the 27th of this month to the 10th of September i was from home, and therefore cannot be ſure that i ſaw the firſt blow of the plants during that interval.

Graſs

September
5. Grafs of Parnaffus, 355. Parnaffia *paluftris*, F.
10. *Catkins of the hafel formed.*
Thermom. 17. *The loweft from the 10th to the end of this month.*
11. *Catkins of the birch formed.*
Leaves of the Scotch fir fall.
Bramble ftill in blow, though fome of the fruit has been ripe fome time; fo that there are green, red, and black berries on the fame individual plant at the fame time.
Ivy, 459. Hedera *helix*, f.
14. *Leaves of the fycomore, birch, lime, mountain afh, elm, begin to change.*
16. Furze, 475. Ulex *Europæus*, F.
Catkins of the alder formed.
Thermom. 36.75. *The higheft from the 10th to the end of this month.*
CHAFFINCH, 88. Fringilla *cælebs*, *chirps*.
17. *Herrings.*
20. FERN, FEMALE, 124.1. Pteris *aquilina*, *turned brown.*
Afh, *mountain*, 452.2. Sorbus *aucuparia*, F. R.
Laurel, 1549. H. Prunus *laurocerafus*, f. r.
Hops, humulus *lupulus*, 137.1. f. r.
21. SWALLOWS *gone. Full moon.*
23. *Autumnal æquinox.*
25. WOOD LARK, 69.2. Alauda *arborea*, *fings.*
FIELD FARE, 64.3. Turdus *pilaris*, *appears.*

Leaves

September

25. *Leaves of the plane tree, tawny---of the hafel, yellow---of the oak, yellowifh green ---of the fycomore, dirty brown---of the maple, pale yellow---of the afh, fine lemon ---of the elm, orange---of the hawthorn, tawny yellow---of the cherry, red---of the hornbeam, bright yellow---of the willow, ftill hoary.*

27. BLACK BIRD *fings.*

29. THRUSH, 64.2. Turdus *muficus, fings.*

30. *Bramble, 467.1. Rubus *fruticofus,* F.

---

*Autumnal heat, according to Dr, Hales, at a medium, is 18.25,

---

X. MONTH.

Arife, ye winds, 'tis now your time to blow,
And aid the work of nature. On your wings
The pregnant feeds convey'd fhall plant a race
Far from their native foil.

October

1. Bryony, *black,* 262. Tamus *communis,* F. R.
Elder, *marfh,* 460.1. Viburnum *opulus,* F.R.
Elder, 461.1. Sambucus *nigra,* F. R.
Briar, 454.1. Rofa *canina,* F. R.
Alder, *black,* 465. Rhamnus *frangula,* F.R.
Holly, 466. Ilex *aquifolium,* F. R.
Barberry, 465. Berberis *vulgaris,* F. R.
Nightfhade, *woody,* 265. Solanum *dulcamara.* F. R.

2. Thorn, *black,* 462.1. Prunus *fpinofa,* F.R.

CROW,

October

2. *CROW, ROYSTON, 39. 4. Corvus *cornix, returns.*

5. *Catkins of fallows formed.*

6. *Leaves of afp almoft all off---of chefnut, yellow---of birch, gold-coloured.*
Thermom. 26.50. *Higheft this month.*

7. BLACK BIRD, 65.1. Turdus *merula, fings.*
Wind high; rooks fport and dafh about as in play, and repair their nefts.

9. Spindle tree, 468.1. Euvonymus *Europæus,* F. R.
Some afh trees quite ftripped of their leaves. Leaves of marfh elder of a beautiful red, or rather pink colour.

10. WOOD LARK *fings.*
† RING DOVE *cooes.*

14. WOOD LARK *fings.*
Several plants ftill in flower, as panfy, white behn, black nonefuch, hawkweed, buglofs, gentian, fmall ftitchwort, &c. in grounds not broken up.
A great mift and perfect calm; not fo much as a leaf falls. Spiders webs innumerable appear every where. Woodlark fings. Rooks do not ftir but fit quietly on their neft trees.

16. GEESE, WILD, 136 4. Anas, *anfer, leave the fens and go to the rye lands.*

October
22. WOODCOCK, 104. Scolopax *rufticola*,
   returns.
   Some afh trees ftill green.
24. LARK, SKY, 69.1. Alauda *arvenfis, fings.*
   Privet, 465.1 Liguftrum *vulgare,* F. R.
26. *Thermom.* 7. *Loweft this month.*
   Honeyfuckle, 458.1, 2 *Lomicera periclymen.*
   ftill in flower in the hedges, and mallow
   and feverfew.
   WILD GEESE *continue going to the rye*
   lands.

Now from the north
Of Norumbega, and the Samoeïd fhore,
Burfting their brazen dungeons, arm'd with ice,
And fnow and hail, and ftormy guft, and flaw,
Boreas, and Cæcias, and Argeftes loud,
And Thrafcias rend the woods, and feas up-turn:
MILTON.

Here ends the Calendar, being interrupt-
ed by my going to London. During
the whole time it was kept, the ba-
rometer fluctuated between 29.1. and
29.9. except a few days, when it funk
to 28.6. and rofe to 30½.

A SIBI-

A Sibirian or Lapland Year.

June
    23. Snow melts.
July 1. Snow gone.
    9. Fields quite green.
    17. Plants at full growth.
    25. Plants in full blow.
Auguſt
    2. Fruits ripe.
    10. Plants ſhed their ſeeds.
    18. Snow.
    From this time to June 23, ſnow and ice; ſo that by this account, plants, from the coming out of the ground to the ripening of their ſeeds, take but a month. And the ſpring, ſummer and autumn, are crouded into the ſpace of 56 days. This account is taken from a treatiſe publiſhed in the Amæn. Academ. vol. iv. and agrees with one i have ſeen quoted out of Gmelin, who was in Sibiria many years.

THE

THE

CALENDAR of FLORA.

By THEOPHRASTUS.

At ATHENS, Latitude 37° 25′.

INTRODUCTION.

THE following Calendar was extracted chiefly from Theophraftus's Hiftory of plants, and put together in the beft manner i was able from imperfect materials. Any one who looks into the original, will fee that accuracy ought not to be expected; the manner of marking the times being often very indeterminate.

I am fenfible that objections may be made to many parts of this Calendar, but i thought it not worth while to give my reafons for what i have done, and thereby load a piece of mere curiofity with pompous quotations.

It has always feemed extraordinary to me, that when difciples of Linnæus have been fent into fo many parts of the world, in order to make difcoveries in natural hiftory, viz. Afia, Penfylvania, Lapland, Ægypt, Paleftine, Malabar, Surat, China, Java, Spain, America, Gotland, Italy, Apulia, Surinam, and St. Euftatia, that Greece fhould have been overlooked. It is true, Monfieur Tournefort was fent into the Levant by Lewis the Fourteenth to fearch for plants, and fpent fome years there; it is alfo as true, that he had all the knowledge and zeal neceffary for fuch a commiffion; but the country was too extenfive for one man to examine thoroughiy in that fpace of time. He rambled over moft of the Greek iflands, Armenia, and other parts of Afia; and though he enriched the royal gardens with many new plants, yet feveral muft have efcaped him for want of time, or a proper feafon.

It were to be wifhed, therefore, that fome perfons properly qualified, might be fent to Greece, and be enjoyned to make Attica, particularly, their place of refidence for a year at leaft. This might furnifh a Fiora and Fauna Attica, that

would

would be extreemly curious to all lovers of natural
hiftory; and tend to clear up many paffages in
thofe authors, who firft opened that branch of
knowledge, as well as carried fome parts of it
much farther, than is generally known, or at leaft
acknowledged; and from whofe writings much
more benefit might ftill be reaped, were they
better underftood, efpecially in the medicinal way.

As the Englifh nation will have the honour of
firft making known to the world the true and
accurate proportions of the ancient Greek archi-
tecture, fo i hope it is referved for us to bring the
reft of Europe thoroughly acquainted with the nature of the foil, climate, productions, animals,
&c. of a country, whofe ancient glory fo much
refembles our own, and in a great meafure has
been the caufe of it, by furnifhing us with the
beft models of good fenfe, tafte, and juft fentiments
in every branch of human knowledge. We therefore ought in a particular manner to look upon
Attica, from whence, as Cicero fays, *Humanitas,*
doctrina, fruges, jura, leges ortæ, atque in omnes
terras diftributa putantur, with the veneration due
to a mother country. Should fuch a fceme take
place, i could name a perfon, perfectly well qualified, by his youth and abilities, and zealoufly inclined upon proper encouragement, to be one of
the party. France, Sweden*, and Ruffia have
fet us examples of this kind, and why this great
and flourifhing nation fhould not follow them, i
cannot fee. We have had our fhare in advancing
natural hiftory, it is true, but hitherto without any
public encouragement.

---

* Amongft many inftances of this fort, there is one that deferves
particular notice mentioned Amæn. Academ. p. 445. the author fays,
that Haffelquift was fent into Ægypt at the expence of his country-
men the Eaft Gothlanders, of the heads of the univerfity, and of the
Eaft India company, for the ftudy of natural hiftory; and ftaid above
a year at Cairo.

THE

CALENDAR of FLORA.

By THEOPHRASTUS.

Feb.

1. —* Violet, *early bulbous*, 1144. H. Leucoium *vernum*, λευκοιον, F.

Wall flower, 291.2. Cheiranthus, *cheiri*, φλογιον, F.

Cornel tree, 1536, H. Cornus, *mas*, κρανεια, L.

Dogberry, 460. Cornus, *sanguinea*, θηλυκρανεια, L.

14. — Bay tree, 1688. H. Laurus *nobilis*, δαφνη, L.

Alder, 442. Betula *alnus*, κληθρα, L.

Abele, 446.3. Populus *alba*, λευκη, L.

Elm, 468. Ulmus *campestris*, πιελεα, L.

Sallow, Salix, ιῖεα, L.

Poplar, *black*, 446.1. Populus *nigra*, αιγειρος, L.

Plane tree, 1706. H. Platanus *orient*. πλαῖανος, L.

* This mark—after some of the figures, denotes that the time is only determined within certain limits.
All the other marks mean the same as in my own Calendar.

Beginning

March
12 — *Beginning of S P R I N G.
Fig tree, 1431. H. Ficus *carica*, ερινεος, L.
Alaternus, 1608.1. Rhamnus *alatern.*
φιλυκη, L.
Hawthorn, 453.3. Cratægus *oxyacanth.*
οξυακανθος, L.
Chrift's thorn, 1708. H. Rhamnus *pali-
urus*, παλιacος, L.
Turpentine tree, 1577. H. Piftacia *te-
rebin.* τερμινθος, L.
Chefnut-tree, 1382. H. Fagus *caftanea*,
διος βαλανος, L.
Walnut tree, 1376. H. Juglans *regia*,
καρυα, L.
Lilly of the valley, 264. Convallaria
Maialis, ενανθη. F.
Narciffus, C. B 49. ατερ ωνη λειμωνια, F.
Daffodil, 1131. H. Narciffus *pfeudo-narc.*
ξυλεοκωσιον, F.
Corn flag, 1169.2. H. Gladiolus *com-
munis*, F.
Hyacinth, 1162.31. Hyacinthus *comofus*,
υακινθος, F.
Rofe, rofa, ροδον, F.
20. † Elder tree, 461.1. Sambucus *nigra*,
ακ.η, L.

---

* Between February 28 and March 12, the Ornithian winds blow,
and SWALLOW appears.
+ Between March 11 and 26, the *kite* and *nightingale* appear, that
is in the leafing feafon. The appearance of the hawk is confonant to
what Ariftotle fays, as quoted in the preface, but is determined upon
a different kind of teftimony; which is a proof that this part of the
Calendar at leaft is tolerably well ftated.

Fleawort,

March

20. Fleawort, 881. H.. Plantago *pfyllium,*
κυν;↓. F.

Oak, 442. Quercus, robur, Ϟρυϟ, L.

Fig tree, 1431. H. Ficus *carica,* συκη, L.

Oak, 1386. H. Quercus, *efculus,* φηγος, L.

Lime tree, 473. Tilia *Europæa,* φιλυρα, L.

Maple, 470.2. Acer *campeftris,* ζυγια, L.

Apple tree, 451. Pyrus *malus,* μηλεα, L.

Ivy, 459. Hedera, *helix,* ιϟος, L.

Beam tree, *white,* 453. Cratægus *aria,*
αρια, L.

26. Tree of life, 1408. H. Thuia *occident.*
ϧυϧα, L.

April

4. — Succory, 172. Cichorium *intybus,* κιχορειον,
F.

May 12.   Beginning of S U M M E R.

15 — *Wheat harveft.*

Turpentine tree, 1557. H. Piftacia *te-*
rebin, τερμιν϶Ϫ, F. R.

Flower of Conftantinople, 992.1. H.
Lychnis *Chalced.* λυχνιϟ, F.

Rofe campion, 993.2. H. Lychnis *co-*
ronar. δ ιϦ ανϧϦ, F.

Afphodel, *yellow,* 1192.4. H. Afphodelus
luteus, αμαραϰϦ, F.

Afh tree, 468. Fraxinus *excelfior,* μελια,
F. R.

Maple, 470.2. Acer *pfcudo-platanus,*
σφενϟαμνϦ, F. R.

Pine, 1398. H. Pinus *fylveftris,* πιυϟ, F.

Fir tree, *common,* 1396.2. Pinus *abics,*
πευϰη, F.

Y 3   Fir

June
20 — *Fir tree, *yew leaved*, 1394. Pinus *picea*,
ελαἴη, F.
Yew tree, 445. Taxus *baccata*, μιλ⊙, F.
R.
Cornel tree, 1536. H. Cornus *mas*,
κρανεια, F. R.
Midsummer shoots of the oak.
The fig, the vine, and the pomegranate,
shoot later.
July
23. *Cuckow disappears.*
30. *Etesian winds blow.*

---

* Botanists doubt which of these two firs is the πευκη and which
the ελαἴη. Theophrastus says expresly that the πευκη flowers
some days before the ελαἴη, and therefore this question might be probably decided.

Auguſt
19 — Beginning of A U T U M N.
Lilly, Lilium, λειριον, F.
Crocus, 1173.3. Crocus *autumnal.* κροκ⊙,
F.
Dogberry, 460. Cornus *sanguinea*,
θηλυκρανεια, F. R.
Alder, 442. Betula *alnus*, κληθρα, F. R.
Quail, 58.6. Tetrao, *coturnix*, ορ͵υξ, *de-*
parts.
Sept.
20 — Crane, 95. Ardea, *grus*, γερανος, *departs.*
Autumn shoots of trees.
October
12 — Oak, 440. Quercus, *robur*, δρυς, F. R.
Chefnut,

October

12 — Chefnut, 1382. H. Fagus, *caftanea*, διος
βαλανος, F. R.
Chrift's thorn, 1708. H.Rhamnus *paliur*.
παλιδους, F. R.
Hawthorn, 453.3. Cratægus *oxyacantha*,
οξυακανθος, F. R.
Holm oak, 1391. H. Quercus *coccifer*,
πρινος, F. R.
Alaternus, 1608.1. H. Rhamnus *alatern*.
φιλυκη, F. R.
29 — Venice fumach, 1696. H. Rhus *cotinus*,
κοκκομηλεα, F.
Apple tree, 451. Pyrus *malus*, μηλεα, F. R.
Beam tree, *white*, 453. Cratægus *aria*,
αρια, F. R.
Lime tree, 473. Tilia *Europæa*, φιλυρη,
F. R.
Box tree, 445. Buxus *fempervivens*, πυξος,
F. R.

Beginning of W I N T E R.

Novem.
15 — Ivy, 459. Hedera *helix*, κιτλος, F. R.
Juniper, 444. H. Juniperus *communis*,
αρκευθος, F. R.
Tree of life, 1408. H. Thuia *occident.*
θυεια, F. R.
Yew tree, 445. Taxus *baccata*, μιλο, F. R.
Pear tree, 1450. Pyrus *communis*, αχρας,
F. R.
Arbutus, 1577.2. H. αδραχνη, F. R.

Y 4   INDEX.

INDEX.

☞ The large Roman Numerals refer to the Months of both Galen-
dars; the fmall Numerals to the Days of the Month of the Swedifh; the common Figures to the Englifh.

A.

ACER, IV. 6. 13.18.25. V. 2.
Achellea, VI. xxiii. xxix. VII.
vi, vii. VI. 18.
Aɛ̃æa, VI. vii.
Adonis, VI. xiii. ix. i.
Adoxa, V. viii.
Aegopodium, VI. 6.
Aefculus, V. xvi. IV. 1. V. 12.
Agrimonia, VII. vi. IV. 24. V. 17.
Agroftema, VII. v. VI. 13.
Ajuga, V. xxx. IV. 29.
Alauda, III. xx. II. 4. IX. 25.
X. 10. 14. 24.
Alchemilla, V. xxv.
Alifma, VII. 28.
Allium, V. 6. VIII. 5.
Alopeurus, VI. iv.
Alnus, III. 26.
Alfine, I. 26.
Amaranthus, VII. 24.
Amygdalus, IV. 6.
Anagallis, VI. 2.
Anas, IV. vii. II. 12. X. 16. 26.
Anemone, IV. xvi. V. iii. IV.
10. V. 20.
Anethum, VII. 9.
Angelica, VII. 9.
Anthemis, VI. xxiii. xxix. VI. 2.
Anthericum, VI. ii.
Anthyllis, VI. xii.
Anthoxanthum, VI. 7.
Antirrhinum, VI. xxviii.
Apis, III. 2. IV. 10.
Apium, VII. 10. VIII. 29.
Aquifolium, IV. 3.
Aquilegia, VI. vii. V. 25.
Arɛ̃ium, VII. ix. VII. 28.
Ardea, IV. 14.
Artemifia, VII. x. VIII. xiv. IX.
vi. IV. 9. V. 1. VII. 16. VIII. 9.
Arum, IV. 26.
Afparagus, VII. 16.

Afperula V. 8.
Atriplex, IX. xxii.
Atropa, VI. xviii. IV. 18. V. 21.
Afarum, V. iii.
Aftragalus, VI. xxiv.
Avena, VI. 28. VIII. 2.

B.

Ballota, VII. x.
Bellis, 1. 26.
Berberis, V. xiii. VI. viii. V. 12.
X. 1.
Betonica, V. v.
Betula, V. xiii. xiv. IV. 1. 7. 27.
Bidens, VII. 18.
Braffica, IV. 15.
Briza, VI. xviii.
Bryonia, VI. xxviii. IV. 27. VI. 6.
Bunium, V. 20.

C.

Caltha, V. xxi. IV. 16.
Campanula, VI. xi. xvi. xxix.
VII. i. ii. vi. VII. 11.
Cannabis, VII. ix.
Caprimulgus, V. 5. VIII. 15.
Cardamine, V. xxviii. IV. 18.
V. 20.
Carduus, VI. xxii. VII. ix. xvii.
VIII. 12.
Carpinus, V. xvi. III. 29. IV.
10. 13. 25.
Caftanea, IV. 16.
Centaurea, VI. xxii. xxiv. VII.
i. vi. xxii. VI. 28. VII. 13.
Chærophillum, V. xxv. VII. vii.
IV. 25. 29. V. 28. VI. 5.
Charadrius, VIII. 14.
Cheiranthus, IV. 21.
Chelidonium, V. xxvii. V. 5. 10.
Chenopodium, IV. 24. VI. 21.
VIII. 17.
Chryfanthemum, VI. xvii. xxix.
VI. 23.
Chryfoplenium, V. iii.

Cicorium,

I N D E X.

Cichorium. VII. xii. VI. 28.
Ciconia, V. ix.
Circæa, VII. x. VII. iv.
Ciftus, VI. xx.
Clematis, IX. vi. IX. 2.
Clinopodium, VII. x.
Cochlearia, III. 21. VI. ſ.
Colchicum, VII. xviii. VIII. xxviii.
Columba, III. 5. VII. 30. X. 10.
Comarum, VI. xx. VI. 12.
Conium, VI. 16.
Convallaria, V. xxx. V. 3. 10.
Convolvulus, VII. i. iv. IV. 2'5.
VII. 27.
Conyza, VII. xxiii.
Cornus, V. xxx.
Corvus, II. 12. III. 2. VIII. 17.
X. 2.
Corylus, IV. xii. V. ix. I. 23. II.
22. IV. 7.
Cratægus, V. xv. VI. xii. xvii.
III. 29. IV. 28. V. 10.
Crepis, VI. xxix.
Crocus, IV. xiii.
Cucubalus, VIII. i.
Cuculus, V. xii. IV. 17.
Cygnus, IV. x.
Cynogloſſum, IV. 10. V. 4.
Cyprinus, V. xxv. xxx.
Cytiſus, IV. xiii.
D.
Daƈtylis, VII. xxii.
Daphne, IV. xiii. IV. 16.
Daucus, VII. vi. VII. 2.
Delphinium, VI. 23.
Dianthus, VI. xxiv. xxix. VII.
viii. VII, 7.
Dies Chalybæati, II. xxii.
Digitalis, VII. iv.
Dipſacus, VII. xviii. xx. VIII. 29.
Draba, IV. xv.
Droſera, VII. x.
E.
Echium, VI. 6.
Elymus, VI. xxviii.
Empetrum, IV. xxx.
Epilobium, VI. xxiv. xxvi. VII.
xii. xv. VI. 13. VII. 28.
Erica, VI. xxix. VI. 9.
Erigeron, VII. xv.

Eriophorum, V. xxx.
Eryſimum, V. xxv. IV. 10. 16.
V. 16.
Eſox, IV. x.
Euonymus, V. xiv. X. 9.
Eupatorium, VII. xv.
Euphorbia, IV. 25.
Euphraſia, VI. xvii. VI. 9. VII. 6.
F.
Fagus, V. xvi. IV. 18. 21. V. 9.
VII. 2.
Ficus, IX. iv. IV. 16. 21. 22. VII.
11.
Filipendula, VI. xxii.
Fragaria, VI. xxvi. IV. 13. VII. 9.
Frankenia, VII. ix.
Fraxinus, V. xxi. IV. 18. 22. V. 6.
Fringilla, II. 16. IX. 16.
G.
Galanthus, IV. xiii. I 26.
Galeopſis, VI. 25.
Galium, VI. xvi. VII. vi. IV. 3.
V. 13. VII. 8. VIII. 1.
Geniſta, IV. 22.
Gentiana, VI. xxii. VII. 26. VII. 2.
Geranium, V. xxvi. xxx. VI. v.
ix. xi. xiv. IV. 23. 27. V. 15.
Geum, VI. ii. xiii. V. 1. 28.
Glechoma, V. xxvi. IV. 16.
Gnaphalium, V. xxvi.
H.
Hedera, VIII. 9. IX. 11.
Helenium, VII. 24.
Helleborus, IV. xxi.
Hemerocallis, VI. xx. VII. vii. xvi.
Heracleum, VII. i. III. 28. IV.
29. VI. 3. 13.
Herniaria, VI. xxix.
Heſperis, VI. vii.
Hieracium, VII. xvi.
Hippophae, V. xiv.
Hirundo, V. ix. IV. 6. IX. 31.
Holcus, VII. v.
Hordeum, V. xiii. V. 6. VIII. 5.
Hottonia, V. 3.
Humulus, VII. vi. IV. 14. IX. 20.
Hyacinthus, VII. 26.
Hybernacula, V. viii.
Hydrocotyle, VI. xxvii.
Hyoſcyamus, VI. xii. V. 26.

Hypericum,

INDEX.

Hypericum, VI. xxix. VII. vi. xii.
IV. 27. VI. 21.
Hypochæris, VI. xxvii.
Hyffopus, VII. 11.

I.

Jafminus, IV. 28. VII. 11.
Ilex, I. 23. IV. 24. 26. X. 1.
Impatiens, VII. xviii.
Inula, VII. xiii. xxiv. IX. xvii.
Iris, VI. x. VII. vi. VI 2.
Ifatis, VI. xxix.
Juglans, IV. xiv. xviii. V. 15.
Juniperus, VI. iii. IV. 28.

L.

Lamium, I. 23. V. 6. VI. 16.
Lapfana, VI. 15.
Lathyrus. VI. xvii. xxix.
Lavandula, VII. vi.
Laurus, III. 11. IV. 10. 29. V. 1.
Leontodon, VI. vii. IV. 3. 10.
VIII. 21.
Leonurus, VII. vii.
Lepidium, V. iii. VII. xiii.
Leucoium, IV. xiii.
Libellula, V. xxi.
Ligufticum, VII. vii.
Liguftrum, V. xiv. X. 24.
Lilium, VI. xviii. VII. xx. VII.
10. 11.
Linum, VI. vii. xxiv. VII. 18.
Liriodendron, IV. 16. V. 4.
Lithofpermum, VII. 6.
Lonicera, IV. xv. VII. xii. I. 11.
23. VI. 15. X. 26.
Lotus, VI. vii.
Lychnis, V. xxx. VI. xiv. xvii.
IV. 22. V. 26. 30.
Lycopodium, IV. i.
Lycopfis, VIII. xii.
Lycopus, VIII. xii.
Lyfimachia, VI. xxii. VII. iv. V.
25. IX. 2.
Lythrum, VII. ii. VII. 18.

M.

Malva, VII. xii. IV. 13. VI. 6.
15. VIII. 15. X. 26.
Marrubium, VIII. 7.
Matricaria, VI. xi. IV. 10. VI.
25. X. 26.
Medicago, VI. xxvii.

Meleagris, IV. xv.
Melica, VI. vii.
Meliffa, VII. xxvi.
Mentha, VII. xv. VII. 22. 28.
VIII. 7. 9.
Menyanthes, VI. xiii. IV. 22.
Mercurialis, V. 1 IV. 12.
Mefpilus, IV. 22. VI. 5.
Mirabilis, VII. xvi.
Morus, IX. i. IV. 12. 18. V. 14.
20.
Motacilla, IV. xiii. V. iii xv. II.
12. IV. 9. 16. 28. VIII. 26.
Myofotis, V. 13.
Myrica, V. xiv. VIII. 26.

N.

Narciffus, V. xv. IV. 1.
Noctes, V. xxiv. VI. 20.
Nymphæa, IV. xvii. VI. xiv. xvi.
VI. 2.

O.

Oenothera, VII. v.
Ononis, VII. vi. VII. 11.
Ophrys, VI. xxii. V. 5.
Origanum, VII. x.
Orchis, VI. vii. xiv. xv. VI. 12.
Ornithogalum, IV. xv.
Orobus, V. xiii.
Ofmunda, VI. xxiv.
Oxalis, V. xiii. IV. 16.

P.

Pæonia, VI. ii. xvi.
Papaver, VI. xxiv. VII. vii. VI.
7. 22.
Papilio, IV. vii.
Parietaria, V. xxiii.
Paris, VI. vii.
Parnaffia, VI. xvi. IX. 5.
Paftinaca, VI. 22.
Pavo, VI. xxix.
Perdix, VII. 18.
Phafeolus, VII. 10.
Phellandrium, VI. 17.
Philadelphus, V. xiv. VI. xxiv.
Phyllerea, IV. 22.
Picris, VII. xii.
Pimpinella, VI. xviii. VII. 28.
Pinguicula, V. xxx.
Pinus, VI. i. III. 29. IV. 17. 18.
21. 22. 25. 29. V. 7. VI. 16.

Pifum.

INDEX.

Pisum, IV. 29. VIII. 21.
Plantago, V. xxviii. VI. v. IV.
26. VII. 2.
Platanus, IV. 14. 18.
Polygala, V. xxv. V. 15.
Polygonum, VI. 3. 7. VI. 8. VII.
13. 20.
Populus, XII. xxiii. IV. xix. xxx.
V. ix. xvi. xx. III. 21. IV. 16.
17. 21. 25. V. 14.
Potentilla, V. xvi. VI. xi. xiv. xvi.
xviii. V. 26. VII. 4.
Prenanthes, VII. x.
Primula, V. i. xiv. xv. III. 29.
IV. 9. V. 4.
Prunella, VI. xxii. VI. 21.
Prunus, V. ix. xv. xxv. xxviii. III.
11. 29. IV. 1. 6. 13. 16, 18,
IX. 20. X. ii.
Pteris, VIII. xxviii, IX. 20,
Pyrus, V. xv. xxvi. VI. ii, IV.
4. 6. 10. 14. 18. 23, V. 13.
Q.
Quercus, V. xxi. IV. 7. 18. V. 6.
R.
Rallus, IV. x.
Rana, IV. xiii.
Ranunculus, IV. xv. V. xxvi. VI.
vij. xvii. VII, vi. III. 28. IV.
28. V. 14.
Reseda, VI. 25.
Rhamnus, V. xv. xxi. VI. xv. xvi.
IV. 11. V. 31. X. 1.
Rheum, VI. xvi.
Rhinanthus, V. 4.
Ribes, V. xxv. VI. vii. II. 25. III,
2. IV. 3. 6. 13.
Robinia, V. xv. IV. 12. 21. VI.
17.
Rosa, V. xv. VI. xv. VII. vii.
xxiv. IV. 4. V. 11. VI. 6.
X. 1.
Rosmarinus, I. 5. IV. 22. VI. 24.
Rubus, V. vii. xxvii. VI. vii. xxiv.
IV. 3. 28. V. 24. VI. 5. 6, VII.
11. 22. VIII. 30.
Ruta, VIII. 1.
S.
Sagina, VII. 2,
Salix, III. xix. IV. xxi. V. vii. xiii.
xvi, III. 11, IV. 1. 7. 10. 17.

Salmo, V. xxi.
Salvia, VI. 13. VIII. 14.
Sambucus, VI. xxix. VII, xvii,
II. 4. IV. 25. VI. 6. X. 1.
Sanguisorba, VII. vii.
Sanicula, VI. 8.
Saponaria, VII. xxii. VIII. 1.
Satyrium, VI. xx.
Saxifraga, V. xxvi. V, 6.
Scabiosa, VI. xxix. VIII. iv. VI.
12. VII. 28.
Scolopax, X. 22.
Scrophularia, VII. x. IV. 27. VI,
13.
Scutellaria, VI. xxvi.
Secale, V. xxv. VI. xviii. VIII.
iv. V. 21. VI. 21.
Sedum, VI. xx. VII. vi. xiv. xv,
VIII. 1. IV. 4. VII. 13. 22,
VIII. 7.
Semina, V. viii. xiii.
Senecio, VI. vii. IV. 12. VIII. 26.
Serapias, VII. ii.
Serpentes, IV. vi.
Serratula, VII. xv. xxvii,
Silene, VI. 13. 28.
Sisymbrium, IV. 14. V. 30. VI.
6. VIII. 1.
Sitta, VIII. 8.
Solanum, VI. xxiv. VI. 16. VII,
11. 30. X 1.
Solidago, V. xxiv.
Sonchus, VII. xi. xxi. VII. 28.
Sorbus, VI. iii. IV. 1. 13. V. 6.
VI. 3. IX. 28.
Spartium, IV. 18. 22. 23. VI. 9.
Spergula, I. 26. V. 31.
Spinacia, VII. 8.
Spiraea, VII. v. IV. 22. VI. 12.
27. VII. 11.
Stachys, VI. xxv. VII. ix. VI.
9. 22.
Stellaria, IV. 22. V. 20. VI. 6.
Sturnus, V. vii.
Syringa, V. xiv. VI. xviii. xxv,
IV. 9. 27.
T.
Tamus, V. 20. 30. X. 1.
Tanacetum, VII. xv. III. 29. VII.
8. VIII. 5.

Tegmenta

Tegmenta, IV. xi.
Tetrao, II. 22.
Teucrium, VII. x. VII. 8.
Thymus, VI. 3.
Tilia, V. xxi. VII. xi. IV. 12.
  18. V. 15. VII. 13.
Tinunculus, IV. xiii.
Thalictrum, VII. 2.
Tipula, IV. vi.
Tordylium, VI. xxvii. VI. 21.
  VII. 6.
Tormentilla, VI. ii. IV. 22. V. 5.
Trifolium, VII. x. V. 27. VIII.1.
Tringa, IV. vi.
Triticum, IV. 3. VI. 12. 21. 25.
' VII. 2. 13. VIII. 21.
Trollius, V. xxvi.
Tulipa, V. xxv.
Turdus, II. 16. III. 4. IV. 23.
  IX. 25. X. 7.
Tuffilago, IV. xii. xxx.

V.

Vaccinium, V. xxx. VI. vii. xxix.
Valantia, V. 1.
Valeriana, VI. xvii. V. 4. VI. 12.
Vaporaria, IV. xix.
Verbafcum, VII. i. ii. VI. 22.VII.
  11.
Verbena, VI. 17.
Veronica, V. xxx. VII. v. III. 26.
  IV. 26. V. 30.
Viburnum, V. xiv. VI. xiv. I. 23.
  III. 11. 29. IV. 4. 11. 16. VI.
  2. VII. 22. X. 1.
Vicia, VI. xxii. xxiv.
Viola, V. iii. III. 28. IV. 18. V.
  20.
Vipera, VIII. 7.
Vitis, IV. 15. VI. 6. 25.
Ulex, IV. 24. VII. 6. IX. 16.
Ulmus, V. viii. xv. IV. 1. 10. 12.
Urtica, IV. 25. VIII. 7.

INDEX.

A.

A Bele, IV. xix. IV. 16. 17.
Acacia, V. xv. IV. 12. 21.
  VI. 17.
Adonis, VI. xiii. IX. i.
Agrimony, VII. vi. xv. VI. 24.
  VI. 17. VII. 18.
Alder, V. xiv. xxi. VI. xvi. III.
  26. IV. 7. 11. V. 31. IX. 16.
  X. 1.
Amcranth, VII. 24.
Anemone, V. iii. IV. 10. V. 20.
Apple tree, V. xv. VI. ii. IV. 4.
  14. 23.
Apricot, IV. 1. 6. 16. 22.
Archangel, I. 2. 3. VI. 16. 25.
Arfmart, VI. 3. VII. 20.
Afh, V. xxi. IV. 18. 22. V. 6.
  20. IX. 20. 22.
Afp, XII. xxiii. IV. xix. V. xx.
  III. 21. IV. 25. V. 14. X. 1.
  22.
Afparagus, VII. 16.
Afphodel, VII. ii.
Affarabacca, VI. ii. xiii.
Avens, VI. ii. xiii. V. 28.

B.

Barberry, V. xiii. VI. viii. IV. 12.
  X. 1.
Barley, IV. xvi. V. xiii. VII. vii.
  VIII. xvi. V. 6. VI. 28. VIII. 3.
Bafil, VII. x.
Bay, III. 11. V. 1. IX. 10. 29.
Beam tree, VI. xv.
Bean, IV. 29. VII. 20.
Bees, III. 11. IV. 10.
Bedftraw, VII. vi. VII. 8. VIII. 1.
Beech, V. xvi. IV. 21. VII. 2.
Bellflower, VI. xi. VII. 11.
Betony, VII. x. IV. 27. V. 5. VI.
  13 VII. 4.
Bilberry, VI. vii. xxix. VII. viii.
Bindweed, VII. i. iv. IV. 25.
  VI. 25. VII. 27.
Birch, V. xiii. IV. 1. 27. IX. 11.
Birds, VIII. iv.
Bittern. IV. 4.

Black cap, IV. 28.

Blackbird, IX. 27. X. 7.
Bluebottle, VI. xxii. VI. 28.
Bramble, V. vii. VI. vii. IV. 3.
  V. 24. VI. 5. VII. 22. IX. 11.
  30.
Brafs nights, VI. xxi.
Bream, V. xxx.
Briar, VI. xv. VII. vii. IV. 4. X. 1.
Brooklime, V. 30.
Broom, IV. 18. 22. 23. VI. 9.
Bryony, VI. xxviii. IV. 27. V.
  20. 30. X. 1.
Buckbean, IV. 22.
Buckwheat, VI. 7.
Bugle, V. xxx. IV. 29.
Buglofs, V. 12. VI. 6.
Bur, IV. xxx.
Burdock, VII. ix. VII. 28. VIII.
  12.
Burnet, VII. vii.
Buttercups, VI. 14.
Butterfly, IV. vii.
Butterwort, V. xxx.

C.

Camomile, VI. xi.
Campion, VI. xiv. xxviii. IV. 22.
  V. 27.
Carrot, VII. vi. VII. ii.
Catchfly, V. xxx. VI. xiii.
Cats foot, V. ix. xxvii.
Cedar, IV. 17.
Celandine, V. xxvii. V. 5. 10.
Chaffinch, II. 16. IX. 16.
Cherry tree, V. xv. xxv. xxviii.
  III. 29, IV. 8.
Chervil, VII. vii. V. 28. VI. 5.
Chefnut, V. xvi. IV. 1. 16. 28. V.
  9. 12. X. 6.
Chickweed, VIII. i. I. 26.
Chriftopher herb, VI. vii.
Cicely, V. xxv. IV. 25.
Cinquefoil, V. xvi. VI. xi. xiv.
  xviii. xx. VI. 12.
Ciftus, VI. xx.
Clary, VIII. 14.
Cleavers, IV. 3. V. 13.

               Clover 2

INDEX.

Clover, VII. x. V. 27. VI. 27.
Cockle, VII. v. VI. 13.
Cold, XII. v. xv.
Coltsfoor, IV. 12.
Columbine, VI. vii. V. xxv.
Comfrey, V. vii.
Cowflips, V. 4.
Crab, IV. 23.
Crakeberry, IV. xxx.
Cranes bill, V. xxvii. xxx. VI. v.
　ix. xi. IV. 27. V. 15.
Crefles, V. 30.
Crow, X. 2.
Crowfoot, VI. vii. IV. 28. V. 14.
Cuckow, V. xii. VII. xv. IV. 17.
Cuckow flower, V. xxviii. IV. 18.
　V. 20. 30.
Curlew, VIII. 14.
Currants, V. xxv. VII. ix. II.
　25. III. 29. IV. 3. 13. 25. VI.
　30.

D.

Daffodil, V. xv. IV. 1.
Daify, VI. xvii. I. 26.
Dakerhen, IV. x.
Dandelion, IV. x. IV. 3. 10.
Darnel, VI. vii.
Devils bit, VIII. iv. VII. 28.
　VIII. 21.
Dewberry, VI. xxiv.
Dove, III. 5. VII. 30. X. 10.
Dropwort, VI. xxii.
Duck, IV. vii.

E.

Earth nut, V. 20.
Elder, V. iv. VI. xiv. xxix. VII.
　xvii. II. 4. III. 29. IV. 11.
　12. 17. 25. VI. 2. 6. X. 1. 9.
Elecampane, VII. xxiv. VII. 24.
Elm, V. viii. xv. IV. 1. 10. 12.

F.

Fennel, VII. 9.
Fern, VIII. xxviii. IX. 20.
Feverfew, VI. xxix. IV. 10. V. 25.
Fieldfare, IV. 23. IX. 25.
Fig tree, IX. iv. IV. 6. 21. 22. VII.
　11.
Filberd, V. ix. IV. vii.
Fir, VI. i. IV. 18. 21. 22. 25. V.
　4. 7. VI. 16. IX. 11.
Flax, VI. vii. xxiv. VII. 20.

Fleabane, VII. iv. xiii.
Flixweed, IV. 14. VI. 6.
Flower de luce, VI. 2.
Foxglove, VII. iv.
Frog, IV. xi. xii.
Furze, IV. 22. 24. VII. 6. IX.
　16.

G.

Game black, IV. vi.
Gentian, V. xxii.
Germander, V. xxx. IV. 26.
Gladdon, VII. vi.
Goat fucker, VI. 5. VIII. 15. 17.
Golden rod, VI. xxiv. VII. xv.
　VIII. 26.
Goldilocks, V. xxvi.
Goofeberry, II. vii. xx. 25. IV.
　6. 13. 25.
Goule, V. xiv. VIII. 26.
Grafs, IV. xv. V. xx. VI. iv. vii.
　xvi. xviii. xxviii. VII. v. xxii.
　III. 21. V. 13. VI. 7. 21. VII.
　2. 13. IX. 5.
Greenhoufe, V. viii. xxiv. VIII.
　xxviii. X. vi.
Gromil, VII. 2.
Groundfel, V. xvii.

H.

Harebells, IV. 26.
Harts tongue, VII. xxii.
Hafel, IV. xii. I. 23. II. 22. IX.
　10.
Hawkweed, VI. xxvii. xxix. VII.
　xvi.
Hay harveft, VII. vii. xvi.
Heat, VI. xxix.
Heath, VI. ix.
Hedges, VI. xxi.
Hellebore, VII. ii.
Hemlock, VI. 16. 17.
Hemp, VII. xi.
Hen, VII. xx.
Henbane, VI. xii. V. 26.
Herring, IX. 17.
Holly, I. 23. IV. 3. 24. 26. X. 1.
Honeyfuckle, IV. xv. V. xxx. II.
　23. X. 26.
Hops, VII. vi. IV 14. IX. 20.
Horehound, VII. ix. x. VI. 22.
　VIII. 7. 12.

Hornbeam,

I N D E X.

Hornbeam, V. vi. III. 29. IV. 10.
13. 25.
Hot beds, IV. xi. xix.
Hounds tongue, IV. 10,
Hyffop, VII. xi.

I.

Jack by the hedge, V. xxv. IV.
10. 17.
Ice, V. 4.
Jeffamine, IV. 28. VII. 11.
Iron nights, VIII. xxviii.
Juniper, IV. 8. 28.
Iva, X. xxviii.
Ivy, V. 26. VII. 9. IX. 11.
Ivy, ground, IV. 16.

K.

Keftrell, IV. xii.
Knapweed, VI. xxii. VII. i. vi.
xxii. VI. 28. VII. 13.

L.

Laburnum, IV. 13.
Lady's mantle, V. xxv.
Langue de boeuf. VII. xvi.
Lapwing, IV. vi.
Larch, III. 29.
Lark, III. xxix. II. 4. IX. 25.
X. 10. 14. 24.
Larkfpur, VI. 23.
Lavender, VII. 6.
Laurel, III. 11. IV. 13. 16. IX.
20.
Lauruftinus, I. 23. III. 1. IV. 4.
VII. 22.
Lead nights, V. xxiv.
Lilac, V. xiv. VI. viii. xxv. IV.
7. 9. 27. VI. 2.
Lilly, IV. xvii. V. xxx. VI. xiv.
xvi. xviii. VII. vii. V. 3. VII.
10. 11.
Lilly day, VI. xx.
Lime, V. xxi. VII. ii. IV. 12. 18.
VII. 13.
Liquorice, VI. xxiv.
Loofeftrite, VI. xxii.
Liverwort, VI. xvi.

M.

Mallow, VII. xii. IV. 13. VI. 6.
15. VIII. 15.
Maple, IV. 6. 18. V. 11.
Marjoram, VII. x. xi.

Marvel, VII. xvi.
Marygold, V. xx. VI. 29. IV. 16.
VI. 23.
Mayweed, VI. xxiii. VI. 6.
Meadow fweet, VII. v. IV. 22.
VI. 12. 27.
Medic, VI. xxvii.
Melilot, VIII. i.
Mercury, V. i. IV. 12. 24.
Mezereon, IV. xv.
Milkwort, V. xxv. V. 15.
Milleria, XI. ii.
Mint, VII. xv. VII. xxviii. VIII.
vii. ix.
Moneywort, VI. iv. V. 25.
Moonwort, VI. xxiv.
Mofcatel, V. viii.
Moffes, IV. i. XI. 5.
Motherwort, VII. vii.
Mugwort, V. 1. VII. 16.
Mulberry, IX. i. IV. 18. V. 14.
20.
Mullein, VII. i. ii. VI. 22. VII.
11.
Muftard, V. 16.

N.

Narciffus, IV. 1.
Nettle, VI. xxv. IV. 25. V. 6. VI.
9. VIII. 7.
Nightingale, V. xv. IV. 9. VI. 15.
Nightfhade, VI. xviii. xxiv. VII.
x. V. 18. 21. VII. 4. 30. X. 1.
Nuthatch, VIII. 7.

O.

Oak, V. xxi. IV. 7. 18. V. 6. 20.
Oats, VI. 28.
Onion, VIII. v.
Orach, IX. xxii. VIII. 17.
Orange, V. xiv. VI. xxiv. VII.
viii.
Orchis, VI. vii. xv. xx. xxii.
Orpine, VIII. i. VIII. 7.
Ofier, V. vii. xiii.
Oxeye, VI. xxix.

P.

Paris herb, VI. vii.
Parfley, VI. 21. VII. 6. 10.
Parfnep, VII. i. III. 28. VI. 3.
13. 22. VIII. 1.
Partridge, II. 22, VII. 18.

Peach,

I N D E X:

Peach, IV. 6. 16.
Peacock, VI. xxix.
Pear, V. xxvi. IV. 6. 18.
Pearlwort, VII. 2.
Pease, V. xxviii. VI. xxix. IV. 29. VIII. 21.
Peiony, VI. i. xvi.
Pellitory, V. 23.
Pennyroyal, VII. 22.
Pennywort, VI. 27.
Pepper, wall, VI. xx. VII. xv.
Phyllerea, IV. 22.
Pike, IV. x.
Pilewort, IV. xv. III. 28.
Pimpernel, VI. 2.
Pine, VII. x.
Pink, VI. xvii. xxix. VII. viii. VII. 7.
Plantain, V. xxviii. VI. v. IV. 26. VII. 1. 24.
Plane tree, IV. 14. 21.
Plumb tree, V. xxviii. IV. 6. 16.
Polyanthus, V. i.
Pondweed, VI. viii.
Poplar, IV. xxx. V. xvi. IV. 21. 22.
Poppy, VI. xxiv. VII. vii. VI. 7. 22.
Potatoe, VII. xi.
Primrose, V. xv. VII. v. III. 29.
Privet, V. xiv. X. 24.

Q.
Quicken tree, VI. iii. IV. i. xiii. V. vi. VI. iii.
Quince, IV. 10. 28. V. 13.

R.
Radish, VI. 3.
Ragweed, IV. 12.
Rampions, VI. xvi. VII. i.
Ramsons, V. 6.
Rasberry, IV. 13. 28. VI. 6. 24. VII. 11.
Rattle, VII. vii. V. 4.
Redstart, IV. 16.
Rest harrow, VII. vi. VII. 11.
Rhapontic, VI. xvi.
Robert herb, VI. xiv. IV. 23.
Robin, VIII. 26.
Roche, V. xxv.
Rocket, VI. 25.

Rook, II. 12. III. 2. VI. 21. VIII. 12. 17. X. 7.
Rose, V. xv. VI. xv. VII. vii. VIII. vii. V. 11. VI. 6.
Rosemary, I. 5. IV. 22. VI. 24.
Rue, VII. iii. VIII. 1.
Rupture wort, V. xxix.
Rush, V. xxx.
Rye, V. xxv. VI. xviii. VIII. iv. V. 21. VI. 21.

S.
Saffron, IV. xii. VII. xviii. VIII. xxviii.
Sage, VII. viii.
Saint John's wort, VI. xxix. VII. vi. xii. IV. 27. VI. 22.
Sallow, III. xix. V. xvi. X. xxviii. III. xi. IV. 6. 7. X. 5.
Salmon, V. xxi. xxviii.
Sampire, IX. xvii.
Sanicle, VI. 8.
Saw-wort, VII. xv.
Saxifrage, V. iii. xxvi. VI. xviii. V. 6. VI. 9. VII. 28.
Scabius, VI. xxix. VI. 12.
Seeds, IX. xiv.
Self heal, VI. xxii. VI. 21.
Serpents, IV. vi.
Sheep, V. iii.
Shoots, VI. 28. VII. 11.
Silverweed, VII. 4.
Smallage, VIII. 29.
Smelt, IV. xxi.
Sneezewort, VI. xxix. VII. vii.
Snow, V. xviii. IV. 29.
Snowdrops, IV. xii. I. 26.
Soapwort, VII. xxii. VIII. 1.
Solomon's seal, V. 10.
Sorrel, V. xiii. IV. 16.
Sowing, V. viii. xiii.
Spearwort, VI. xvii. VII. 6.
Speedwell, VII. v. III. 26.
Spider, IV. vi.
Spikenard, VII. xxiii.
Spindle tree, V. xiv. X. 9.
Spurge, IV. xxv.
Spurrey, I. 26. V. 31.
Star of Bethlehem, IV. xv.
Starling, V. vii.
Steel nights, II. xxii.
Stitchwort,

Stitchwort, IV. 22. V. 20. VII. 6.
Stonecrop, VII. vi. xiv. VII. 13.
Strawberry,VI.xxvi.IV.13.VII.9
Succory, VII. xii. VI. 28;
Sundew, VII. x.
Swallow, V. ix. IX. xvii; IV. 6.
   IX. 21.
Swan, V. ix. IX. xvii.
Sycomore, IV. 13; 25;
   T.
Tanfey, VI. xvi. VII. xv. III.
   29. V. 26. VII. 8. VIII. 5;
Tare, VI. 6.
Teafel, VII. xviii. VII. 29.
Thermometer, II. 20. 25. 26. III.
   2. 28. IV. 20. 29. V. 4. 30.
   VI. 19. 25. VII. 8. 15. VIII.
   8. 16. IX. 10. 16. X. 6.
Thiftle, VI. xxii. VII. ix. x. xi.
   xvii. xxi. xxvii. VII. 29. VIII.
   12.
Thorn, V. iv. xv. xxviii. VI. xv.
   xvii. III. 29. IV. 18. 22. 28.
   V. 10. VI. 5. X. 2.
Throatwort, VI. xxix. VII. ii. vi.
Thyme, VI. 3.
Thrufh, II. 16. III.4. IX. 29.
Toad flax, VI. xxviii.
Tormentil, VI. ii. IV. 22. V. 5.
Touch me not, VII. xviii.
Travellers joy, IX. 2.
Trefoil, VI. vii.
Tulip, V. xxv.
Tulip tree, IV. 16. V.4.
Turkey, IV; xv. V; 15;

Turneps, IV. 15.
Tway blade, VI. xxvi. V. 5.
   V.
Valerian, VI. xvii. V. 4. VI. 12.
Vervain, VI. 17.
Vetch, VI. xii. xvii. xxii. xxiv.
Vine, IV. 15. VI. 6. 25.
Violet, IV. xii. V. iii. vii. VII.
   xxvi. III. 28. IV. 18. V. 3. 20.
   VII. 2.
Viper, VIII. xxix.
   W.
Wagtail, IV. xii. V. iii. IX.
   xvii. II. 12.
Wallflower, IV. 2.
Wallnut, IV. 14. V. 15.
Wheat, IV. 3. VI. 12. 21. 25.
   VII. 11. VIII. 21.
Wheat ear, V. iii.
Whorts, V. iii.
William, fweet, V. xxiv.
Willow, IV. xxi. IV. 1. 7. 10.
   17. VII. 11.
Willow herb, VI. xxii. xxiv. xxvi.
   VII. i. ii. xii. VI. 13. VII. 18.
   28. VIII. 21. IX. 2.
Woad, VI. xxix. VI. 25.
Woodbind, VII. xii. VI. 15.
Woodcock, X. 22.
Wormwood, VIII. xiv. IX. vi. IV.
   9. VIII. 9.
   Y.
Yarrow, VI. xxiii. VII. vi. VI.
   18.
Yew tree, III. xxix. IV. 24.

Z

T H E

THE

SWEDISH PAN.

~~~~~~~~~~~~~~~~~~~~~ ❉ ~~~~~~~~~~~~~~~~~~~~~

THE

SWEDISH PAN.

BY

NICOLAS HASSELGREN.

Upſal, 1749. Decem. 9.

Amænit. Academ. vol. 2.

§. I.

THE antients attributed the paſtoral life to *Pan*, the care of flowers to *Flora*, hunting to *Diana*, and the cultivation of grain to *Ceres*. We, tho' acknowledging only one Deity, who governs all things, yet often uſe theſe names to denote the ſubject we undertake to treat upon. What word is now more known among botaniſts than the word *Flora*; by which they mean all thoſe plants, which grow within a certain compaſs of ground; as our Fauna Suecica

Z 3   takes

takes in all thofe animals, which are natives of
Sweden ? For a like reafon we have entitled this
fmall tract the *Swedifh Pan*; intending thereby
to denote the five domeftic quadrupeds, which
live upon plants growing in Sweden ; or the de-
vouring army of *Pan*, which lays wafte the provinces of the *Swedifh Flora*. We choofe by this
means to avoid a prolix definition, which is always difagreeable for the title of a book.

§. 2.

The paftoral life, by the teftimony of both
facred, and prophane hiftory, is nearly as old
as man himfelf; fo that i would willingly derive
the knowledge, which i am going to deliver, from
the moft ancient times. But altho' plants have
been conftantly obvious to the eyes of every man;
yet i am obliged to declare, that we have nothing delivered down to us in any book concerning the kinds of plants proper for the different kinds of cattle ; fo that i may be fure of
not difgufting my reader with ftale matter new
dreffed up. For the whole of what i prefent to
him is new.—Our illuftrious prefident in his
journey thro' Dalecarlia ann. 1734, made the
firft attempt this way, as may be feen Flor.
Lapp.

Lapp. p. 158: where he fays thus. ' In my
' journey thro' Dalecarlia, when we had climbed
' up the mountains, and were got into Norway,
' my fellow travellers being tired, and afleep, i
' wandered about in a difmal wood, and per-
' ceived that the horfes eafily diftinguifhed
' wholefome from noxious food; for being very
' hungry, they devoured all forts of plants, ex-
' cept the following; *meadow fweet, valerian,*
' *lilly of the valley, angelica, loofe-ftrife, marfh-*
' *cinquefoil, cranes bill, hellebore, monks-hood,* and
' many fhrubs. This gave me a hint to re-
' commend to the curious, that they would fet
' about examining what plants fuch animals, as
' live on vegetables, viz. *the cow,* the *fheep,* the
' *goat,* the *deer,* the *horfe,* the *hog,* the *monkey*
' and their fpecies will not touch. An examina-
' tion which would not be without its ufe, were
' it properly made.' Notwithftanding this re-
commendation no enquiry was made, till our
prefident returned home from his travels thro'
forreign countries, and made a progrefs thro'
our own provinces. Afterwards profeffor Kalm,
that worthy difciple of fo great a mafter, follow-
ed his example; fo that in his journey to Bahus
we find mention made of fome plants, which
cattle either eat, or refufe. Ann. 1747 and

Z 4   1748

1748 our prefident undertook with great diligence not only to make experiments himfelf,
but to excite his difciples, and auditors to do the
fame ; of which number i was one. Thus at
laft many experiments were made, and repeated, efpecially by D. D. Hagftrom, Mag.
E. G. Liidbeck, E. Ekelund, J. G. Wahlbom,
L. Montin, F. Oldbers, J. C. Forfkahl, A.
Fornander ; not to mention others, who ftrove,
as it were, to out-do one another in finding the
plants, which were fuitable to different animals,

§. 3.

The difficulty however of examining all the
Swedifh plants, and getting animals proper for
experiments, which ought all to be repeated,
has hindered us from being able to give a
compleat work on this fubject. But the greateft part, and the moft common vegetables of
Sweden being now determined by us ; what is
wanting may be fupplied from time to time.
We hinted that animals proper for experiments,
which ought to be taken from among *cows*,
goats, *fheep*, *horfes*, and *fwine*, are difficult to be
found, for thefe reafons ; firft, becaufe fome
plants are eaten by them in the fpring, which

they
2

they will not touch all the fummer; when they are apt to grow rank in tafte, and fmell, and become ftalky and hard. Thus many people eat the *nettle* in the fpring; but who could bear it afterwards? Again, becaufe fome kinds of animals eat the flower, and will not eat the ftalks; others eat the leaves and will not eat the ftalks. N. B. When they eat the leaves, we fay in general they eat the plant, otherwife there would be few graffes they could be faid to eat. Œcon. Nat. Next, the animals ought not to be over hungry, when we make our experiments, if we intend to make them properly. For they will greedily devour moft kinds of plants at fuch a time, which they will abfolutely refufe at another. Thus when they come immediately out of the houfe, they are not fit to make experiments upon; for then they are ravenous after every green thing that comes in their way. The beft method is to make the experiments when their bellies are almoft full, for they are hardly ever fo intirely. Moreover the plants ought not to be handled by fweaty hands; fome animals will refufe the moft pleafing, and tafteful in that cafe. We ought to throw them on the ground, and if we find the animal refufes to eat them, we muft mix them

with

with others that we know they like ; and if they
ftill refufe them, we have a fure proof; efpecially if the fame be tryed with many individuals.

§. 4.

Our views do not extend beyond the Swedifh
plants, and that for the fake of our own œconomy. Let forreigners look to that part which
concerns themfelves, and thus our work will be
confined within moderate bounds. We can produce above 2000 certain experiments, fome of
which were repeated ten times over, fome twice
as often. If we take the *Flora Suecia* Holm.
1745. and put to any herb the generical name,
adding the number, and fome epithet by way
of difference, our work will be very much
abridged.

§. 5.

It is manifeft that the vegetable world was intended for the fupport of the animal world; infomuch that altho' not a few animals are carnivorous, yet thefe animals which they devour
cannot fubfift without vegetables. In this fpe-

culation

culation we behold with admiration the wifdom
of the Creator, which has made fome vegetables
abfolutely difagreable to fome animals that live
upon plants, while thefe plants are agreeable to
others. And there are plants, which are poifonous to fome animals, which are very wholefome to others, and on the contrary. This did
not happen by chance, but was contrived for
wife purpofes. For if the Author of nature
had made all plants equally grateful to all kinds
of quadrupeds, it muft neceffarily have happened, that one fpecies of them being remarkably increafed, another fpecies muft have pe-
rifhed with hunger, before it could have got
into better pafture; the vegetables being confumed over a large tract of ground. But as it
is ordained every fpecies muft by force leave
certain plants to certain animals, fo that they
always find fomething to live upon, till they
meet with better pafture; in the like manner we
find it contrived in relation to the plants themfelves, which do not all grow in the fame countrey, and climate; but every plant has its place
appointed by the Creator, in which it grows
more abundantly, than any where elfe. From
hence we may obferve, that thofe animals,
which chiefly live upon particular plants, chiefly
abound

abound in certain places. Thus the *lichen* or
liverwort, Fl. 980. is found in greateſt plenty
on the cold alps, and therefore the *rhen deer*,
which all winter live moſtly upon this plant,
are obliged to live there. The feſtuca, Fl. 94.
which floriſhes and ſpreads moſt on dry paſtures,
draws the ſheep thither, which above all things
delight in that kind of graſs. The ſeeds of
the *dwarf birch*, Fl. 777. which afford the beſt
ſort of food to the *rough-legg'd partridge*, and the
Norway rat, Fn. 26. tempt them to dwell in
theſe northern parts of the world. *Camels hay*,
Mat. Med. 312. which above all plants, thrives
on looſe ſand, draws the camel to chooſe thoſe
barren places, as they there find food moſt
agreeable to them ; not to mention many other
ſimilar inſtances. Trees, whoſe heads ſhoot up
ſo high, that quadrupeds cannot eaſily reach
them, afford nouriſhment for that reaſon to
more numerous tribes of infects, as the *fallow*,
the *oak*, the *pear*, &c. The Creator, who moſt
wiſely eſtabliſhed this law, has as it were im-
printed it on the organs of animals, that they
might not offend againſt it thro' ignorance ;
and as every tranſgreſſion has its puniſhment
allotted, ſo alſo no offence againſt the law of
nature

nature can efcape. Animals, which violate this law are punifhed by difeafes or death; and hence we behold with admiration that brutes, which were defigned to be guided by inftinct, can by no means whatever be prevailed upon to act againft it. If by chance it happens that any animal offends this way, and fuffers for it, we vulgarly fay it has taken poifon; fo that ig-norant people wonder, not to fay murmur at the wife difpofition of the Creator, who has pro-duced fo many noxious plants; but without fufficient reafon, for no one plant in the world is univerfally poifonous, but all things are good, as they came from the hands of the Creator. Phyficians often mention that this or that plant is deadly, becaufe its particles are of a nature apt to wound the fibres of the body or corrupt the juices. But this is only refpectively to the fpecies of animals, e. g. the *fun-fpurge*, Fl. 536. has a milky juice, which caufes blotches in our fkin and hurts our fibres, and therefore it is faid to be poifonons; yet the *moth*, Fn. 825. almoft entirely lives upon this plant, and prefers it both for tafte and nourifhment to all others, as it thrives beft upon it. Thus one animal leaves that, which to itfelf is poifonous, to ano-ther animal, which feeds upon it delicioufly.

Long-

Long-leaved water hemlock will kill a *cow*, whereas the *goat* browſes upon it greedily. *Monks-hood* kills a *goat*, but will not hurt a *horſe*; and the *bitter almond* kills a *dog*, but is wholeſome food for *man*. *Parſley* is ,deadly ⁻to *ſmall birds*; while *ſwine* eat it ſafely; and *pepper* is mortal to *ſwine*, and wholeſome to *poultry*. *Thus every creature has its allotted portion.* Animals diſtinguiſh the noxious from the ſalutary by ſmell and taſte. Younger animals have theſe ſenſes more acute, and therefore are more nice in diſtinguiſhing plants. An empty ſtomach will often drive animals to feed upon plants, that were not intended for them by nature. But whenever this has happened they become more cautious for the future, and acquire a certain kind of experience; e. g. *the monks-hood*, which grows near Fahluna, is generally left untouched by all the animals, that are accuſtomed to theſe places; but if forreign càttle are brought thither and meet with this vegetable, they venture to take too large a quantity of it, and are killed [b]. The cattle that have

[b] The ſame thing has been told me by the countrey people in Herefordſhire in relation to *mcadow-ſaffron*, which grows in plenty in ſome parts of that county. Gmelin, Flor. Sibirica, p. 76. ſays that cattle eat the leaves of the *hellebore*, 40. when they firſt ſpring out of the grou ɩd, and are thereby killed.

been

been reared in the plains of Schonen,· and Weftrogothia, commonly fall into a dyfentery when they come into the woodland parts, becaufe they feed upon fome plants, which cattle ufed to thofe places have learned to avoid. In the fpring, when the *water hemlock* is under water, fo that the cows cannot fmell it, they dye in heaps ᶜ. But when the fummer comes on

and

ᶜ This affair is of fo much confequence to the farmer, that i think it right to tranfcribe a paffage out of Linnæus upon this fubject.

" When I arrived, fays he, at Tornea, the inhabitants complained of a terrible difeafe, that raged among the horned cattle, which upon being let into the paftures in the fpring dyed by hundreds. They defired that i would confider this affair, and give my advice what was to be done in order to put a ftop to this evil. After a proper examination i thought the following circumftances worth obferving.

1. That the cattle dyed as foon as they left off their winter fodder, and returned to grazing.

2. That the difeafe diminifhed as the fummer came on, at which time, as well as in the autumn, few dyed.

3. That this diftemper was progagated irregularly, and not by contagion.

4. That in the fpring the cows were driven into a meadow near the city, and that they chiefly dyed there.

5. That the fymptoms varied much, yet agreed in this, that the cattle, upon grazing indifcriminately on all forts of herbs, had their bellies fwelled, were feized with convulfions, and in a few days expired with horrible bellowings.

6. That

and has dryed the ground, they are very care-full not to touch it. It is alfo true, that all vegetables prohibited by nature to particular animals are not equally pernicious; and therefore though through neceffity and hunger they eat them,

6. That no man dared to flea the recent carcafes, as they found by experience, that not only the hands of fuch as attempted it, but their faces too had been inflamed, and mortified, and that death had enfued.

7. The people enquired of me, whether there were any kinds of poifonous fpiders in that meadow, or whether the water which had a yellowifh tint was not noxious.

8. That it was not a murrain was clear, becaufe the dif-temper was not contagious, and becaufe that diftemper is not peculiar to the fpring. I faw no fpiders but what are common all over Sweden ; and as to the water, the fediment at the bottom, that caufed the yellownefs, was nothing but what came from iron.

9. I was fcarcely got out of the boat, which carried me over the river into the meadow, before i gueffed the real caufe of the difeafe. For i there beheld the *long-leaved water hemlock*. My reafons for gueffing this were as follow.

10. Becaufe in that meadow, where the cattle firft fell ill, this poifonous plant grows in great plenty, chiefly near the banks of the river. In other places it was fcarce.

11. The leaft attention will convince us that brutes fhun whatever is hurtfull to them, and diftinguifh poifonous plants from falutary by natural inftinct ; fo that this plant is not eat by them in the fummer, and autumn, which is the reafon that in thofe feafons few cattle dye, viz. only fuch as either accidentally, or preffed by extreme hunger, eat of it.

12. But

them, yet they do not immediately dye; but it is certain that they cannot have from thence good and proper nourifhment.

§. 6.

The end of this kind of knowledge is not

12. But when they are let into the paftures in fpring, partly from their greedinefs after frefh herbs, and partly from the emptinefs and hunger which they have undergone during a long winter, they devour every green thing which comes in their way. It happens moreover that herbs at this time are fmall, and fcarcely fupply food in fufficient quantity. They are befides more juicy, are covered with water, and fmell lefs ftrong, fo that what is noxious is not eafily difcerned from what is wholefome. I obferved likewife, that the radical leaves were always bitten, the others not; which confirms what I have juft faid.

13. I faw this plant in an adjoining meadow mowed along with grafs for winter fodder; and therefore it is not wonderfull, that fome cattle, tho' but a few, fhould dye of it in winter.

14. After i left Tornea i faw no more of this plant till i came to the vaft meadows near Limmingen, where it appeared along the road, and when i got into the town i heard the fame complaints, as at Tornea, of the annual lofs of cattle with the fame circumftances.

15. It would therefore be worth while to eradicate carefully thefe plants, which might eafily be done, as they grow in marfhy grounds; and are not hard to find, as they grow by the fides of pools or rivers. Or if this could not be done, the cattle fhould not be fuffered to go into fuch places, at leaft during the fpring. For i am perfuaded, that later in the year they can diftinguifh this plant by the fmell alone.

A a   bare

bare curiofity, although were this the cafe every part of knowledge, which fets forth the ftupendous works of the Creator, is never to be looked upon as of no confequence. On the other hand we do not pretend to gain any medicinal advantages from thefe fpeculations, namely, to be able from hence to conclude, that this or that plant is noxious to man, becaufe it is fo to this or that brute animal. Nor do we for that reafon approve of Wepfer's experiments upon dogs, and other animals, as if any knowledge can be thence gained in regard to man. No, the end we aim at is merely œconomical.

α. From thefe experiments we may know whether certain paftures afford good nourifhment for this or that fpecies of animals. We fee e. g. *heifers* wafte away in enclofures, where the *meadow-fweet* grows in abundance, and covers the ground fo that they can fcarce make their way through it ; the countrey people are amazed, and imagine that the pafture is too rich for them ; not dreaming that the *meadow-fweet* affords them no nourifhment. Whereas the *goat*, which is bleating on the other fide of the hedge, is not fuffered to go in, though he longs to be browfing upon this plant, which to him is a moft delicate and nourifhing food.

β. From

β. From thefe experiments we may almoſt be ſure by affinity and analogy, whether mea-dows or paſtures are ſalutary or noxious to par-ticular animals; e. g. long experience has taught us that our *ſheep* take up poiſon in marſhy grounds, though no one till lately knew what was the particular poiſon. Yet the *ſpiderwort* 267. the *mouſe-ear ſcorpion graſs* 149. the *mer-cury* 823. the *ſun-dew* 257,8. the *hairy wood graſs* 287. the *leſſer ſpearwort* 458. the *butter-wort* 21. have evidently ſuſpicious marks[c]. I will therefore propoſe a new experiment. The *andromeda* Fl. Virgin. 160. is known to be a moſt rank poiſon to ſheep in Virginia. The *andromeda*, called by the people of New York *dwarf laurel*, Cold. Act. Upſal. 1743. p. 123. is very fatal to the ſheep in New York. Theſe two plants are of a different ſpecies, but of the ſame natural genus, and therefore have the ſame vertues. Amongſt us, eſpecially in the northern parts, the wild *roſemary*, *andromeda*

[c] There is great reaſon to think that what makes low grounds ſo noxious to ſheep is not the moiſture, but the plants that grow there. For it is obſerved by ſhepherds that the great danger to ſheep is immediately after a freſh ſpring of graſs, which i imagine is owing to their licking up the young and tender ſhoots of poiſonous plants, along with their proper food, not being able to diſtinguiſh them.

335. grows every where in marſhy grounds, which being of the ſame natural genus with the foregoing, we may reaſonably conclude that it deſtroys our ſheep. To this we may add, that it is on account of three other ſpecies of *andromeda* 336,7,8. which grow on the Lapland mountains, that the ſheep there never are healthy ; and laſtly although the *ciſtus ledon* 341. is not a ſpecies of *andromeda*, yet being of the ſame natural claſs, it is not unlikely but that this plant is far from affording good nouriſhment to ſheep. This conjecture gives our ſhepherds an unexpected opportunity of making experiments with their ſheep ; and indeed they cannot omit to do it without being juſtly blameable, ſince on this the health of their whole flock depends. It is particularly to be noted upon this occaſion, that the botany of America, a countrey ſo far disjoyned from us, gives a hint for conſidering things of the greateſt uſe, of which the antients did not ſo much as dream.

ꝛ. From hence the œconomiſt may truly judge of his meadows, and know that ſome are vaſtly preferable to others for certain animals. For although cattle, preſſed by neceſſity and hunger, will feed upon vegetables leſs gratefull to them ; yet it is not to be doubted but that they

they are not equally well nourifhed by thefe as by others. Thus the Dalecarlians are obliged in a fcarcity of wheat to fupport themfelves by *bread* made of the *bark* of the *pine* ; yet it does by no means follow from hence that this affords proper nourifhment. We fee that *horfes* in time of war, when preffed by extreme hunger, will eat *dead hedges*, but we cannot hence conclude, that wood is good food for them.

♪. The induftrious farmer may judge from hence, when he fows his meadows with hay feeds for pafture, that it is not indifferent what kinds of feeds he choofes, as the vulgar think. For fome are fit for *horfes*, others for *cows*, &c. *Horfes* are nicer in choofing than any of our cattle ; *filiquofe* and *filiculofe* plants particularly are not relifhed by them. *Goats* feed upon a greater variety of plants than any other cattle, but then they chiefly hunt after the extremities and flowers. *Sheep* on the contrary pafs by the flowers and eat the leaves. Not to mention the different difpofition in different animals as to grazing near the ground or not. The countreyman who underftands thefe things, and knows . how in confequence to difpofe of his grounds, and affign each kind of cattle to its propereft food, muft neceffarily have them more healthy

and

and fat, than he who is deftitute of thefe principles.   The good œconomift will obferve the
fame of his hay.   For although many herbs,
when dry, are eat, which when green would
be refufed, it does not follow from hence that
they yield good nourifhment.   Much might be
added concerning the propenfion of cattle to
this or that plant, which the compafs of this
fmall tract will not admit of; e. g. that *fheep*
above all things delight in the *feftuca* 95. and
grow fatter upon it than any other kind of
grafs ; that *goats* prefer certain plants, but
being led by an inftinct peculiar to themfelves,
they fearch more after variety, and do not long
willingly ftick to any one kind of food whatever;
that *geefe* are particularly fond of the feeds of
the *feftuca,* Fl. 90 ; that *fwine* greedily hunt
after the roots of the *bull-rufh* 40. while they
are frefh, but will not touch them when dry.
Hence it appears that it is in vain to contrive
engines to extract the roots of the *bull-rufh* out
of the water, and dry them for the ufe of thefe
animals in winter.   Becaufe thefe animals fpoil
the meadows, where the *fcorzonera* grows, in
order to come at its root, which they delight
in ; and alfo the fields, to get at the roots of
clowns-all-heal, the hufbandman imagines they
do

do good to his fields by ploughing the ground and eating the roots of *couch-grafs*, whereas they never touch them, but when preffed by the utmoft neceffity [d].

§. 7.

To give a view of my defign in a few words. I have difpofed the plants mentioned in the Flora Suecica according to their numbers; and to be as fhort as poffible, it was neceffary to add the generical name with a fhort and incompleat

[d] In the fame way with us it is a notion that prevails commonly that *cows* eat the *crow-foot* that abounds in many meadows, and that this occafions the butter to be yellow, from whence i fuppofe it is generally known by the name of the *butter-flower*. But this i believe is all a miftake, for i never could obferve that any part of that plant was touched by *cows* or any other cattle. Thus Linnæus obferves, Fl. Lapp. p. 195. that it was believed by fome people that the *marfh marygold* made the butter yellow, but he denies that cows ever touch that plant. Yet he thinks that all kinds of pafture will not give that yellownefs, and then obferves that the beft and yelloweft butter he knows, and which is preferred by the dealers in thofe parts to all other butter, was made where the *cow-wheat* grew in greater plenty than he ever faw any where elfe. This fhews how very incurious the countrey people are in relation to things they are every day converfant with, and which it concerns them fo much to know.

epithet,

epithet, which however may be illuftrated out of the Flora itfelf. I have diftinguifhed the cattle againft every plant into five columns. The firft of which contains *oxen*. The fecond *goats*. The third *fheep*. The fourth *horfes*. The fifth *fwine*. By the mark (1) i have denoted thofe plants which are eaten; by the mark (o) thofe which are not eaten; by both together thofe which are fometimes eaten, fometimes refufed; or are eaten when cattle are more ufed to them, and are more hungry, otherwife not.

§. 8.

Upon the firft view of this fubject the reader will perceive, that it is not treated compleatly, fo that every Swedifh plant is pointed out, and by what animals it is eaten. What generally happens upon breaking up old pafture lands, viz. that for the firft years it cannot be cleanfed from all ufelefs weeds, and be laid down fine like a garden, but will here and there have rough tumps and hard clods, unlefs we will let it lye fallow for a very long time; the fame or fomething like it has happened upon this occafion.

I am

I am apt to believe however that the reader will be better pleafed that I have opened this new fcene, than if I had waited longer in order to gain farther light. For fince there are many people here curious in botany and œconomy, i hope they will all lend a helping hand, that i may one day be enabled to give a more compleat edition of this piece[e].

[e] After this in the original follows a long table of experiments, of which i fhall only give a fmall fpecimen ; as the whole would increafe the bulk but not the value of this piece to fuch readers as this tranflation is intended for, fince they would neither know the plants by the names the author has given them, nor by any i could put in their room. However i fhall for curiofity give a fpecimen, and add the general refult of his experiments, juft as he has marked it at the end of his table ; which is as follows. ' Thus far,' fays he, ' we have given 2314 experiments. From thefe it appears ' that

Oxen eat	276	refufe	218	plants
Goats	449		126	
Sheep	387		141	
Horfes	262		212	
Swine	72		171	

' And thus thefe animals leave untouched 886 plants.
' Thefe animals will not eat any kind of *mofs*.
' The goats are very fond of the *algæ*.
' Some of them greedily devour the *fungi*, others will ' not tafte them. But we recommend farther trials in rela- ' tion to thefe matters.'

Then follows an account of fome trials made by Dr. Q. Hagftrom to the fame purpofe in relation to *rhen deer*,

but

but as they no ways concern us, i have omitted to mention them.

N. B. For the table i have chofen not to take fuch plants as occurred firſt in my author, but to feleƈt the graſſes of our own countrey, and have given Engliſh names to them of my own invention, the reaſon of which will appear in the following obſervations.

	O.	G.	S.	H.	Sw.
Spring grafs	I	I	I	I	-
Mat grafs	10	I	I	I	O
Canary grafs, *reed*	I	I	I	I	O
Cat's-tail, *meadow*	I	I	O	I	O
Fox-tail, *meadow*	10	I	I	I	10
———*flote*	I	I	I	I	O
Millet grafs	I	I	I	-	-
Bent grafs, *ſilky*	-	I	O	I	-
———*fine*	I	I	-	I	-
Hair grafs, *ſmall leaved*	I	I	I	I	-
———*water*	I	-	I	I	-
Meadow, *creeping*	I	I	I	I	O
———*annual*	I	I	I	I	I
———*great*	I	I	I	I	I
——— *narrow leaved*	I	I	I	I	I
———*common*	I	I	I	I	I
Cock's-foot grafs, *rough*	O	I	I	I	O
Dogs-tail grafs, *creſted*	-	-	I	-	-
———*blue*	-	I	I	I	O
Fefcue grafs, *flote*	O	I	I	I	10
———*purple*	I	I	I	I	-
———*ſheep's*	I	I	11	I	-
Brome grafs, *field*	I	I	I	I	-
———*ſpiked*	-	I	I	I	-
Oat grafs, *meadow*	I	I	I	I	-
——— *bearded*	-	10	-	-	-

2

Obſervations on GRASSES.

Obſervations on GRASSES.

AS the foregoing treatiſe contains ſome obſervations on graſſes [f], that are quite new,
and as this affair is of the utmoſt importance to
the huſbandman, i ſhall ſubjoyn ſome obſervations of my own relating to the ſame ſubjeſt.

It is wonderfull to ſee how long mankind has
neglečted to make a proper advantage of plants
of ſuch importanee, and which in almoſt every
countrey are the chief food of cattle. The farmer for want of diſtinguiſhing, and ſelečting
graſſes for ſeed, fills his paſtures either with
weeds, or bad, or improper graſſes ; when by
making a right choice, after ſome trials he might
be ſure of the beſt graſs, and in the greateſt
abundance that his land admits of. At preſent
if a farmer wants to lay down his land to graſs,

---

[f] *By graſſes are meant all thoſe plants, which have a round,
jointed and hollow ſtem, ſurrounded at each joint with a ſingle
leaf, long, narrow and pointed, and whoſe ſeeds are contained in
chaffy huſks. It appears by this definition, which is Ray's, that
all the kinds of grain, as wheat, oats, barley, &c. are properly
graſſes, and that the broad, the white, the hop, &c. clovers are
not graſſes, though ſo frequently called by that name.*

what

what does he do ? he either takes his feeds indif-criminately from his own foul hayrick, or fends to his next neighbour for a fupply. By this means, befides a certain mixture of all forts of rubbifh, which muft neceffarily happen ; if he chances to have a large proportion of good feeds, it is not unlikely, but that what he intends for dry land may come from moift, where it grew naturally, and the contrary ᵍ. This is fuch a flovenly

ᵍ *Since the firft edition of thefe tracts i have had feveral op-portunities of obferving inftances of this flovenly kind of hufbandry, and its effects. Inftead of covering the ground in one year with a good turf, i have feen it filled with weeds not natural to it, and which never would have fprung up, if they had not been brought there.*

Arguments are never wanting in fupport of ancient cuftoms, and i am no ftranger to the arguments, fuch as they are, which prejudice and indolence have made ufe of on this occafion.

1. Some fay then, that if you manure your ground properly, good graffes will come of themfelves. I own they will. But the queftion is how long it will be before that happens, and why be at the expence of fowing what you muft afterwards try to kill by manuring ? which muft be the cafe, as long as people fow all kinds of rubbifh under the name of hay feeds. Again, if the beft way is to let the ground take its chance, why is the farmer at the expence of procuring the feeds of the white, and broad clo-ver, which come up in almoft all parts of England fpontaneoufly ? but if this is allowed not to be the beft way in relation to clover of any kind, what reafon can be in nature, why grafs feeds only ought not to be fown pure?

2. Others

flovenly method of proceeding, as one would think could not poffibly prevail univerfally ; yet this is the cafe as to all graffes except the darnel grafs, and what is known in fome few counties by the name of the Suffolk grafs ; and this latter inftance is owing, i believe, more to the foil than any care of the hufbandman. Now would the farmer be at the pains of feparating once in his life half a pint, or a pint of the different kinds of grafs feeds [h], and take care

2. *Others fay, that it is better to have a mixture of different feeds. I will fuppofe this to be true. But cannot a mixture be had though the feeds be gathered, and feparated ? and is not a mixture by choice more likely to be proper, than one by chance ? efpecially after a fufficient experience has been had of the particular virtues of each fort, the different kinds of cattle each grafs is moft adapted to, the different grounds where they will thrive beft, &c. all which cicumftances are now in general wholly unknown, though of the utmoft confequence.*

3. *It is faid by fome, that weeds will come up along with the grafs. No doubt of it. Can any one imagine that grafs feeds fhould be exempted above from what happens to every other kind of feed. But i will venture to fay, that not near the quantity of weeds will fpring up which they imagine, if it be fown very thick. Men muft be very much put to it, when they make fuch objections as this laft, or indeed any of the others. I am almoft inclined to fay with a great writer, ' It is a fimple thing to ' take much pains to anfwer fimple objections.'*

[h] *I have had frequent experience how eafy it is to gather the feeds of graffes, having employed children of ten or eleven years*

old

care to fow them feparately; in a very little
time he would have wherewithal to ftock his
farm properly, according to the nature of each
foil, and might at the fame time fpread thefe
feeds feparately over the nation by fupplying

*eld feveral times, who have gathered many forts for me without
making any miftakes, after i had once fhewn them the forts i
wanted.*

*I have procured thus the creeping bent, the fine bent, the fheep's
fefcue, the crefted dog-tail, &c. in fufficient quantities to begin a
ftock, but for want of a proper opportunity of cultivating them
myfelf, or meeting with any one who had zeal enough to beftow
a proper care on them, my collections of this kind hitherto have
only proved that the fcheme is in itfelf feafible.*

*This very year 1761, a little boy by my direction gathered as
much of the crefted dog-tail in 3 hours by the fide of a road, as
when fhed, yielded upon weighing above a quarter of a pound
averdupois, perfectly free from hufks.   As this feed is fmall the
fkillfull will eafily judge how far fuch a quantity would go if
properly employed.*

*My very eftimable and ingenious friend Mr. Aldworth, who
was witnefs of the fact which i laft mentioned, at my defire ordered a fmall part of a meadow, near his feat at Stanlake,
which had better graffes and lefs mixed than the reft, to be left
unmowed till the feeds were fit for gathering.   This piece yielded
upon threfhing and fifting a full bufhel by meafure of almoft
pure feed of the crefted dog-tail.   In cafe any one fhould be inclined to follow this example, i think it highly neceffary to obferve that care muft be taken to mow the grafs before it fheds ;
that it be mowed very early in the morning before the dew is
off the ground, and that it ought not be fpread as in making hay,
but left as it falls from the fcythe a fufficient time, and then gently
turned over.*

the

the feed-fhops. The number of graffes fit for the farmer is, i believe, fmall; perhaps half a dozen, or half a fcore are all he need to culti- vate; and how fmall the trouble would be of fuch a tafk, and how great the benefit, muft be obvious to every one at firft fight. Would not any one be looked on as wild who fhould fow *wheat, barley, oats, rye, peas, beans, vetches, buck-wheat, turneps* and weeds of all forts to- gether? yet how is it much lefs abfurd to do what is equivalent in relation to graffes? does it not import the farmer to have good hay and grafs in plenty? and will cattle thrive equally on all forts of food? we know the contrary. Horfes will fcarcely eat hay, that will do well enough for oxen and cows. Sheep are parti- cularly fond of one fort of grafs, and fatten upon it fafter, than on any other in Sweden, if we may give credit to Linnæus. And may they not do the fame in England? How fhall we know till we have tryed? Nor can we fay that what is valuable in Sweden may be inferior to many other graffes in England; fince it ap- pears by the Flora Suecica that they have all the good ones that we have. But however this may be i fhould rather choofe to make experi- ments, than conjectures.

B b   I now

I now propofe to add a few obfervations on
fome of our graffes, as far as i have been able to
make any with fome appearance of probability;
but as there has reigned hitherto the greateft
confufion in the Englifh names of thefe moft
valuable plants, and as they have never been
properly ranged but by Linnæus, i fhall firft,
in imitation of that great author in his Flora
Suecica, give new generical names with trivial
ones to diftinguifh the fpecies of all our Englifh
graffes [i]. I mean all thofe which are found in
that author; as for the reft, fince fome are
omitted by him, their names may be eafily fupplyed when their genera are fettled by the
learned [k]. It happens very luckily, that our
common people know fcarce any of the graffes
by names, as far as i could ever find by converfing with farmers, hufbandmen, &c. fo that
fomething may be done to remove this confufion, if a lift of names be fettled and agreed

[i] Mr. Hudfon having thought proper to adopt my names
with fome alterations; and having cleared up many of the
fpecies of graffes in a better manner than has been done before; i have referred throughout to his Flora Britannica,
which is likely to be in the hands of all who are curious in
botany.

[k] This has fince been done in fome meafure in the afore-
mentioned Flora Britannica.

on

4

on by fuch as are likely to have influence fufficient in thefe matters. As to my own lift, it
is only meant as a hint for others to work upon.

In giving names i have had two things in
view. Firft to retain as much as poffible fuch
as have hitherto been ufed for fome fpecies of the
genus. Secondly, where that could not be done,
to give fuch as are of eafy and familiar pronun-
ciation to our common people, and at the fame
time approach as near as poffible to the Latin
names in found where they could not be in-
terpreted. This was done for the fake of the
learned for the more eafy recollecting the botanical name. Thus i have called the *aira hair*-
grafs, the *bromus brome*-grafs, &c. in others i
have merely tranflated the Latin name, as
alopecurus *fox-tail* grafs, cynofurus *dog-tail*
grafs, &c.

After thefe preliminary obfervations i hope
it will not be neceffary to make any apology for
the liberty i have taken. I am certain that till
names properly adapted to the purpofe be invented, we have little chance of feeing any general reformation made in this part of hufbandry; and even after this without fome perfon
properly qualified to direct the countrey people, and fhew them the graffes with their names,

nothing

nothing will come of that moſt uſeful doctrine delivered in the foregoing treatiſe of Haſſelgren [1]. But it is to be hoped that gentlemen at leaſt will not be ſo incurious as to remain ignorant of what imports them ſo much to know. Nor is the mere botaniſt leſs concerned in the ſucceſs of this ſcheme, for there is great reaſon to think that many of the graſſes are not thoroughly ſettled, varieties perhaps being put for different ſpecies [m]; now this uncertainty can never be better cleared up than by ſowing the ſame kind of feeds on different ſoils.

[1] Many people having expreſſed a deſire that i ſhould have plates of ſome of the profitable graſſes added to this piece, that moſt excellent man, the late Mr. Price of Foxley, whoſe extraordinary character i ſhall always revere, and do intend to give a ſketch of on ſome future occaſion, kindly condeſcended to employ his pencil, which in the opinion of the beſt judges was equal to things of a much ſuperior nature, in making me ſeveral drawings from the plants themſelves, and a very able hand has ſupplied the reſt and engraved them all.

[m] Thus Gmelin Flor. Lapp. mentions four of the meadow graſſes which he ſays have for a long time perplexed botaniſts of great reputation. And the editor of Ray's Synopſis, p. 402. doubts whether five graſſes which are put down as different by Petiver be not only varieties of a graſs mentioned before. I have many ſpecimens of this graſs in my collection differing in color, ſtature and outward aſpect, which yet moſt likely are of the ſame ſpecies.

A Table

A Table of Englifh G R A S S E S.

G E N U S 1.

VERNAL grafs, *Tab.* 1. Anthoxanthum *Odoratum* *H. 10. R. 398.1.

G E N U S 2.

MAT grafs   Nardus *Striƈta*

H. 20. R. 393.2.

G E N U S 3.

Manured   CANARY grafs Phalaris *Canarienfiṣ*

H. 20. R. 394.

Sea   CANARY   Phalaris *Arenaria*

H. 21. R. 398.4.

Reed   CANARY   Phalaris *Arundinacea*

H. 21. R. 400.1.

Ribband   CANARY   Phalaris *ibid. b. ibid.*

G E N U S 4.

Green   PANIC grafs   Panicum *Viride*

H. 21. R. 393.1.

Loofe   PANIC   Panicum *Crufgalli*

H. 22. R. 394.2.

Cock's-foot PANIC   Panicum *Sanguinale*

H. 22. R. 399.2.

Creeping   PANIC   Panicum *Daƈtylon*

H. 22. R. 399.1.

*N. B. H refers to the Flora Britannica of Mr. Hudfon.

B b 3   G E-

G E N U S 5.

Meadow CAT's-TAIL grafs Phleum *Pra-*
tenfe H. 22. R. 398.1.

Branched CAT's-TAIL Phleum *Paniculatum*
H. 23.

Bulbous CAT's-TAIL Phleum *Nodofum*
H. 23. R. 398.3

G E N U S 6.

Meadow FOX-TAIL grafs, *Tab.* 2. Alopecurus
Pratenfis H. 23. R. 396.1.

Field FOX-TAIL Alopecurus *Myofuroides*
H. 23. R. 397.

Bulbous FOX-TAIL Alopecurus *Bulbofus*
H. 24. R. 397.3.

Flote FOX-TAIL Alopecurus *Geniculatus*
H. 24. R. 396.2.

G E N U S 7.

FEATHER grafs Stipa *Pennata*
H. 24. R. 393.3.

G E N U S 8.

Smooth COCK's-FOOT grafs Dactylis *Cy-*
nofuroides H. 25. R. 393.4.

Rough COCK's-FOOT Dactylis *Glomeratus*
H. 25. R. 400.2.

G E N U S 9.

MILLET grafs Milium *Effufum*
H. 25. R. 402. 1.

G E-

GENUS 10.

Silky	BENT grafs	Agroftis *Spica venti*
	H. 26. R. 405.17.	
Brown	BENT	Agroftis *Canina*
	H. 26.	
Red	BENT	Agroftis *Rubra*
	H. 26. R. 394.4.	
Creeping	BENT	Agroftis *Stolonifera*
	H. 27. R. 402. 2.	
Marſh	BENT	Agroftis *Paluſtris*
	H. 27, R. 404.11.	
Fine	BENT *Tab. 3.*	Agroftis *Capillaris*
	H. 27. R. 402.4.	
Wood	BENT	Agroftis *Sylvatica*
	H. 28. R. 404.13.	
Small	BENT	Agroftis *Minima*
	H. 28. R. appendix.	

GENUS 11.

Creſted	HAIR grafs	Aira *Criſtata*
	H. 28. R. 396.3.	
Purple	HAIR	Aira *Cærulea*
	H. 29. R. 404.8.	
Water	HAIR	Aira *Aquatica*
	H. 29. R. 402.3.	
Turfy	HAIR	Aira *Cefpitofa*
	H. 29. R. 403.5.	

Bb 4   *Mountain*

Mountain	HAIR *Tab.* 4.	Aira *Flexuofa*
	H. 30. R. 407.8,9.	
Small-leaved	HAIR	Aira *Setacea*
	H. 30.	
Grey	HAIR	Aira *Canefcens*
	H. 30. R. 405.16.	
Early	HAIR	Aira *Præcox*
	H. 31. R. 407.10.	
Silver	HAIR *Tab.* 5.	Aira *Caryophillea*
	H. 31. R. 407.7.	

G E N U S 12.

	MELIC grafs Melica	*Nutans*
	H. 31. R. 403.6.	

G E N U S 13.

Middle	QUAKING grafs	Briza *Media*
	H. 32. R. 412.1.	
Small	QUAKING	Briza *Minor*
	H. 32. R. 412.2.	

G E N U S 14.

Water	MEADOW grafs	Poa *Aquatica*
	H. 32. R. 411.13.	
Common	MEADOW	Poa *Trivialis*
	H. 33. R. 409.2.	
Great	MEADOW *Tab.* 6.	Poa *Pratenfis*
	H. 33. R. 409. 3.	
Creeping	MEADOW	Poa *Compreffa*
	H. 33. R. 409.5.	

Narrow-

Narrow-leaved MEADOW	Poa *Anguſtifolia*	
H. 34. R. 409. 4.		
Bulbous MEADOW	Poa *Bulbofa*	
H. 34. R. 411.12.		
Hair-leaved MEADOW	Poa *Setacea*	
H. 34.		
Annual MEADOW *Tab.* 7.	Poa *Annua*	
H. 34. R. 408 1.		
Wood MEADOW	Poa *Nemoralis*	
H. 34.		
Sea MEADOW	Poa *Maritima*	
H. 35. R. 410.7.		
Hard MEADOW	Poa *Rigida*	
H. 35. R. 410.8.		
Spiked MEADOW	Poa *Loliacea*	
H. 35. R. 395.4.		

G E N U S 15.

Sheep's FESCUE grafs, *Tab.* 8.	Feſtuca *Ovina*
H. 36. R. 410.9.	
FESCUE	Feſtuca *Vivipara*
ibid. *b.*	
Hard FESCUE	Feſtuca *Duriufcula*
H. 36. R. 413.4.	
Purple FESCUE *Tab.* 9.	Feſtuca *Rubra*
H. 36.	
Barren FESCUE	Feſtuca *Bromoides*
H. 37. R. 415.13.	

Wall

Wall	FESCUE	Feſtuca *Myurus*
	H. 37. R. 411.16.	
Tall	FESCUE	Feſtuca *Elatior*
	H. 37. R. 411.15.	
Small	FESCUE	Feſtuca *Decumbens*
	H. 38. R. 408. 11.	
Flote	FESCUE *Tab.* 10.	Feſtuca *Fluitans*
	H. 38. R. 412.17.	
Spiked	FESCUE	Feſtuca *Loliacea*
	H. 38.	
Wood	FESCUE	Feſtuca *Sylvatica*
	H. 38. R. 394.	

G E N U S 16.

Field	BROME graſs	Bromus *Secalinus*
	H. 39. R. 413.5. 414.7,8.	
Corn	BROME	Bromus *Arvenſis*
	H. 39. R. 414.9.	
Upright	BROME	Bromus *Erectus*
	H. 39.	
Wall	BROME	Bromus *Ciliatus*
	H. 40. R. 413.2.	
Barren	BROME	Bromus *Sterilis*
	H. 40. R. 412.1.	
Tall	BROME	Bromus *Giganteus*
	H. 40. R. 415.11.	
Wood	BROME	Bromus *Ramoſus*
	H. 40. R. 415.10.	

Spiked

Spiked	BROME	Bromus *Pinnatus*
	H. 41. R. 392.	

GENUS 17.

Naked	OAT grafs	Avena *Nuda*
	H. 41. R. 389. *b:*	
Bearded	OAT	Avena *Fatua*
	H. 41. R. 389.7.	
Meadow	OAT	Avena *Pratenfis*
	H. 42. R. 405.1.	
Rough	OAT	Avena *Pubefcens*
	H. 42. R. 406.2.	
Tall	OAT	Avena *Elatior*
	H. 42. R. 406.4.	
Yellow	OAT	Avena *Flavefcens*
	H. 42. R. 407.5.	

GENUS 18.

Common	REED grafs	Arundo *Phragmites*
	H. 43. R. 401.1.	
Branched	REED	Arundo *Calamagroftis*
	H. 43. R. 401.2.	
Small	REED	Arundo *Epigeios*
	H. 43. R. 401.3.	
Sea	REED	Arundo *Arenaria*
	H. 43. R. 393.1.	

GENUS 19.

Perennial	DARNEL grafs	Lolium *Perenne*
	H. 44. R. 395.2.	

Annual

Annual DARNEL Lolium *Temulentum*

H. 44. R. 395.1.

G E N U S 20.

LYME grafs Elymus *Arenarius*

H. 44. R. 390.3.

G E N U S 21.

Common WHEAT grafs Triticum *Repens*

H. 45. R. 390.1.

Bearded WHEAT   Triticum *Caninum*

H. 45. R. 390.2.

Sea   WHEAT   Triticum*Junceum*

H. 45. R. 391.5.

G E N U S 22.

BARLEY grafs Hordeum *Murinum*

H. 46. R. 392.3.

G E N U S 23.

RYE grafs   Secale *Villofum*

H. 46. R. 392.4:

G E N U S 24.

Crefted DOG's-TAIL,grafs*Tab.*11.Cynofurus

Criftatus H. 47. R. 398.2. 399.3.

Rough DOG's-TAIL Cynofurus *Echinatus*

H. 47. R. 397.5.

Blue DOG's-TAIL Cynofurus *Cæruleus*

H. 47. R. 399.4.

Bearded DOG's-TAIL Cynofurus *Paniceus*

H. 47. R. 396.4.

G E-

Tab. 1.

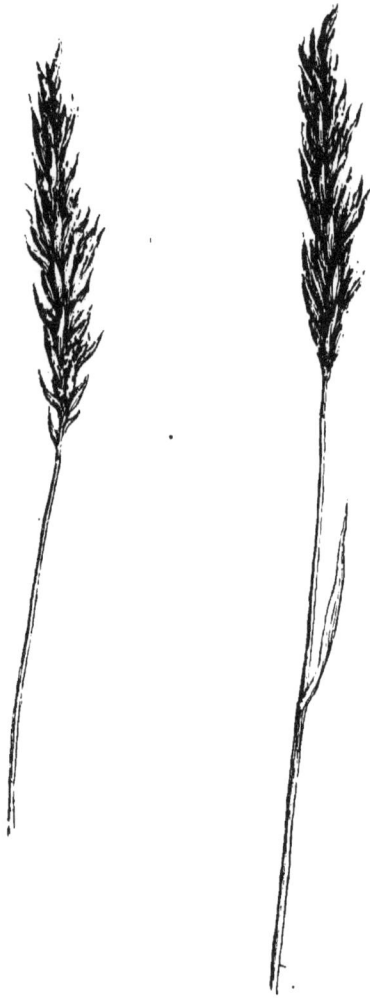

Vernal Grass.

Tab. 2.

R. Price delin. *Meadow Fox-tail Grass.*

GENUS 25.

SOFT grafs   Holcus *Lanatus*

H.   R. 404.14.

Genus the firſt. VERNAL. *Tab.* 1.

This graſs grows very commonly on dry hills, and likewiſe on ſound rich meadow land. It is one of the earlieſt graſſes we have, and from its being found on ſuch kinds of paſtures as ſheep are fond of, and from whence excellent mutton comes, it is moſt likely to be a good graſs for ſheep paſtures. It gives a grateful odor to hay.

ADDITION. *This graſs i have found on all kinds of grounds, from the moſt ſandy and dry to the moſt ſtiff and moiſt, and even in bogs. It is very plentiful in the beſt meadows about London, viz. towards Hampſtead and Hendon. It is very eaſy to gather, as i have found by experience; as it ſheds its ſeeds upon the leaſt rubbing.*

Genus the ſixth. *Meadow* FOX-TAIL. *Tab.* 2.

This graſs as well as the foregoing is found in great plenty in our beſt meadows about London, and i believe makes very good hay. Linnæus ſays that it is a proper graſs to ſow on grounds that have been drained.

ADDITION. *I am informed that the beſt*

hay which comes to London is from the meadows, where this grafs abounds. I faw this fpring a meadow not far from Hampftead, which confifted of this grafs chiefly with fome of the vernal grafs and the corn brome grafs. This grafs is fcarce in many parts of England, particularly Herefordfhire, Berkfhire and Norfolk. It might be gathered at almoft any time of the year from hay ricks, as it does not fhed its feeds without rubbing, which is the cafe of but few graffes.

Water FOX-TAIL.

This is alfo found in the meadows about town, that are found but lye under water in the winter, and perhaps might be proper to fow on fuch grounds.

Genus the tenth. *Marfh* BENT.

ADDITION. *This grafs grows very common- ly in moift grounds and ditches in many parts of England, where i have been. I fhall fay more of it under article Flote FESCUE grafs.*

Fine BENT. *Tab.* 3.

This grafs i have always found in great plenty on the beft fheep paftures, as on Malvern hills and on all the high grounds in Herefordfhire, that are remarkable for good mutton.

ADDITION. *I may add on Bagfhot heath] and the beft fheep paftures in Berkfhire, Oxfordfhire and Norfolk.*

Fine Bent Grass

Tab. 4.

Mountain Hair Grass.

R. Price delin

Tab. 5.

Silver Hair-Grass.

J. Miller del. et sc.

Tab. 6.

Great Meadow Grass.

R. Price delin.

Tab. 7.

Annual Meadow Grafs.

S. Miller del. et Sc

Genus the eleventh. *Mountain* HAIR. *Tab.* 4.

The fame may be faid of this grafs as of the foregoing. It grows in great plenty on Bagfhot heath.

Silver HAIR. *Tab.* 5.

This alfo is found on the fame kind of pafture as the two foregoing.

Genus the fourteenth. *Great* and *narrow-leaved*

MEADOW. *Tab.* 6.

Thefe graffes are common in our beft meadow grounds, and i believe make good pafture and hay.

ADDITION. *I have found them frequently on banks by the road fide, and near ditches, even where they were not to be found in the adjoyning meadows, and paftures.*

Annual MEADOW. *Tab.* 7.

This grafs makes the fineft of turfs. It grows every where by way fides, and on rich found commons. It is called in fome parts the Suffolk grafs. I have feen whole fields of it in High Suffolk without any mixture of other graffes, and as fome of the beft falt butter we have in London comes from that county, it is moft likely to be the beft grafs for the dairy. I have feen a whole park in Suffolk covered with this grafs, but whether it affords good venifon i cannot tell, having never tafted of any from it. I fhould rather

think

think not, and that the beſt paſture for ſheep is alſo the beſt for deer. However this wants trial. I remarked on Malvern hill ſomething particular in relation to this graſs. A walk that was made there for the convenience of the water drinkers, in leſs than a year was covered in many places with it, tho' i could not find one ſingle plant of it beſides in any part of the hill. This was no doubt, owing to the frequent treading, which above all things makes this graſs floriſh, and therefore it is evident that rolling muſt be very ſerviceable to it.

ADDITION. *It has been objected that this graſs is not free from bents, by which word is meant the flowering ſtems. I anſwer that this is moſt certainly true, and that there is no graſs without them. But the flowers and ſtems do not grow ſo ſoon brown as thoſe of other graſſes, and being much ſhorter they do not cover the radical leaves ſo much, and therefore this graſs affords a more agreeable turf without mowing than any other whatever that i know of.*

Sheeps FESCUE. *Tab.* 8.

This is the graſs ſo much eſteemed in Sweden for ſheep.

Gmelin, Flor. Sibir. ſays that the Tartars chooſe to fix during the ſummer in thoſe places where there is the greateſt plenty of this graſs; becauſe

Tab. 8.

Sheeps Fescue Grass.

R. Price delin.

becaufe it affords a moft wholefome nourifhment to all kinds of cattle, but chiefly fheep; and he obferves that the fepulchral monuments of the antient Tartars are moftly found in places that abound with this grafs, which fhews, adds he, that it has long been valued amongft them.

I have among my graffes a fpecimen of it, but do not remember where i found it. I am certain it is not common in any of the places where i have been. Perhaps upon examination it may be found on places famous for our beft mutton, as Banftead Downs, Church-Stretton in Shrop-fhire, fome parts of Wales &c.

ADDITION. *I have fince found this grafs in great plenty in many parts of England and Wales; indeed on all the fineft fheep paftures in Hereford-fhire, Berkfhire, Oxfordfhire, Norfolk &c. The reafon why i thought it not common was, that it is an early grafs, and had fhed its feeds, before i ufually made my fearches in thofe places where it only grows. I muft alfo obferve that, contrary to what Linnæus fays, either the fheep or fome other animals do eat the flowering ftems of this grafs, for upon Banftead Downs there was nothing to be feen but the radical leaves of it, unlefs amongft the bufhes near the hedges, where it was guarded from the fheep.*

C c   Genus

Genus the fifteenth. *Purple* FESCUE. *Tab.* 9.

ADDITION. *This grafs i have always found along with the fine* BENT *and filver* HAIR-GRASS, *particularly on Banftead Downs in great plenty in a place inclofed in order to keep the fheep out. From hence i am inclined to think that this is the chief grafs all over the Downs, but as the flowering ftems in the other parts were intirely gone, unlefs along the hedges, i could not be certain.*

Flote FESCUE. *Tab.* 10.

I have no knowledge of the qualities of this grafs from my own experience, but fhall quote fomething concerning it out of a piece publifhed in the Amæn. Academ. vol. 3. entitled Plantæ Efculentæ. The author fays there, artic. 90. that the feeds of this grafs are gathered yearly in Poland, and from thence carried into Ger-many and fometimes into Sweden, and fold under the name of manna feeds. Thefe are much ufed at the tables of the great on account of their nourifhing quality and agreeable tafte. It is wonderfull, adds the author, that amongft us thefe feeds have hitherto been neglected, fince they are fo eafily collected and cleanfed.

ADDITION. *Mr. Dean, a very fenfible farmer at Rufcomb, Berkfhire, affured me that a field always lying under water of about four acres,*

that

Tab. 9.

Purple Fescue Grass.

J. Miller del. et sc.

Flote Fescue Grass.

J. Miller del. et sc.

that was occupied by his father when he was a boy, was covered with a kind of grafs, that maintained five farm-horfes in good heart from April to the end of harveſt without giving them any other kind of food, and that it yielded more than they could eat. He at my deſire brought me ſome of the grafs, which proved to be the flote FESCUE *with a mixture of the marſh* BENT ; *whether this laſt contributes much towards furniſhing ſo good paſture for horfes i cannot ſay. They both throw out roots at the joynts of the ſtalks, and therefore likely to grow to a great length. In the index of dubious plants at the end of Ray's Synopſis, there is mention made of a grafs under the name of Gramen caninum ſupinum longiſſimum, growing not far from Saliſbury* 24 *feet long. This muſt by its length be a grafs with a creeping ſtalk ; and that there is a grafs in Wiltſhire growing in watery meadows ſo valuable, that an acre of it lets from* 10 *to* 12 *pounds, i have been informed by ſeveral perſons. Theſe circumſtances incline me to think it muſt be the flote fefcue ; but whatever grafs it be, it certainly muſt deſerve to be inquired after.*

There is a clamminefs on the ear of the flote fefcue when the ſeeds are ripe that taſtes like honey, as i have often found, and for this reafon perhaps they are called manna ſeeds.

Linnæus

Linnæus Flor. Suec. art. 95. *fays, that the bran of this grafs will cure horfes troubled with bots, if kept from drinking for fome hours.*

Genus the feventeenth. *Yellow* OAT.

This grafs is found in great pleaty in fome grounds where the fheep's FESCUE, *the fine* BENT, *and the crefted* DOG-TAIL *grow, and therefore likely to be good for fheep. It is alfo not uncommon in good meadows.*

Genus the nineteenth. *Perennial* DARNEL.

This grafs is well known, and cultivated all over England; and it is to be hoped the fuccefs we have had with it will in time encourage our farmers to take the fame pains about fome others that are no lefs valuable, and are full as eafy to be feparated. It makes a moft excellent turf on found rich land where it will remain.

If i may judge by the venifon i have eat out of a paddock, that was chiefly filled with this grafs, i would by no means recommend it for parks. I know it will be faid that venifon is never good out of a paddock, that the deer muft have room to range, trees to browfe on, &c. I grant there is fome reafon for faying this, but i believe in general it is more owing to want of proper food, viz. good grafs, than merely to confinement; for paddocks are generally made

by

Tab. 11.

Crested Dogs - tail Grass.

R. Price delin.

by converting fome rich fpot near the houfe, that has conftantly been manured, and of courfe is full of graffes fitter for the dairy or the ftable than for deer, which hardly ever is the cafe of large parks. No man will, i fuppofe, pretend to make good pork from a hog fed with grains inftead of peas, tho' he has the liberty of choofing as much ground as he pleafes, and where he pleafes.

This grafs is called in many counties *rye* grafs. It were to be wifhed that the old name might prevail, becaufe there is a genus of grafs, viz. the 22d. known by the name of *rye* all over the kingdom, of which genus there is a fpecies that ought to bear the fame generical name.

ADDITION. *I have fince eaten venifon out of a large park, where there was much of this grafs, and it was no better than that out of the paddock. I fhould be apt to think from hence that this grafs would not be proper for fheep, as i have always obferved that the fame kind of ground which yeilds good venifon yields alfo good mutton. For what particular ufes it is good, wants to be tryed, whether for the dairy, for fatting cattle, or for horfes. Many are tempted by the facility of procuring the feed of this grafs to lay down grounds near their houfes, where they want to have a fine*

turf

turf with it ; for which purpose unless the soil be very rich a worse grass cannot be sown, as it will certainly die off in a very few years intirely.

Genus the twenty fourth. *Crested* DOG-TAIL. *Tab.* 11.

This grafs i imagine is proper for parks. I know one where this abounds, that is famous for excellent venifon. It may perhaps be as good for fheep.

ADDITION. *That it is good for sheep i have since found by experience. The best mutton i have tasted, next to that which comes from hills where the purple and sheep's fescue, the fine bent, and the silver hair grasses abound, having been from sheep fed with it.*

It makes a very fine turf upon dry sandy or chalky soils, as i have seen in many parts of Berkshire, but unless swept over with the scythe, its flowering stems will look brown ; which is the case of all grasses, which are not fed by variety of animals. For that some animals will eat the flowering stems is evident by commons, where scarcely any parts of grasses appear but the radical leaves.

Order of coming into ear of the above mentioned grafses.

Annual MEADOW

Meadow FOX-TAIL

VERNAL

VERNAL

Great MEADOW

Narrow-leaved MEADOW

Crested DOG-TAIL

Sheep's FESCUE

Purple FESCUE

Fine BENT

Marsh BENT

Silver HAIR

Yellow OAT

Flote FESCUE

The whole time from the beginning of May
till about the middle of June.

Ει—κεν και σμικρον επι σμικρω καταθειο
Και θαμα τεθ'ερδοις, ταχα κεν μεγα και το γενοιλο.

Hesiod.

F I N I S.

www.ingramcontent.com/pod-product-compliance
Lightning Source LLC
Chambersburg PA
CBHW031828270326
41932CB00008B/590